Gospels and Tradition

Gospels and Tradition

Studies on Redaction Criticism
of the Synoptic Gospels

Robert H. Stein

BAKER BOOK HOUSE
Grand Rapids, Michigan 49516

Library of Congress Cataloging-in-Publication Data

Stein, Robert H., 1935–
    Gospels and tradition : studies on redaction criticism of the Synoptic
Gospels / Robert H. Stein.
        p.   cm.
    Includes bibliographical references and index.
    ISBN 0-8010-8326-5
    1. Bible. N.T. Gospels—Criticism, Redaction. 2. Bible. N.T. Mark—
Criticism, Redaction. I. Title.
BS2555.2.S727   1991
226'.06—dc20   91-37424
                                          CIP

To Professors:
  Bertil Gärtner
  J. Christiaan Beker
  Bruce M. Metzger

Contents

Abbreviations

ATR	*Anglican Theological Review*
BDF	Blass, Debrunner, Funk, *Greek Grammar*
BiL	*Bibel und Leben*
BJRL	*Bulletin of the John Rylands University Library of Manchester*
BR	*Biblical Research*
BZ	*Biblische Zeitschrift*
CBQ	*Catholic Biblical Quarterly*
ExpT	*Expository Times*
Greg	*Gregorium*
Interp	*Interpretation: A Journal of Bible and Theology*
JBL	*Journal of Biblical Literature*
JBR	*Journal of Bible and Religion*
JETS	*Journal of the Evangelical Theological Society*
JR	*Journal of Religion*
JSNT	*Journal for the Study of the New Testament*
JTS	*Journal of Theological Studies*
LCL	Loeb Classical Library
LXX	Septuagint
NIV	New International Version
NovT	*Novum Testamentum*
NTS	*New Testament Studies*
RGG	*Religion in Geschichte und Gegenwart*
RSV	Revised Standard Version
SJT	*Scottish Journal of Theology*
TDNT	*Theological Dictionary of the New Testament*
TLZ	*Theologische Literaturzeitung*
TR	*Theologische Revue*
TZ	*Theologische Zeitschrift*
ZKG	*Zeitschrift für Kirchengeschichte*
ZKT	*Zeitschrift für katholische Theologie*
ZNW	*Zeitschrift für die neutestamentliche Wissenschaft*
ZTK	*Zeitschrift für Theologie und Kirche*

Preface

The beginning of my interest in redaction criticism can be dated to a doctoral seminar on the Gospel of Mark in which I participated as a student at Princeton Theological Seminary. As I read Willi Marxsen's *Der Evangelist Markus*, I realized that the Gospel traditions did in fact contain three separate *Sitze im Leben* and that the Evangelists were to be taken seriously as theologians of the Gospel materials rather than as mere editors. Nevertheless the particular problems associated with the investigation of a Marcan redaction criticism troubled me, for neither Marxsen nor the other redaction critics had clearly defined what a proper methodology for ascertaining a Marcan redaction criticism involved. As a result I chose as my dissertation subject, "The Proper Methodology for Ascertaining a Marcan Redaktionsgeschichte." I had the unique privilege of working under the supervision of Professors Bertil Gärtner, J. Christian Beker, and Bruce M. Metzger. Few doctoral students have been as fortunate as I to work under such capable and knowledgeable teachers. I shall always be indebted to these men for what I learned from them.

Following graduation my interest in Marcan redaction criticism continued unabated. Three articles distilled from my dissertation were published in successive years. The first (Chapter 1—"What Is Redaktionsgeschichte?" *JBL* 88 [1969]: 45–56) was concerned with a definition of the new discipline, whereas the other two discussed the methodology needed to apply this discipline to the study of the Gospel of Mark (Chapter 4—"The 'redaktionsgeschichtlich' Investigation of a Markan Seam [Mc

1:21ff.]," *ZNW* 61 [1970]: 70–94; Chapter 3—"The Proper Methodology for Ascertaining a Markan Redaction History," *NovT* 13 [1971]: 181–98). Thereafter, due to my continued interest in the subject as well as the stimulation of the Markan Task Force of the Society of Biblical Literature, I worked on several key passages in Mark that were at the center of Marcan redaction-critical investigation (Chapter 5—"Is the Transfiguration [Mark 9:2–8] a Misplaced Resurrection-Account?" *JBL* 95 [1975]: 79–96; Chapter 6—"The Cleansing of the Temple in Mark—Reformation or Judgment?"; Chapter 7—"A Short Note on Mark XIV.28 and XVI.7," *NTS* 20 [1973]: 445–52). To these have been added a paper on Luke 1:1–4 read at the annual meeting of the Evangelical Theological Society in 1982 in which I discuss the Evangelist's description of the various *Sitze im Leben* of the Gospel traditions ("Luke 1:1–4 and *Traditionsgeschichte*," *JETS* 26 [1983]: 421–30) and two essays involving the "quest" for the *ipsissima verba* of Jesus. The first deals with the terminology used in the discussion ("'Authentic' or 'Authoritative'? What Is the Difference?" *JETS* 24 [1981]: 127–30), and the other seeks to organize and discuss the various criteria being used in this "quest" ("The 'Criteria' for Authenticity," in *Gospel Perspectives: Studies of History and Tradition in the Four Gospels*, ed. R. T. France and David Wenham [Sheffield: JSOT, 1980), 1:225–63).

The reprinting of previously published articles is both flattering and encouraging to any author. The value of reprinting such essays, however, is somewhat questionable, for as the years go by, new insights are gained and past errors are more clearly seen. Yet, although the bibliography of these essays is now dated, I believe that the essential arguments and theses are still sound and deserve repeating. There is another value in such a collection in that it brings together into one place related materials found scattered in various journals over a period of years. I would like to thank Jim Weaver, Editor of Academic and Reference Books, and Baker Book House for making this collection of essays available.

Acknowledgments

Permission to reprint the following essays, which originally appeared in the sources indicated, is gratefully acknowledged:

"What Is Redaktionsgeschichte?" *JBL* 88 (1969): 45–56. Reprinted by permission of the Society of Biblical Literature.

"Luke 1:1–4 and *Traditionsgeschichte*." *JETS* 26 (1983): 421–30. Reprinted by permission of the Evangelical Theological Society.

"The Proper Methodology for Ascertaining a Markan Redaction History." *NovT* 13 (1971): 181–98.

"The 'redaktionsgeschichtlich' Investigation of a Markan Seam (Mc 1:21ff.)." *ZNW* 61 (1970): 70–94.

"Is the Transfiguration (Mark 9:2–8) a Misplaced Resurrection-Account?" *JBL* 95 (1976): 79–96. Reprinted by permission of the Society of Biblical Literature.

"A Short Note on Mark XIV.28 and XVI.7." *NTS* 20 (1973): 445–52. Reprinted by permission of Cambridge University Press.

"'Authentic' or 'Authoritative'? What Is the Difference?" *JETS* 24 (1981): 127–30. Reprinted by permission of the Evangelical Theological Society.

"The 'Criteria' for Authenticity." In *Gospel Perspectives,* ed. R. T. France and David Wenham (Sheffield: JSOT, 1980), 1:225–63. Reprinted by permission of Sheffield Academic Press.

Introduction

During the last three decades no subject has dominated Gospel research more than redaction criticism, and during those years a plethora of articles, books, and seminars on the subject have appeared. Scholarly journals were filled with articles devoted to the investigation of the third *Sitz im Leben* of the Gospel materials. The enthusiasm for this new discipline often brought forth creative and imaginative reconstructions of the situation in which and for which the individual Evangelists were writing. At times, however, some reconstructions, due to a lack of sound methodological controls, resembled more the writing of fiction than careful exegetical investigation. Few scholars could resist the attractive, compelling call of the siren of redaction criticism. There were several reasons for this.

First, redaction criticism offered a corrective to the one-sided approach of form criticism. The sociological orientation of form criticism either lost sight of or ignored the role of the Evangelists in the recording of the Gospel traditions. Redaction criticism responded to this basic flaw of form criticism, and the Evangelists were now regarded as individual authors possessing their own theological emphases rather than simply "scissors and paste" editors of the Gospel traditions. No longer could their role in the composition of the Gospels be ignored. The rise of redaction criticism was greeted with great excitement in part because the final lacuna of *Traditionsgeschichte* was now filled. This gap was always present in form-critical discussion, but

13

until the rise of redaction criticism it was never remedied.[1] Form criticism correctly recognized in the history of the Gospel traditions the *Sitz im Leben* of Jesus and the *Sitz im Leben* of the church during the oral period, but it never completed tradition history by acknowledging that the writing down of this tradition provided a third *Sitz im Leben*. There were several possible reasons for this. The sociological orientation of form criticism had difficulty coming to grips with the individuality of the Evangelists,[2] even though there were sufficient clues that the Gospel writers were more than bland editors of the tradition. It may also be that form criticism sought to minimize the variable factors in investigating the Gospel traditions. Two *Sitze im Leben* were far easier to deal with than three. Redaction criticism, however, was not a refutation of or threat to form-critical investigation. Rather it was viewed as its ally in completing the spectrum of tradition history; and in the investigation of Marcan redaction criticism, form-critical research was heavily involved.

A second impetus to redaction-critical studies was the fact that certain earlier results of Gospel studies, which had pointed out the particular emphases of the Evangelists, no longer needed to be ignored. Matthew's emphasis that the life and teachings of Jesus were the fulfillment of the Old Testament could now be fully appreciated. The logical implication of the messianic secret in Mark, about which all form critics knew, could now be accepted, namely, that Mark was indeed an interpreter, not just a typesetter of the Gospel traditions. The recognition of

1. It is the lasting contribution of Willi Marxsen that he clearly revealed the gap in tradition criticism that form criticism left.

2. This was clearly experienced by the present writer at one of the Society of Biblical Literature's Markan Seminars held in the 1970s. As we discussed the theology of "Mark," a leading redaction critic kept referring to the theology of the "Marcan community." When I suggested that it would be more proper to refer to the theology of Mark since we know that the author of Mark believed this but could not guarantee that his "community" (whether there was such a community is another question) also believed this, he simply could not fully accept the individuality of the Evangelist. The Evangelist must represent a "community." Yet Mark's own theological emphasis may or may not have represented a community's theology. Does Paul's theology in Galatians represent the theology of the "Galatian community"? If it does, he would never have written Galatians! Was Mark or Luke commissioned by a community to write their Gospels? Clearly the only thing we can say with certainty is that the Gospel of Mark represents Mark's theology.

Luke's theological emphases in Acts could be extended to his Gospel as well. Now his Gospel could be treated as the first volume of the great theological work, Luke–Acts. A great deal of information existed as to unique theological emphases of the individual Synoptic Gospels, and with the rise of redaction criticism these no longer needed to be minimized or ignored as form-critical research did. The Synoptic Gospels could now be investigated for their theological emphases just as the Gospel of John had been. This approach, which emphasized the theology of the Synoptic Gospels rather than their history, found a warm welcome among kerygmatic theologians.

A third factor that caused interest in this discipline was the fact that it was a "new discovery." To a certain extent the fraternity of biblical scholars was like the Athenians "who . . . spent their time in nothing except telling or hearing something new" (Acts 17:21). Young doctoral students, the present writer included, in seeking something "new" to write on for their dissertations found redaction criticism a most fruitful area. Thus it is not surprising that much of New Testament scholarship became involved in the new movement. It would have been most surprising if it had not.

Today redaction criticism has fallen on hard times. In part this is to be expected, since the fever pitch of redaction-critical studies could not maintain itself. Like other movements in biblical research, this one would also peak and recede. This was only natural, and the excess of some redaction-critical studies, the lack of a clear methodology (especially with regard to Marcan studies), and the narrow focus of redaction criticism aided in its receding from the dominating position in New Testament scholarship. As new interests, such as literary criticism, sociological studies, and feminist theology, came on the scene, it was not unnatural that the fraternity of scholars would switch their attention to these new disciplines.

A basic presupposition underlying most Marcan redaction criticism is the priority of Mark. This has been aggressively challenged by William Farmer and the new Griesbach School.[3] If Mark indeed had copies of Matthew and Luke before him as he wrote his Gospel, then Marcan redactional investigation would proceed quite differently than if Mark brought together

3. See Stein, *Synoptic Problem*, 129–38.

isolated pieces or collections of tradition. Yet it is the practice of Marcan redaction criticism that provides some of the most weighty arguments in favor of Marcan priority, and those scholars who have investigated this area are as a result strong advocates of Marcan priority. Elsewhere I have sought to show how two Matthean emphases (the use of the title "Son of David" and the use of the fulfillment quotations) can easily be explained by the author's having added them to his Marcan source, but there is no acceptable explanation of why, if Matthew were used by Mark and Luke, that the latter two writers would have omitted this material. The fulfillment emphasis would have fit Luke's own similar emphasis especially well. I have also demonstrated that two clear Marcan emphases (his use of "immediately" and of explanatory clauses introduced by a γάρ) are found disproportionately in the material Matthew has in common with Mark but not elsewhere in Matthew's Gospel. This makes perfectly good sense if Matthew were using Mark but defies explanation if Mark used Matthew.[4] It is true that most redactional investigation of Mark is built upon the presupposition that Mark did not know any of the other Gospels, but this presupposition seems to be supported time and time again by the results of such investigation. The paucity of a meaningful Marcan redaction criticism based upon the Griesbach Hypothesis can also be mentioned in this regard.

There is a great deal of criticism today directed at studies in Marcan redaction criticism.[5] Much of it is deserved. All too frequently the study of the third *Sitz im Leben* of Mark was pursued without carefully defining the parameters under which such investigation should proceed.[6] Marxsen would not have argued that the Gospel was written to Jewish Christians in Judea telling them to flee to Pella if he had observed how the Evangelist explains Jewish customs (Mark 7:3–4; 14:12; 15:42) and Aramaic terms (Mark 3:17; 5:41; 7:11, 34; 14:36; 15:22, 34) to his readers. Similarly the thesis that Mark was seeking to combat a divine-man Christology, which almost dominated Marcan studies in the 1970s,[7]

4. See ibid., 76–86.
5. See Black, "Quest of Mark the Redactor," 19–39, and *Disciples*; Marshall, *Faith as a Theme*, 9–14; Muddiman, "End of Markan Redaction Criticism?" 307–9.
6. See Black, *Disciples*, 183–248.
7. See especially Weeden, *Mark*.

would never have gained such notoriety if it had been observed that Mark in his summaries and insertions emphasizes the miracles of Jesus and the great astonishment and amazement they caused (Mark 1:22, 32–34, 39; 3:7–12; 5:20, 42; 6:13, 53–56; 7:37; etc.). It cannot be denied therefore that Marcan studies have often suffered due to an unclear methodology. As a doctoral student this was apparent to me, and as a result I devoted my doctoral dissertation to "The Proper Methodology for Ascertaining a Marcan Redaktionsgeschichte." Several of the chapters that appear in this volume are devoted to this subject—"Ascertaining a Marcan Redaction History: The Proper Methodology"[8]; "A Seam in Mark (1:21–22): A Redactional Investigation"[9]; and "The Transfiguration in Mark (9:2–8): A Misplaced Resurrection Account?"[10]

Another reason for the "demise" of redaction criticism is that for many the limited goals and aims of redaction criticism were not properly understood. Many redaction critics mistakenly equated Marcan redactional emphases with the "theology of Mark." It is an error, however, to assume that the theological uniqueness of Mark is equivalent to the total theology of Mark. Redaction criticism properly defined involves the former not the latter. Marcan theology, on the other hand, consists of all that Mark teaches in his Gospel, and a great deal of this he shares with the other Evangelists. Some redaction critics seem to have ignored this material that Mark shared with the other Evangelists, and which makes up the majority of his Gospel, and they assumed that Mark only sought to teach what was unique to his Gospel. As a result some redaction critics made the same kind of mistake that those using the criterion of dissimilarity made in seeking the authentic sayings of Jesus. They assumed that what was unique to Jesus or Mark was the major part or even the totality of his message.[11] I argued in "What Is Redaktionsgeschichte?" that redaction criticism seeks: (1) what unique theological views the Evangelist presents that are foreign to his sources; (2) what unusual theological emphasis or emphases the Evangelist places upon the sources he received; (3) what theological purpose or purposes the Evangelist has in writ-

8. See pp. 49–67.
9. See pp. 69–96.
10. See pp. 97–119.
11. See pp. 175–76.

ing his Gospel; and (4) out of what *Sitz im Leben* the Evangelist writes his Gospel. The limited nature of redactional research is thus clear.[12] Even though redaction criticism treats the Gospels holistically, rather than atomistically as in form criticism, it does not seek the whole theology of the Evangelists but rather that which is unique to them.[13]

Of these aims (3) and especially (4) are the most elusive and hypothetical. Yet much of redaction criticism has concentrated on these.[14] Today I am more pessimistic about reconstructing the hypothetical purpose and *Sitz im Leben* of the Evangelists than I was when I wrote "What Is Redaktionsgeschichte?" Whereas the "what" that an author seeks to convey is reasonably accessible to the reader, the "why" often is not. The "what" that an author willed to convey to his readers is available in the words of his text. We, as readers, have access to this, but the "why" is a step, a large step, removed. For those who confidently think that they can reconstruct this "why" of the author, C. S. Lewis's *Fern-seed and Elephants* should be required reading.[15] If Lewis is anywhere near correct, all New Testament studies—and not just redaction criticism—should content itself primarily with investigating the "what" that an author seeks to convey rather than in pursuing the more subjective and less accessible reconstruction of "why" an author wrote.

Is redaction criticism dead? That it has "peaked" is evident. The limitations of this discipline have now finally been recognized. Yet scholarship will never be able to retreat from redaction criticism's great contribution—the recognition of the Evangelists as theologians who have interpreted the Gospel traditions for their readers. Thus redaction criticism will continue for as long as scholarship is interested in ascertaining the meaning

12. See pp. 30–31.

13. It is evident that this narrower understanding of redaction criticism conflicts with what I have said in note 35 of "Luke 1:1–4 and *Traditionsgeschichte*." See below p. 47. I disclaim this definition of redaction criticism found in the note.

14. See Perrin, *What Is Redaction Criticism?* vi: "Its [Redaction criticism's] goals are to understand why the items from the tradition were modified and connected as they were, to identify the theological motifs that were at work in composing a finished Gospel, and to elucidate the theological point of view which is expressed in and through the composition."

15. *Fern-seed and Elephants and Other Essays on Christianity* (Glasgow: William Collins Sons, 1975), 104–25, especially 114–17.

of the Gospel writers. As one observes Luke's use of Mark and how the Evangelist emphasizes the role of the Spirit in Jesus' ministry (see Luke 3:22; 4:1, 14, 18; 5:17), one is better able to see what Luke is trying to convey to his readers. Similarly as one sees in the Marcan editorial framework various theological emphases, one is likewise better able to understand Mark's message as well. Presently "new" interests dominate the landscape of Gospel studies, but long after scholarly interest wanes with regard to employing sociological theory, reader response techniques, anthropological insights, and the like to the Gospels, the church will continue to study the Gospels in order to understand what their divinely inspired authors meant. At present there is a tendency to treat the Gospels as autonomous texts torn away from their first-century authors, but such an approach in which meaning tends to be determined by the reader, will eventually be seen as a kind of idolatrous self-worship in which the reader becomes the "divine" creator and determiner of meaning. The church, on the other hand, will always be interested in redaction-critical studies because the church will always be interested in hearing the divine word brought to her by God's ordained spokesmen—the Evangelists. Thus redaction criticism will neither die nor fade away. Every good commentary will always have a section dealing with "The Theology of the Evangelist" and in that section the unique emphases of the Evangelist will be discussed.

1

What Is
Redaction Criticism?

The Rise of Redaktionsgeschichte

The value of the form-critical method for the investigation of the Gospels is recognized today by all (or almost all) scholars. Despite its great value, however, form criticism possesses certain limitations. One of these limitations was in reality a glaring oversight. Whereas the form critics dealt intimately with the individual pericopes and even blocks of material that make up the Gospel tradition, they neglected to treat the Gospels themselves as individual entities.[1] In its investigation of the indi-

1. "Aber in diesem ersten Stadium hatte die Formgeschichte tatsächlich eine Schwäche, die sie ergänzungsbedürftig macht: sie drohte—indem sie den einzelnen Traditionsstücken nachging—das Evangelium als Ganzes aus den Augen zu verlieren . . . als eine neue Lösung für die synoptische Forschung ist diese Betrachtungsweise, die sich dem Evangelisten und seinem Werk als einem Ganzen zuwendet, erst in den 50er Jahren zur Geltung gekommen" (Haenchen, *Der Weg Jesus*, 23). See also Schille, "Bemerkungen zur Formgeschichte des Evangeliums," 1; Frör, *Biblische Hermeneutik*, 246; Koch, *Was Ist Formgeschichte?* 68–71. For an early protest against form criticism's neglect of the individual Evangelists, see Dobschütz, "Zur Erzählerkunst des Markus," 193f. For an unsuccessful attempt to deny that form criticism neglected the Gospels as complete

21

vidual trees making up the forest form criticism lost sight of the forest itself. As a result the form critics forgot that the individual Gospels are also units that demand consideration and must be investigated as individual entities. This error was due in part to the fact that the form critics looked upon the Gospel writers as merely collectors or *Sammler*,[2] "scissors and paste men" who assembled together the various pericopes. As a result the first three books of the New Testament were viewed not as "Gospels" but as "pericope collections." Form critics therefore felt justified in treating each pericope as an individual gem. Each bit of tradition was treated as a separate pearl and carefully analyzed. But what of the setting into which these gems were placed? The form critics overlooked the fact that the setting provided by the Evangelists gave a distinct appearance to these gems. They overlooked the fact that these pearls of tradition were strung together in a particular manner and revealed a particular design.

It is now generally recognized that the Evangelists were not merely "scissors and paste men." On the contrary the "scissors" were manipulated by a theological hand and the "paste" was impregnated with a particular theology. In contrast to the anti-individualistic view of the form critics, today the Evangelists are recognized as individual theologians. It is true that they collected the Gospel traditions and were limited by them, but each had a theological purpose in writing his Gospel.[3] The first major work that aroused interest in viewing the writers of the Gospels as individual theologians was Hans Conzelmann's

---

entities, see Klein, *Die Zwölf Apostel*, 15; and Bultmann, "Study of the Synoptic Gospels," 4.

2. Dibelius (*From Tradition to Gospel*, 3) states: "The composers are only to the smallest extent authors. They are principally collectors, vehicles of tradition, editors." Frör (*Wege zur Schriftauslegung*, 254) sums up the view of the form critics as follows: "Die Evangelisten wurden im wesentlichen als Sammler der überlieferten Stoffe gewertet." See also Ibers, "Zur Formgeschichte der Evangelien," 337; and Rohde, *Die redaktionsgeschichtliche Methode*, 20. For an unsuccessful attempt to deny the "individualism" of the Evangelists and to return to the pre-*redaktionsgeschichtlich* view of them as *Sammler*, see Strecker, *Der Weg der Gerechtigkeit*, 10.

3. Cf. Frör (*Biblische Hermeneutik*, 254): "Inzwischen wurde aber deutlicher gesehen, dass die Arbeit der Evangelisten sich nicht in ihrer Sammlertätigkeit erschöpft, sondern als selbständige theologische Leistung zu werten ist." See also Schelke, *Das Neue Testament*, 33; Karnetzki, "Die Galiläische Redaktion im Markus-evangelium," 238; and Grundmann, *Die Geschichte Jesu Christi*, 15.

Die Mitte der Zeit, which appeared in 1954.[4] In this well-received work Conzelmann investigated Luke's unique understanding and use of his sources.[5] Shortly thereafter Willi Marxsen published his *Der Evangelist Markus.* What Conzelmann sought to do with Luke, Marxsen sought to do with Mark. It is interesting to note that these two works were written independently of each other.[6] Even as form-critical thinking was in the air at the end of the 1920s, so in the mid-1950s *redaktionsgeschichtlich* thinking was in the air. With the publication of these two works *Redaktionsgeschichte* became increasingly the major concern of synoptic investigation, and the host of works that have since appeared indicates that *Redaktionsgeschichte* has today become the most important area of Gospel studies.[7]

It should not be thought that other scholars had not realized that the Gospel writers contributed their own thoughts to their works and sought to investigate this. William Wrede in his *Das Messiasgeheimnis in den Evangelien* did just this over fifty years before the work of Conzelmann and Marxsen.[8] Johannes Weiss also realized the importance of the investigation of the particular views of the Evangelists.[9] Some other writers who

4. The English translation by Geoffrey Buswell appeared in 1960 under the title *The Theology of St. Luke.*

5. *Theology of St. Luke,* 9, 95.

6. *Der Evangelist Markus,* 5.

7. Ibers ("Zur Formgeschichte der Evangelien," 285) states that form criticism is no longer the most important area of Gospel studies: "Sie ist heute kein Brennpunkt wissenschaftlicher Diskussion mehr. Mit Recht hat man von einer 'Stagnation der formgeschichtlichen Arbeit' gesprochen." To this can be added a statement by Karnetzki ("Die Galiläische Redaktion im Markus-evangelium," 238): "Sie ist heute die Zeit der redaktionsgeschichtlichen Untersuchungen." For a similar view, see Suhl, *Die Funktion,* 9.

8. Wrede's work was published in 1901. It is clear that Wrede saw the importance of investigating the unique theology of the Evangelists. See pp. 2–3, 71, 129, 131, 145. Because of Wrede's interest in the individual Evangelists Schreiber (*Theologische Erkenntnis,* 9) maintains that he is the true father of *Redaktiongeschichte.*

9. In his *Die Schriften des Neuen Testaments,* 1:62, Weiss states: "Die Aufgabe des Erklärers der Evangelien ist eine vielseitige: Es gilt erstens, den Schriftsteller zu verstehen, zu erkennen, was er seinen Lesern sagen will, und wie er diese Worte und Geschichte auffasst. Zweitens gilt es dann, die von ihm benutzte Überlieferung selber in ihrer ursprünglichen Eigenart auf sich wirken zu lassen, die volkstümlichen Erzählungen aus der Seele der alten Gemeinden heraus mit zu empfinden. Schliesslich werden wir versuchen, die Stoffe nutzbar zu machen für das Verständnis der Geschichte und der Person Jesu."

investigated the redactional work and theology of the Evangelists are Ernst Lohmeyer,[10] Karl Kundsin,[11] A. Schlatter,[12] Robert Henry Lightfoot,[13] and James M. Robinson.[14] As can be seen *redaktionsgeschichtlich* investigation did not begin with Conzelmann and Marxsen. The question can therefore be raised as to what is new about *Redaktionsgeschichte*. In reply to this question it can be said first of all that the work of Conzelmann and Marxsen must be understood in the light of the then present view of the Evangelists as pictured by the form critics. The sociological orientation of the form critics had resulted in an anti-individualistic attitude toward the Evangelists. Conzelmann and Marxsen were prophetic voices protesting against this view and claiming that the Evangelists were not merely *Sammler* but individual theologians. Second, *Redaktionsgeschichte* builds much of its investigation upon the work of form criticism. Through form criticism's successful isolation of the Gospel pericopes, *Redaktionsgeschichte* has been better able to ascertain the editorial work of the Evangelists. As a result, it was not until form criticism separated the pericopes from the redaction that *Redaktionsgeschichte* was really possible. This is especially true with regard to the *redaktionsgeschichtlich* investigation of Mark. Third, *Redaktionsgeschichte* can be said to have started with Conzelmann and Marxsen because it was through their works that the importance of this area of study became clear. As a result history will credit these two men with the "discovery" of *Redaktionsgeschichte* even though they had their forerunners, just as Columbus is credited with the discovery of America even though he, too, had his forerunners.

A *Definition* of Redaktionsgeschichte[15]

Although Conzelmann's *Die Mitte der Zeit* was the first major work on *Redaktionsgeschichte* to appear in the mid-1950s, he neither used the term *Redaktionsgeschichte* nor systematically

10. *Galiläa und Jerusalem.*
11. *Topologische Überlieferungsstoffe im Johannes-Evangelium.*
12. *Der Evangelist Matthäus.*
13. *Locality and Doctrine in the Gospels.*
14. *Problem of History in Mark.* One work that has gone unnoticed up until now is Nicolardot, *Les procédés de rédaction.*
15. Although this term was used before Marxsen, it has become a *terminus technicus* through his use of it.

defined what the investigation of the unique theology of Luke involves or is. *Redaktionsgeschichte* for Conzelmann is simply the attempt to ascertain that which "distinguishes him [the Evangelist]"[16] from his sources. Marxsen on the other hand began his work by defining what *Redaktionsgeschichte* is, and all the subsequent discussion has centered around his definition. Marxsen speaks of three separate *Sitze im Leben* that must be distinguished in the investigation of the Gospels. The first refers to the "einmaligen Situation der Wirksamkeit Jesu," [17] that is, the relationship of our Gospels to the historical or earthly Jesus. The second *Sitz im Leben* refers to "die Situation der Urkirche,"[18] that is, form criticism and its attempt to ascertain the theology of the early church by the investigation of the units handed down by the tradition. Up to this point Marxsen has said nothing new or unique. This is exactly what the form critics have said all along. Marxsen, however, speaks of a third *Sitz im Leben*, which he calls *Redaktionsgeschichte* and which he defines as the attempt to ascertain the unique view of the Gospel writers.[19] Whereas form criticism is primarily concerned with the shaping of and formation of the oral traditions, *Redaktionsgeschichte* is primarily concerned with what the individual writers of the Gospels did with the materials (both oral and written) available to them.[20] It therefore looks at the Evangelists as writers and not as mere *Sammler* as form criticism was prone to do.[21]

Some scholars have maintained that Marxsen's definition is misleading because there cannot be three *Sitze im Leben* but only two—the earthly Jesus and the early church. The second

16. *Theology of St. Luke*, 13. See also pp. 9, 12–14, 95.

17. *Der Evangelist Markus*, 12.

18. Ibid.

19. Best (*Temptation and the Passion*, xii) is in close agreement with Marxsen when he says that "Any full study of a Gospel involves an examination of three factors: the Evangelist's theology, the early Church's modification of the tradition, and the original event." Koch (*Was Ist Formgeschichte?* 63), Grundmann (*Das Evangelium nach Markus*, 23), and Vögtle ("Die historische und theologische Tragweite," 393) also agree with the view of Marxsen.

20. Marxsen, *Der Evangelist Markus*, 13.

21. Koch (*Was Ist Formgeschichte?* 62) points out that the Evangelists can neither be viewed as *Verfasser*, because they were limited by their material, nor *Sammler*, because they are more than mere editors. He also dislikes the term *Redaktor*. Perhaps the least misleading term in German is *Schriftsteller*.

Sitz im Leben, however, is seen as twofold. It consists of (1) the transmission of the oral traditions by the early church and (2) the editorial redaction of the Evangelists.[22] Seen in this light the second *Sitz im Leben* is not as misleading as the form critics have often portrayed it. Yet we must not lose sight of the fact that the writing of the Gospels was a unique event. This is especially true in the case of Mark. The writing of the Gospels was a major step in the transmission of the Gospel materials. It gave a definite pattern to the materials, so that from the time of Mark the Gospel materials had received a definite framework. The writing of the first Gospel therefore marked the twilight of the oral period. Another problem in including both form criticism and *Redaktionsgeschichte* in the same *Sitz im Leben* is that the form critics have tended to speak of the oral period as an anonymous one. Usually it is the "religious community" that is thought of as shaping the material. With the writing of the Gospels, however, we leave the stage of "anonymity." We are here dealing with individual authors, not with the "community." This is certainly the case with regard to the Gospel of Luke. This Gospel is clearly the product of the reflection and thinking of Luke. It is perhaps somewhat less so with regard to Mark, and it is quite possible that in the case of Matthew we are dealing with a school.[23] It cannot be denied that a Gospel such as Mark represents the views of Mark's church, for no one writes in a vacuum, and it would certainly be false to assume that Mark wrote an apologetic against the views of his church. If Mark were written, at least in part, for catechetical purposes, then we would expect that Mark closely reflects the views of his church. Yet it is best to think of the Gospel of Mark as portraying the views of the Evangelist rather than those of the Evangelist's church. This would avoid the danger of transferring the particular theology of Mark, which we can ascertain, to Mark's church, which we cannot directly know. An example of this danger is the "messianic secret" found in Mark. We know that the secrecy motif in our first Gospel is a Marcan emphasis, but it would be an unwarranted step to conclude that this was also an emphasis of Mark's church. It seems best

22. This is the view of Trilling (*Das Wahre Israel*, 13).

23. For the opposing view that the Gospel of Matthew is not the product of a school but of an individual, see Fuller, *Critical Introduction to the New Testament*, 114.

therefore to consider the Gospel of Mark as reflecting the views and the attitudes of the Evangelist even though it is probably true that it reflects closely the views of his church.[24] It should also be noted that the creation of the Gospel form by Mark was a unique event. The creation of such a form is the work of an individual rather than of a church. With the writing of the Gospels we have passed from a sociological *Sitz im Leben* (the community) to an individualistic *Sitz im Leben* (the Evangelists). We have reached a new stage in the transmission of the Gospel materials. It seems best, therefore, to view the work of the Evangelists as a third *Sitz im Leben* rather than as part of the second, for not only will this indicate that we have come to a third major stage in the transmission of the materials—for the creation of the Gospel form is a major step in the transmission of the Gospel materials—but this will also help in a practical way to overcome the misconception created by the form critics that the Evangelists were merely "scissors and paste men."

Some scholars have sought not only to place *Redaktionsgeschichte* in the second *Sitz im Leben* but also to place it under form criticism. Rudolf Bultmann attempts to do so,[25] as do Georg Strecker,[26] Gottfried Schille,[27] Klaus Koch,[28] E. Dinkler,[29] Donald Guthrie,[30] and Ernst Haenchen.[31] Haenchen speaks of a first and second *Stadium* of form criticism. In the first *Stadium* he places the work of K. L. Schmidt, Martin Dibelius, and Bultmann. In the second he puts the work of Conzelmann, Marxsen, and the other *redaktionsgeschichtlich* scholars.[32] But is there suf-

---

24. The failure to distinguish between the Evangelist and his church is a major weakness in the works of Lohmeyer and Robinson.

25. "Study of the Synoptic Gospels," 4.

26. Strecker, *Der Weg der Gerechtigkeit*, 9.

27. "Der Mangel eines kritischen Geschichtsbildes," 492.

28. Koch, *Was Ist Formgeschichte?* 62 n. 1.

29. "Form Criticism of the New Testament," 683.

30. *New Testament Introduction*, 188.

31. Haenchen, *Der Weg Jesus*, 20f.

32. It would be a mistake to think that Haenchen minimizes the importance of *Redaktionsgeschichte* by placing it under form criticism. On the contrary, he urges that a new name be given to this second *Stadium* in that *Redaktionsgeschichte* does not stress sufficiently enough that the Evangelists were not "scissors and paste men." By using a new term—*Kompositionsgeschichte*—he thinks that the unique contribution of the Evangelists will be seen more clearly.

ficient continuity between form criticism and *Redaktionsgeschichte*
to permit this? Bultmann,[33] Strecker,[34] Günther Klein,[35] and
Conzelmann[36] claim that there is. Marxsen, however, disagrees.
The oral stage tended toward the breaking up and scattering of
material, not toward its synthesis.[37] The Evangelists opposed
this tendency toward scattering that existed in the oral period.
There is not, therefore, a continuity of syntheticism but a decisive movement by the Evangelists against this destructive dis-
persion of the oral period.[38] The implications of what Marxsen
is saying are of great consequence. He is in effect denying that
the redaction of Mark by Luke and Matthew provides a pattern
by which we can judge how the oral transmission of the Gospel
traditions was formed and shaped. R. M. Grant[39] and Koch[40]
agree with Marxsen in this regard.

It seems to the present writer that both Marxsen and his
form-critical opponents have erred. In the oral stage there
already existed a synthesizing tendency. The pre-Marcan passion
narrative, the parable collections, and the sayings collections
prove this, and even Marxsen acknowledges that there were
pre-Marcan blocks of material.[41] Furthermore Marxsen's thesis
would require that originally the Gospel materials must have
stood together. Then in the course of the oral period this
material was scattered. In the writings of the Gospels, it was
once again brought together. But to argue for an original
"togetherness" of the material would require some hypothesis
such as Harald Riesenfeld[42] and Birger Gerhardsson[43] propose;
and this Marxsen rejects.[44] On the other hand, there exists a

33. *History of the Synoptic Tradition*, 321; cf. also McArthur, "Basic Issues,"
48–49.

34. Strecker, *Der Weg der Gerechtigkeit*, 9. See also his review of Marxsen's
Der Evangelist Markus , 143–44.

35. Klein, *Die Zwölf Apostel*, 15–16.

36. Conzelmann, *Die Mitte der Zeit*, 12.

37. Marxsen, *Der Evangelist Markus*, 8–9. See also his *Einleitung in das Neue Testament*, 113.

38. *Der Evangelist Markus*, 9.

39. Grant, *Historical Introduction to the New Testament*, 80.

40. Koch, *Was Ist Formgeschichte?* 63.

41. *Einleitung in das Neue Testament*, 115–17.

42. *Gospel Tradition*.

43. *Memory and Manuscript*.

44. See *Der Evangelist Markus*, 8. It must be acknowledged that Marxsen is
quite unclear as to exactly what he means by "scattering" and "synthesis."

large *Spannung* between the collection of certain materials such as parables, sayings, the passion narrative, and the like, and the writing of a Gospel. The form critics—who seek a continuity between form criticism and *Redaktionsgeschichte*—do not appreciate how great a step the Evangelists took when they composed their Gospels.[45]

It would be an error to make *Redaktionsgeschichte* part of form criticism. Kurt Frör has correctly pointed out that they are primarily concerned with two different things. Form criticism is primarily concerned with the investigation of the individual pericopes and the oral period. *Redaktionsgeschichte* is concerned with the theological conception of each Gospel as an individual entity.[46] Furthermore, whereas there are times when the investigations of *Redaktionsgeschichte* will be intimately related to the same interests of form criticism, there will be other times when they will be quite independent. When we seek a Marcan *Redaktionsgeschichte* we are of necessity involved with form-critical investigation, for we must first isolate the Marcan redaction from the tradition. This can be done only by the form-critical method. We are likewise involved in form-critical investigation when we seek a Matthean *Redaktionsgeschichte* in the M material and a Lukan *Redaktionsgeschichte* in the L material. To a lesser extent we are also involved in form-critical study when we investigate the Q material. When we seek, however, to ascertain a Matthean or a Lukan *Redaktionsgeschichte* in the material that they have in common with Mark, we are not so much concerned with form-critical investigation as with literary analysis. In this area where we can most clearly ascertain

45. Schweizer in his *Das Evangelium nach Markus*, 222, sees clearly how big this step was for Mark: "Dass Markus in dieser Lage als erster ein Evangelium schrieb und damit eine ganz neue literarische Gattung schuf, war eine theologische Leistung ersten Ranges." For a similar appreciation of the great step taken by Mark, see S. Schulz, "Die Bedeutung des Markus," 2:145.

46. Frör, *Wege zur Schriftauslegung*, 254: "Die formgeschichtliche Untersuchung interessierte sich zunächst vor allem für die kleinsten Einheiten, ihre Struktur, ihren Sitz und ihre Überlieferungsgeschichte . . . Die redaktionsgeschichtliche Arbeit versteht jedes Evangelium als einen ganzheitlichen Entwurf, der eine bestimmte theologische Konzeption vertritt. Sie fragt darum gerade nach dem Gesamtzeugnis des einzelnen Evangeliums und nach seiner spezifischen kerygmatischen Intention. Daraus ergibt sich ein profiliertes Bild seiner Eigenart." See also Strecker, "Die Leidens- und Auferstehungsvoraussagen im Markusevangelium," 16.

the *redaktionsgeschichtlich* work of the Evangelist we are quite independent of form-critical research, because in Mark we already possess the source. It seems clear, therefore, that to place *Redaktionsgeschichte* as a subdivision of form criticism would be quite erroneous in that at times they are almost entirely independent. Furthermore we shall later see that these two disciplines have only the first step of form criticism in common.[47] It is best then to view form criticism and *Redaktionsgeschichte* as two independent areas of study even though at times they may be interrelated. We should limit by definition form criticism to the investigation of the oral forms of the tradition and not include in form criticism the investigation of the particular use and interpretation of these traditions by the Evangelist.

It is apparent then that Marxsen is essentially correct. *Redaktionsgeschichte* is the attempt to arrive at the third *Sitz im Leben*, that is, it is the attempt to ascertain the unique theological purpose or purposes, views, and emphases that the Evangelists have imposed upon the materials available to them. It would be an error to define *Redaktionsgeschichte* as simply the attempt to arrive at the theology of the Evangelists. Marcan, Matthean, and Lukan theology differ from Pauline theology in that the latter involves all that the apostle believed. *Redaktionsgeschichte* seeks not the total theology of the Evangelists but primarily their uniqueness in relation to their sources.[48] We are not concerned in the case of Matthew and Luke primarily with what they believe in common with Mark. Our interest lies primarily in how they differ. Pauline theology, on the other hand, is not concerned primarily with the investigation of the sources used, changed, omitted, or uniquely stressed by the apostle.[49] It is concerned with the totality of what Paul believed. Here our

47. See below pp. 33–34. Marxsen (*Der Evangelist Markus,* 12) says, concerning the first step of form criticism (the isolation of the Evangelist's redaction from the tradition), "An diesem Punkt zeigt sich die grosse Nähe der Redaktionsgeschichte zur Formgeschichte."

48. Best (*Temptation and the Passion,* x) is therefore imprecise when he says with regard to the investigation of a Marcan *Redaktionsgeschichte,* "We may state our problem somewhat differently by saying that we are seeking to determine the Markan kerugma."

49. The reason for this different interest is due to the fact that, whereas the apostle's words can only be traced to sources in a few instances, the Evangelists' words are derived primarily from their sources.

task is simpler.[50] We can simply study the Pauline epistles as they are without searching for his sources. For the totality of what the Evangelists believed we would only have to study the totality of their work. *Redaktionsgeschichte* would be useful in helping us to ascertain "part" of what the Evangelists believed. This "part" could, of course, involve the purpose of the Evangelist in writing his Gospel, but it would still be only a "part." In *redaktionsgeschichtlich* studies, however, this "part"[51] has become the focal point of attention. We are not primarily concerned with all that the Evangelists believed. Rather we are concerned with ascertaining the unique contribution to and understanding of the sources by the Evangelists. This will be found in their seams, interpretative comments, summaries, modification of material, selection of material, omission of material, arrangement, introductions, conclusions, vocabulary, Christological titles, and the like.[52] In the *redaktionsgeschichtlich* investigation of the Gospels we do not seek primarily the theology of the Evangelist's sources, as form criticism does, but having ascertained the Evangelist's redaction we seek to answer the following questions. (1) *What unique theological views does the Evangelist present that are foreign to his sources?* *Redaktionsgeschichte* is not primarily concerned with any unique literary style or arrangement that an Evangelist may have used. It seeks rather the unique theological views of the Evangelist. An example of this is the twofold division of Galilee–Jerusalem found in Mark. If this is due to literary and stylistic motives, *Redaktionsgeschichte* is not involved. If this scheme is due to a theological motive, however, then *Redaktionsgeschichte* is very much involved. (2) *What unusual theological emphasis or emphases does the Evangelist place upon the sources he received?* An Evangelist may give to his sources an emphasis that is not necessarily a de novo creation. The Evangelist reveals his *Redaktionsgeschichte* in this instance by the unusual stress he places upon a certain theme found in the tradition. An example of this is the "messianic secret" found

50. The present writer does not mean to imply that Pauline theology is "simple."

51. Since this "part" involves the purpose of the Evangelist, it is clear that *Redaktionsgeschichte* is not concerned only with minutiae.

52. For a detailed discussion of the means for ascertaining a Marcan *Redaktionsgeschichte*, see Stein, "Ascertaining a Marcan Redaction History," pp. 49–67.

in Mark.[53] (3) *What theological purpose or purposes does the Evangelist have in writing his Gospel?*[54] (4) *What is the* Sitz im Leben *out of which the Evangelist writes his Gospel?* It is hoped that the results of (1) and (2) can be systematized, so that the purpose and *Sitz im Leben* of the Evangelist can be ascertained. This will not always be so. Some of the Evangelists' *Redaktionsgeschichte* will concern peripheral matters, for not every change or stress will involve a major problem, concern, or purpose of the Evangelists. As a result some of the results of (1) and (2) may at times not be of great importance or relevance for (3) and (4).

We may conclude our definition of *Redaktionsgeschichte* by saying that *Redaktionsgeschichte* seeks to discover the qualitative and quantitative uniqueness that distinguishes the Evangelists from their sources, and, having ascertained these, it then seeks to ascertain the *Sitz im Leben* out of which each Evangelist wrote and the particular purposes for which he wrote his Gospel.

The Proper Procedure to Follow in the Investigation of the Gospels

The important question must be raised here as to what the first task of the exegete is in the study of the Gospels. In the debate over whether form criticism or *Redaktionsgeschichte* is the first task of the exegete, scholars have lost sight of the fact that all *Traditionsgeschichte* overlaps. All *redaktionsgeschichtlich* and form-critical studies involve in one way or another literary criticism, and literary criticism involves similarly form-critical and *redaktionsgeschichtlich* investigation.[55] It is fallacious

53. Wrede himself argued that the "messianic secret" was already contained in part in the sources Mark used. This has been further demonstrated. See Burkill, "Hidden Son of Man," 189–213; Schweizer, "Zur Frage des Messiasgeheimnisses bei Markus," 1–8; and Sjöberg, *Der Verborgene Menschehsohn.* For an attempt to deny that the "messianic secret" was at least in part pre-Marcan, see Strecker, "Zur Messiasgeheimnistheorie im Markusevangelium," 3:96.

54. If the writers were only *Sammler*, although there could be a number of practical reasons for having written their Gospels (to keep the traditions from becoming lost, a desire to collect the traditions into one corpus, etc.), there would be for the most part only one theological purpose for writing them. This would be to gather together the traditions because of the delay of the parousia.

55. One of the reasons often given for a Marcan priority is that the theology of Mark is more "primitive" than that of Matthew and Luke. When we argue in this manner we are discussing the way the later Evangelists "redacted" their source.

therefore to think that any of these areas of Gospel research can exist independently of the others or deserves preeminence over the others. Each has its own right for existence, and each works together with the others in the investigation of the Gospels.

The question of whether form-critical investigation is to precede *redaktionsgeschichtlich* investigation is much debated.[56] Do we seek first to arrive at the oral stage or do we investigate the work of the final redactor first? How can we investigate the redaction of the Evangelists unless we first of all ascertain the oral traditions that they used? On the other hand, did not Bultmann obtain his "laws" of the oral tradition by first of all investigating the Matthean and Lukan redaction of Mark? Can these two tasks really be separated? Conzelmann has argued that form-critical investigation must precede *redaktionsgeschichtlich* investigation. Therefore form criticism is the first task of the exegete.[57] Long ago Johannes Weiss argued that *Redaktionsgeschichte* is the first task of the exegete.[58] The debate has been vigorous. Koch,[59] Joachim Rohde,[60] Gerhard Ibers,[61] Klein,[62] and Schille[63] agree with Conzelmann, but Austin Farrer[64] and Sherman E. Johnson[65] agree with Weiss. On the other hand, Marxsen[66] maintains that form-critical and *redaktionsgeschichtlich* investigation must be simultaneous. This diversity of opinion is due to each of these scholars having overlooked the fact that these scientific disciplines overlap. It should be remembered that form criticism involves the following steps: (1) isolation of the tradition from the editorial redaction; (2) classification of

56. Austin Farrer stated the problem clearly even before the work of Marxsen and Conzelmann. In his *A Study of St. Mark*, 21, he stated, "Has the man who wishes to understand the unity of thought and plan in the Gospels to wait for the form-critics to do their work, and to go on from there, or is it they, on the contrary, who have to wait for him, and take the question up as he leaves it?"

57. Conzelmann, *Die Mitte der Zeit*, 12.

58. Weiss, *Die Schriften des Neuen Testaments*, 62. See above note 9.

59. Koch, *Was Ist Formgeschichte?* 62 nn. 1, 71.

60. Rohde, *Die redaktionsgeschichtliche Methode*, 22.

61. Ibers, "Zur Formgeschichte der Evangelien," 338.

62. Klein, *Die Zwölf Apostel*, 16.

63. Schille, "Der Mangel eines kritischen Geschichtsbildes," 492.

64. Farrer, *Study in St. Mark*, 23.

65. Johnson, *Theology of the Gospels*, 21.

66. Marxsen, *Der Evangelist Markus*, 10.

the material according to types; (3) determination of the *Sitz im Leben* out of which the material came; and (4) the historical-critical evaluation of the individual pericopes. Once the Synoptic Problem has been resolved, we can proceed to the *redaktionsgeschichtlich* investigation of Mark immediately after the first step of form criticism—separation of the oral units from the redaction of the Evangelists—has been accomplished. In other words, the first step of *Redaktionsgeschichte* is the same as the first step of form criticism in the investigation of Mark, M, and L. Both must first isolate the redaction of the Evangelists.[67] After this is done each discipline concentrates upon its own interests. Form criticism "sets aside" the redaction and concentrates its investigation upon the tradition, whereas *Redaktionsgeschichte* "sets aside" the tradition and concentrates its investigation upon the redaction. It is evident therefore that the relationship between form criticism and *Redaktionsgeschichte* is not a simple first step–second step process. It is more like walking along a common path until one's particular interests bring one to a fork in the path. When one comes to the fork one must then decide whether to take one path or the other. The common path both disciplines must walk involves the separation of the tradition from the redaction of the Evangelist. What to do next brings us to the fork in the road. If we decide to investigate the tradition, we must pursue form-critical studies. If we decide to investigate the redaction, we shall then pursue *redaktionsgeschichtlich* studies.

---

67. This is more true in certain areas of investigation (such as the investigation of the seams, insertions, and summaries of the Evangelists) than in others (such as the arrangement of the pericopes). Yet even in the latter instance, by our assumption that the pericopes existed for the most part as isolated units and that the arrangement is due to the Evangelist, we have "isolated" the tradition from the editorial redaction.

2

Luke 1:1–4 and
Tradition Criticism

Of all the canonical Gospel writers, Luke alone discusses the methodology used in the composition of his Gospel. His prologue therefore is the most explicit statement available as the transmission of the Gospel traditions from the time of the historical Jesus to their incorporation into Luke's Gospel. Scholars would of course like to have had Luke elaborate and comment a great deal more on the subject and to have been more explicit, but our disappointment over the brevity of Luke's statement should not cause us to forget how fortunate we are that he commented at all. Despite its brevity the Lukan prologue provides us with much useful material that enables us to understand what took place during the second and third *Sitze im Leben* of the Gospel tradition.

The prologue itself ranks among the very best Greek literature of the first century. In style and vocabulary it is similar to other writings of the day, and this along with the non-Lukan nature of much of the vocabulary[1] reveals that we have in the Lukan

---

1. Four terms in the prologue are *hapax legomena* in the New Testament: ἐπειδήπερ, ἀνατάξασθαι, διήγησιν, and αὐτόπται. Two additional terms in the

35

prologue a conventional form of introduction that was rather common in Luke's day.[2] The purpose of this chapter is to investigate the Lukan prologue in order to see what light it may shed on the *Traditionsgeschichte* of the Gospel materials. The prologue itself consists of three parts. The first, consisting of verses 1–2, is an explanatory clause in which Luke informs Theophilus of his predecessors in the history of the Gospel traditions; the second, consisting of verse 3, is the main clause of the prologue in which Luke gives his "credentials" for writing his Gospel; and the third, consisting of verse 4, is a purpose clause in which Luke informs Theophilus of his purpose in writing the Gospel of Luke.[3] In this chapter we shall deal with each of these sections selectively and briefly.

The Lukan Predecessors (Verses 1 and 2)

"Inasmuch as many have undertaken to compile a narrative." In the opening words of the prologue Luke speaks of those who have written on the subject before him. Several things should be observed with regard to these opening words. One important issue involves the term πολλοί (many). Does this expression suggest that before Luke "dozens" of people had already written a "life of Christ"? Can we limit "many" to only a couple of sources such as "Mark" and "Q" as the two-source hypothesis suggests, or to "Mark," "Q," "L," and "M" as the four-source hypothesis suggests?[4] Of cardinal importance to this question is the fact that πολλοί and its related expressions appear frequently

---

prologue—πεπληροφορημένων and παρηκολουθηκότι—are found nowhere else in Luke–Acts.

2. See Cadbury, "Preface of Luke," 2:492–510; Du Plessis, "Once More," 259–63; Dillon, "Previewing Luke's Project," 205–6. Perhaps the best example by way of comparison is Josephus, *Jewish War* 1.17. Cadbury, "Preface of Luke," 490, states concerning the Lukan prologue that "its very brevity is an admirable illustration of obedience to ancient maxims on preface writing."

3. It is generally acknowledged that Luke–Acts is better understood as two parts of a single work than as two separate but related works. As a result it is probable that the Lukan prologue alludes at times to the Book of Acts as well. Nevertheless in the light of verses 1–2 it would seem reasonable to conclude that the Lukan prologue has primarily the Gospel of Luke in mind. See Schneider, "Der Zweck des lukanischen Doppelwerks," 47–48. For the view that the Lukan prologue does not in any way refer to Acts, see Haenchen, *Acts of the Apostles,* 136 n. 3.

4. So Dillon, "Previewing Luke's Project," 207.

in rhetorical prefaces. We can see this conventional usage of the term in the New Testament (Acts 24:2, 10; Heb. 1:1; John 20:30; 21:25), the intertestamental literature (Wisdom—prologue), the early church fathers, Josephus (*Jewish War* 1.17), and secular Greek literature.[5] Its use in general introductory formulas indicates that it functioned as a *topos* and that we should therefore beware of placing too great an emphasis on this word. The fact that Luke is using a stylistic convention in his prologue with regard to both vocabulary and style demands this. What is clear is that before Luke wrote his Gospel, others had also written similar accounts. Unfortunately just how many there were is uncertain. Some scholars have suggested that three would have been sufficient for Luke to use πολλοί,[6] but it seems wisest at this point to confess that we simply cannot be certain as to how many predecessors are to be included in the "many" of the prologue.

Another important term in this clause is ἐπεχείρησαν (undertaken). Does this imply that Luke sees these former attempts as having been unsuccessful and that he is seeking to remedy this? Support for such a view can be found in the fact that Luke uses this term in only two other instances (Acts 9:29; 19:13), and both describe unsuccessful attempts. Such an interpretation of this term has an ancient history that dates back at least to Origen.[7] Most scholars today, however, reject a pejorative interpretation of the term and tend to interpret it either positively or at least in a neutral way.[8] This is due to at least four reasons. First, the term also appears to be a *topos* or conventional term used in literary introductions,[9] and as such it was frequently used in a positive or neutral sense. More important still is the fact that Luke associates his own work with that of his predecessors by the κἀμοί (to me also) of verse 3. κἀμοί in this verse is clearly not a reproach of these other attempts but rather

---

5. See Cadbury, "Preface of Luke," 492–93; Du Plessis, "Once More," 261; and especially Bauer, "ΠΟΛΛΑΙ," 263–66.

6. See ibid., 266.

7. Dillon, "Previewing Luke's Project," 207.

8. Ibid., 207–8. Moulton and Milligan, *Vocabulary of the Greek Testament*, 251, after listing a number of examples of the use of this term in the papyri, state: "These examples show that any idea of failure, though often suggested by the context, does not lie in the verb itself." See also Glöckner, *Die Verkündigung*, 11–12.

9. Du Plessis, "Once More," 261–62.

an identification of Luke with them. Perhaps the most important factor that will decide the issue, however, is the question of how one "solves" the Synoptic Problem. If Luke did make use of some of these other attempts such as the two- or four-source hypothesis suggests, then a pejorative interpretation of the verb must be rejected. Finally, the positive attitude of Luke toward the witnesses and ministers of the word found elsewhere in Luke and Acts (see Acts 1:8, 22; 2:32; 3:15; 26:16) means that Luke 1:2 must be understood positively, and this in turn means that Luke 1:1 must be understood positively.

One final term that should be discussed in this section is διήγησιν (narrative). Attempts have been made to distinguish between a "narrative" and a "proclamation." Some scholars have suggested that whereas Mark is a Gospel of proclamation and therefore "kerygmatic," Luke is a Gospel of narration or "salvation history," and thus Luke is guilty of the sin of "historicizing" the gospel. Such an interpretation, however, is based not on exegesis but on an existential hermeneutic whose bias ignores the fact that the verbs "to narrate" (διηγέομαι) and "to preach" (κηρύσσω) are used interchangeably by Luke. This is most evident in Luke 8:39, where the Gergesene maniac is told to "narrate" what God has done for him and goes out "preaching" how Jesus healed him.[10]

"Of the things that have been accomplished among us." The "things" referred to in this clause can be interpreted as a reference to the Old Testament prophecies fulfilled in the life of Christ that the Gospel of Luke records and to the events in the life of the church to which Acts refers. The expression "have been accomplished" (πεπληροφορημένων) then would best be translated "have been fulfilled." It seems better, however, not to restrict the definition of "things" so narrowly but to include with the theme of Old Testament fulfillment[11] all the events of Jesus' life as well, for Luke did not distinguish between them.[12] Furthermore, if the teachings of Jesus found in the Gospel came, in part at least, from the sources mentioned in

10. See Dillon, "Previewing Luke's Project," 208–9.
11. That this is an important theme in Luke is evident from the following: Luke 4:16–21; 18:31; 22:37; Acts 2:16–21, 25–31, 34–36; 3:18–26; 10:43; 13:27, 29, 32–37, 40–41.
12. Du Plessis, "Once More," 263. See also Acts 3:24; 10:43; 13:27.

this verse, these teachings could not be included in any narrow interpretation of the fulfillment of Old Testament promises.

Closely related to this issue is the meaning of the expression "have been accomplished." The term can mean "have been completed or experienced" among us. This would then imply that Luke was claiming to be a personal witness of these things either in the sense of participation in the "we sections" of Acts, or in the events recorded in the Gospel of Luke, or both.[13] One problem with this view is the fact that the subject of the verb is not Luke, however, but rather the "many" already referred to. Furthermore, what value would participation in the events recorded in Acts be for establishing the "certainty" of the accounts recorded in the Gospel? Verse 2 even more clearly forces us to reject such an interpretation, for here Luke distinguishes between these events and himself. The events are not contemporaneous with him but predate his own experience of the Christian faith and even the passing on of those traditions. The term "accomplished" is best understood therefore as an intensive synonym for πληρόω and as referring to the events that have taken place in the church's experience of the coming of Christ (no doubt in fulfillment of the Old Testament) whose salvific effects and consequences still remain.

"Just as they were delivered to us." It is important to note that "delivered" (παρέδοσαν) is a technical term used to describe the passing on of authoritative tradition.[14] Despite the various weaknesses present in the theories of Harald Riesenfeld and Birger Gerhardsson,[15] probably the most helpful analogy available of how the "delivering process" proceeded is the rabbinic model they espouse.

The interpretation of the "us" in verses 1–2 is somewhat debated. If they refer to the same group, this causes several difficulties. The second "us" is clearly a group separated from the events themselves, for why would these "things" be delivered to a group who personally witnessed them? The "us" of verse 2

13. πεπληροφορημένων can also mean "to be fully believed" as Rom. 4:21; 14:5; Col. 4:12 reveal, but one would expect the present tense if such were the case in the Lukan prologue.

14. See Mark 7:13; Acts 6:14, 1 Cor. 11:2, 23; 15:3; 2 Pet. 2:21; Jude 3. The term refers much more readily to the Gospel traditions found in Luke than to the Book of Acts and whatever sources may have been used therein.

15. Riesenfeld, *Gospel Tradition*; Gerhardsson, *Memory and Manuscript*.

is therefore clearly removed from the actual events, in that they were neither "eyewitnesses" nor the "many" who had written. The first "us," however, is involved in the "events" or "things" that have been fulfilled. One attempt to resolve this issue is to interpret the "things fulfilled" as referring to the events of the Book of Acts. By so doing the term "us" can refer to the same specific group of people who have witnessed the fulfillment of these things in the post-Pentecost situation and have also had the pre-Pentecost traditions delivered to them. A better resolution of the problem, however, is to interpret the two uses of "us" in a broader way as referring to the Christian church as a whole. This would enable one to interpret the "things fulfilled among us," as we have done above, as referring to the events of the new covenant that have taken place in the coming of Christ (the first "us") and in which the church now shares personally (the second "us") through the eyewitnesses. Understood in this broad corporate sense, the term "us" can be both specifically different and yet broadly the same.[16]

"By those who from the beginning were eyewitnesses and ministers of the word." Two major issues present themselves in this passage. The first involves the designation "eyewitnesses and ministers of the word" (οἱ ἀπ' ἀρχῆς αὐτόπται καὶ ὑπηρέται), and the second involves the relation of the participle "were" (γενόμενοι) to these two terms. With regard to the latter question the phrase can be interpreted in two ways: (1) "those who were from the beginning eyewitnesses and ministers of the word," or (2) "those who were eyewitnesses from the beginning and became ministers of the word." In respect to the latter interpretation it can be argued that if Luke wanted to say (1) he could have used ὄντες, which would have fit better. His use of γενόμενοι fits the second possibility better. H. J. Cadbury, however, remarks: "The fact that *ginesthai* is almost invariably used in Greek writers with *autoptēs* favours assigning the participle to both nouns rather than merely to the nearest."[17] One other argument in favor of the first reading is the way the terms "servant" and "witness" are related in Acts 26:16. The total expression "servant and witness," which refers to the same person, goes with the relative pronoun (ὧν) that follows, and this style is much like

16. See Marshall, *Gospel of Luke*, 41, for a similar view.
17. Cadbury, "Preface of Luke," 498.

what we find in Luke 1:2. It seems best therefore to translate γενόμενοι as "were" and to connect it to both of the nouns that make up the expression.[18]

The use of the single article for both "eyewitnesses" and "ministers" indicates that Luke is referring to a single group of people. Cadbury points out that Luke's use of "eyewitness" in contrast to "witness" emphasizes the actual presence of such people at the events whose traditions they were delivering.[19] This seems to be a valid conclusion even though the term is somewhat a *topos* in historical works.[20] The claim to be an eyewitness "from the beginning" should not be pressed, however, to include such events as recorded in Luke 1–2 but should be understood in the sense of Acts 1:21–22—the beginning of Jesus' ministry, which Luke locates in his baptism.[21] As in the case of the secular historians, by his use of the term "eyewitness" Luke no doubt sought to gain credence from his readers as to the truthfulness of the events recorded in his Gospel, for these eyewitnesses "could not but speak of what they had seen and heard" (Acts 4:20). It has rightly been pointed out that this group cannot be limited to the Twelve alone,[22] for Luke sees the group of eyewitnesses as more inclusive than that (as is evident from Luke 6:12–13). No doubt Luke would have included in this group the seventy mentioned in Luke 10:1–2, and perhaps others such as Paul and Stephen. It should be noted, however, that Paul is described in similar language in Acts 26:16, but instead of the expression "eyewitness and minister" the expression used for Paul is "minister and witness." There may be here a conscious distinction between Paul and the eyewitnesses on the part of Luke. Even if, however, the expression "eyewitnesses and ministers of the word" cannot be narrowed down to mean the "Twelve," it still remains true that for Luke the

18. It is furthermore difficult to believe that in Luke's mind the followers of Christ became ministers of the word only after Pentecost, for in Luke 24:48 the disciples are called "witnesses," which in Acts 26:16 is a synonym for "minister," and the promise of the Holy Spirit is still future in Luke 24:48. Also it is difficult to understand what the seventy were doing in Luke 10:1–2 if they were not ministers of the word.

19. Cadbury, "Preface of Luke," 499.

20. Du Plessis, "Once More," 265.

21. See Acts 10:36–37.

22. Dillon, "Previewing Luke's Project," 216–17; see also Glöckner, *Die Verkündigung,* 21–23.

Twelve are par excellence "the eyewitnesses and ministers of the word." One cannot help seeing them as standing in the forefront of this group.

The Main Clause (Verse 3)

"It seemed good to me also, having followed all things closely for some time past." With verse 3 Luke begins the second and main clause of the prologue. Here Luke shares with Theophilus his procedure in writing his Gospel. The *crux interpretum* in the entire prologue centers around the phrase "having followed all things closely for some time past." The use of the aorist "seemed" could be interpreted to mean that Luke appended the prologue to his Gospel after he had written the entire work, but Cadbury's suggestion that the aorist refers here to Luke's decision to write, rather than to the actual writing itself, seems more correct.[23] The term "followed" can mean a number of things: (1) the studying or reading of the various narratives referred to in verse 1 (the "things" as they were handed down); (2) having become acquainted with the events that had happened (the "things" as they had happened); (3) having participated in the events themselves.[24] The decision of how to interpret this word depends on a number of issues. One involves how to interpret ἄνωθεν. Should it be translated "for some time past" or "from the beginning"? Is the purpose of Luke in his prologue to show the duration or length of his research (i.e., he followed or investigated for a long time), or to show the extent or scope of his research (i.e., he followed or investigated from the beginning)? In other literature ἄνωθεν is frequently used to mean either.[25] The term appears only one other time in Luke–Acts. In Acts 26:5 Paul tells Agrippa that the Jews have known his Hebraic background "from the beginning." This example is interesting in that the preceding verse contains the prepositional phrase ἀπ' ἀρχῆς, which we likewise find in the verse preceding Luke 1:3. It does not appear that certainty can be reached as to how to interpret this term in the prologue.

23. Cadbury, "Preface of Luke," 500–501.
24. Ibid., 501–2; cf. also Du Plessis, "Once More," 267. Higgins, "Preface to Luke," 82, seeks to combine all three possibilities in Luke's use of the term.
25. See Moulton and Milligan, *Vocabulary of the Greek Testament,* 50.

Scholarship is divided on this issue.[26] To the present writer the context suggests that Luke is primarily concerned in the prologue not so much with telling Theophilus how long he has researched this material but rather with his having covered the entire scope of the subject. The fact that he begins his Gospel immediately after the prologue with the birth narratives supports this view, for certainly this is the story of Jesus "from the beginning." The heavily Semitic nature of Luke 1:5–2:52 also seems to indicate that the "things fulfilled among us" that Luke investigated involved Semitic sources that contained this "from the beginning" kind of material. In light of this it may even be that ἄνωθεν surpasses in scope the ἀπ' ἀρχῆς of Luke 1:2.[27]

"All things" in turn is best understood as referring to the "things accomplished among us" in Luke 1:1. In light of this it would seem best to paraphrase this section as follows: "It seemed good to me as well since I have investigated from the beginning with care[28] all these events and the narratives others have written." This seems the best interpretation of these words, for Luke clearly did not participate in the events of Luke 1–2. The use of ἀκριβῶς (with care), which goes with the participle rather than the infinitive "write," also favors this interpretation, since one cannot participate "with care" whereas one can investigate "with care."[29] Luke's mention of the other written (and oral) accounts of these events in verses 1–2 seems to imply that he has made use of or read them, for to say what he does in verses 1–2 and then conclude "but I paid no attention to them" would clearly have caused a loss of confidence in his own account on the part of his reader(s). Luke "investigated" these things in the sense of having both read carefully what others had written as well as investigating on his own, when possible, the accounts found in his Gospel.[30]

26. In favor of the idea of duration ("for a long time") we can list the RSV and Marshall, *Gospel of Luke,* 43; in favor of the idea of extent ("from the beginning") we can list the NIV; Dillon, "Previewing Luke's Project," 218–19; Kümmel, *Introduction to the New Testament,* 179.

27. So Dillon, "Previewing Luke's Project," 218–19; Schürmann, *Traditionsgeschichtliche Untersuchungen zu den synoptischen Evangelien,* 258; Klein, "Lukas I, 1–4 als theologisches Programm," 208.

28. See Acts 18:25–26; 23:15, 20; 24:22.

29. So Kümmel, *Introduction to the New Testament,* 179.

30. Traditional scholarship has frequently associated such verses as Luke 2:51 with Luke's own "investigative reporting."

"To write an orderly account for you, most excellent Theophilus." Having investigated carefully all these things from the beginning, Luke then sought to write "an orderly account" (καθεξῆς). Here again we have a problem as to exactly what this term means. Generally the term refers to some sort of a sequence or order, but this can be (1) a geographical or temporal sequence (Luke 8:1), (2) a temporal sequence (Acts 3:24), (3) a geographical sequence (Acts 18:23), or (4) a logical sequence (Acts 11:4). The latter is found in the fact that Peter in Acts 11:15 states that the Spirit came upon Cornelius *as* he began to speak, whereas in Acts 10:44–45 the Spirit came *after* Peter had spoken for some time. This indicates that Luke's "sequence" in Acts 11:4 is logical rather than temporal. Since the term καθεξῆς can at times refer to a logical rather than a chronological sequence and since "Luke's actual procedure may seem to rule out the idea of chronological exactitude,"[31] it appears best to interpret "orderly" here as a synonym for "organized" or "logical."

The Purpose of Luke (Verse 4)

"That you may know the truth concerning the things of which you have been informed." In this the third and final section of the prologue, Luke gives his purpose for writing his Gospel. Again our interpretation of this section is not self-contained but dependent on our conclusions as to how the previous section is to be interpreted. If the "orderly" nature of Luke's account involves chronological precision, then Luke seeks to convince Theophilus of the factual exactness of the chronological data as well as its theological exactness. On the other hand if the "orderly" nature of Luke's account refers to a logical precision, then it is more likely that Luke is seeking to convince Theophilus of the truthfulness of the data concerning the life of Christ, and this may not always involve chronological exactness. (In other words some material may be arranged in Luke on a basis other than chronology.) To claim that Luke is not interested in the historical facts or events recorded in his Gospel but only with their kerygmatic value, however, would be to go too far. Such a distinction is frequently found among twentieth-century existentialists, but such a distinction between

31. Marshall, *Gospel of Luke,* 43.

Historie and *Geschichte* would not only be denied by Luke; it would probably not have been understood by him.

One final issue that must be dealt with in verse 4 is the verb "taught" (κατηχήθης). The term can mean "to report (or inform)" or "to instruct."[32] If the latter is intended by Luke, then Theophilus was a Christian. In favor of the former view, however, is the fact that in Acts 21:21, 24 the same verb is used with the preposition περί just as we have in Luke 1:4, and here the verb clearly means "to inform." It is probably best therefore to interpret the verb in Luke 1:4 in a similar manner.

Conclusion

Having investigated rather hurriedly the Lukan prologue, we must now seek to ascertain what the prologue may say concerning the various disciplines of literary criticism, form criticism, redaction criticism, the quest for the *ipsissima verba,* and *Traditionsgeschichte* in general. We must be careful in this regard not to read into the text personally cherished and/or critically accepted conclusions. We must also be aware that the prologue may be ambiguous on certain issues and silent on others. What then can we learn concerning the history of the Gospel materials from the Lukan prologue?

First, Luke knew of at least three separate situations or *Sitze im Leben* of the Gospel materials. These are (1) the situation of the events themselves—the situation of the historical Jesus in which the "things fulfilled among us" took place: (2) the situation in which the eyewitnesses "delivered" orally these things; and (3) the situation in which others wrote down these "things delivered by the eyewitnesses" and to which Luke and his work belong.

Several other things can be mentioned with regard to these three *Sitze im Leben.* Luke's own perception of the oral period is that the process of the transmission of the materials was carried out by eyewitnesses. We have already pointed out that this group cannot be limited to the Twelve, but it must also be pointed out that the term "eyewitness," although a common term in literary introductions, must be taken quite seriously in the Lukan prologue due to the qualifying "from the begin-

---

32. The words "catechism," "catechize," and the like, come from this Greek term.

ning." For Luke, it is quite clear that if a choice has to be made for the bearers of the oral tradition between the "anonymous herd" of the radical form critics and the "collegium of the Jerusalem apostles" of the Swedish school, the latter would clearly be Luke's choice.

It should also be pointed out that to see in the other narratives that Luke has followed or researched either the two-source (Mark and Q) or the four-source (Mark, Q, L, and M) hypotheses is illegitimate, for Luke is simply not specific enough. On the other hand Luke does refer to the investigation of and most probably the use of written sources, and this lends credence to such theories. Clearly such theories of literary dependence on the part of the Evangelists can be neither ignored nor condemned by evangelical scholarship, for Luke, if our exegesis is correct, acknowledges such a dependence.

One final comment must be made with regard to what Luke states concerning the various *Sitze im Leben*. Whereas Luke associates the eyewitnesses with the process of oral tradition in the second *Sitz im Leben*, he distinguishes them from the writers of that tradition in the third *Sitz im Leben*—that is, the "many" of verse 1. Luke knows of no apostle or eyewitness who has written a "narrative" of the Gospel events. This need not exclude apostolic participation in the writing of the Gospels of Matthew and John, but if they are apostolic in part or in the main it would imply that Luke did not know of them. If may be therefore that a Lukan dependence on Matthew, as posited in the Griesbach Hypothesis, can only be maintained on the assumption that Matthew is not apostolic in composition or that Luke was not aware of any apostolic association with that Gospel. On the other hand Luke's use of Mark and Q would not conflict with anything Luke says in the prologue.

A second helpful insight provided by the Lukan prologue is that both Luke and Theophilus were aware of and, at least in the case of Luke, acquainted with both the written and the oral traditions.[33] Gospel studies must become more aware of the fact that for a rather long period of time the Gospel traditions were circulating simultaneously in both oral and written form.

---

33. This is suggested by the ἐπειδήπερ of verse 1. BDF 238 (#456 [3]) states that the term in Luke 1:1 implies a fact already well known.

Papias likewise calls our attention to this fact.[34] No doubt during this period they mutually influenced each other. It may well be that the single most difficult problem facing the hypothesis of Marcan priority, that of the Matthew–Luke agreements against Mark, can best be explained by their independent use of a common oral tradition against Mark. There is a growing consensus that no solution of the Synoptic Problem will prove successful that does not take into consideration the coexistence of both the oral and written forms of the tradition. Luke tells us that he was acquainted with both, and no doubt both played a part in his writing of his Gospel.

A final insight that the prologue provides involves the issue of hermeneutics. Luke in his prologue tells us that he had a specific purpose for writing his Gospel. An evangelical hermeneutic must keep foremost in mind the purpose of the divinely inspired author. This indicates that redaction criticism—and here I mean primarily the aims and goals of the discipline, not the various presuppositions that certain scholars bring with them to it[35]—is not merely an option but a divine mandate for evangelical scholarship. Whatever the value and the legitimacy of the quest of the historical Jesus and the *ipsissima verba*, or source analysis, or form criticism, or *Traditionsgeschichte* in general, the primary hermeneutical goal of the evangelical scholar must always be to seek the verbal meaning of the divinely inspired author as it is revealed in the text. The constant question that the interpreter of the Gospel of Luke must ask himself is this: "How is Luke in this passage seeking to fulfill his divinely inspired purpose for writing this Gospel?" Here, too, the Lukan prologue can be of great help.

---

34. Here the famous quote of Papias found in Eusebius (*Hist. eccl.* 3.39) should be noted: "For I did not suppose that information from books would help me so much as the word of a living and surviving voice" (LCL).

35. To my listing of the goals of redaction criticism in "What Is Redaktionsgeschichte?" I would include under (3) what can be called "the theology of Luke"—that is, all that his Gospel teaches.

3

Ascertaining a Marcan Redaction History
The Proper Methodology

During recent decades two new emphases have dominated the investigation of the Gospel materials. One of these is the "new" quest of the historical Jesus. Receiving its initial impetus from the now famous lecture of Ernst Käsemann,[1] investigators have sought to establish some sort of continuity between the historical Jesus and the Christ of the kerygma. In so doing the "new" quest hopes that it possesses certain bulwarks[2] that will protect it from the errors of the nineteenth-century quests. The second new emphasis in Gospel studies is the *redaktionsgeschichtlich*[3] investigation of the Gospels. Whereas form criticism generally thought of the Evangelists as collectors and "scissors and paste men," Günther Bornkamm,[4] Hans Conzelmann,[5]

1. "Problem of the Historical Jesus."
2. See Jeremias, *Problem of the Historical Jesus,* 15f.
3. See the author's article, "What Is Redaction Criticism?" pp. 21–34 for a definition of this term.
4. Bornkamm's work is contained in *Tradition and Interpretation in Matthew,* which he co-authored with G. Barth and H. J. Held.
5. *Theology of St. Luke.*

49

and Willi Marxsen[6] demonstrated that they were more than
this. Each Evangelist was a theologian in his own right and
possessed a theological purpose for writing his Gospel. As a
result there has been much investigation of the particular the-
ologies of Matthew, Mark, and Luke. Although there has been
a great deal of *redaktionsgeschichtlich* investigation, the question of methodology has frequently been glossed over. Yet a
proper methodology is necessary. This is especially true with
regard to *redaktionsgeschichtlich* investigation of Mark. The purpose of this chapter is to list some of the means by which we
can ascertain a Marcan redaction history.

It is evident from the start that the investigation of a Marcan redaction history is much more difficult than the investigation of a Matthean or Lukan one.[7] The reason for this is
twofold. First, Mark nowhere expressly states his purpose for
writing his Gospel.[8] Second, we do not possess any of the sources
that Mark used, whereas for Matthew and Luke we possess Mark,
their main source,[9] and we can construct, to a certain extent,
the "Q" source that they used. In the case of Mark, however,
we lack any such source to use as a standard for comparison.
Yet such a standard is necessary. We must be able to ascertain
what the sources of Mark were like or else our ability to ascertain
a Marcan redaction history will be severely limited, for before we
proceed to the latter investigation, we must ascertain the Marcan
redaction and this can only be done by comparing Mark with the
sources he used. How then are we to determine what the sources
available to Mark were like? If we could go back in time and
look over the shoulder of the Evangelist to see what his sources
were like (let us assume for the sake of our illustration that the
sources of Mark were all written), our task would be considerably
easier. Unfortunately no such possibility exists. Nevertheless it is
possible, although difficult, by means of form-critical investigation to reconstruct to a certain extent the pre-Marcan tradition.
Having done this, we then can see how Mark joined, arranged,
modified, and selected the traditions available to him. Mark has

6. *Mark the Evangelist.*

7. This was clearly seen and stated already in 1908 by Nicolardot in his *Les
procédés de rédaction,* 215.

8. Cf. Luke 1:1–4 and John 20:31.

9. The present writer believes that Matthew and Luke used a copy of Mark
very much like the one we possess.

made our task more complicated, however, because he has "marcanized" the traditions, both oral and written, which were available to him. He has done this by retelling the traditions in his own words and in his own style. This is unfortunate because it makes the separation of the Marcan redaction from the pre-Marcan tradition all the more difficult.

The primary purpose of this chapter is to list the various ways in which Mark has edited the materials available to him. By the investigation of this editorial redaction we can then ascertain a Marcan redaction history. We cannot, of course, describe in detail the various areas of redaction, so that we shall have to content ourselves with simply listing them. Up to the present time this has not been done, and it is a pressing need.[10]

The Marcan Seams

One of the means most often used to ascertain a Marcan redaction history is the investigation of the Marcan seams.[11] It was because the region of Galilee was so frequently mentioned in the Marcan seams that Ernst Lohmeyer,[12] R. H. Lightfoot,[13] and Marxsen[14] argued for a unique Galilean emphasis and stress on the part of Mark. Ernest Best[15] argued from the frequency with which the terms διδάσκαλος, διδαχή, and διδάσκειν appear in the Marcan seams that the Evangelist desired to portray Jesus as a teacher rather than as an exorcist. The importance of the seams for ascertaining a Marcan redaction history has been recognized by almost all of the scholars interested in the investigation of the third *Sitz im Leben* of Mark.[16]

10. Strecker in his article, "Passion- and Resurrection Predictions," states that the methodological problem of redaction criticism has not yet been clearly presented for Mark and remains a matter of urgent importance.

11. Marxsen, *Mark the Evangelist*, 23, writes: "We grasp Mark's share of the work and thus his actual achievement (as well as that of the other evangelists) not in the material primarily but in the 'framework.'" See also Best, *Temptation and the Passion,* 63: "The most obvious place to look for Mark's hand is in the words, phrases, sentences which join together the various incidents of the Gospel."

12. *Galiläa und Jerusalem,* 26.

13. *Locality and Doctrine in the Gospels,* 112.

14. Marxsen, *Mark the Evangelist,* 54f.

15. Best, *Temptation and the Passion,* 71–72.

16. See Schweizer, *Das Evangelium nach Markus,* 4–5; Johnson, *Theology of the Gospels,* 21; Grundmann, *Die Geschichte Jesu Christi,* 15; Koch, *Growth of the Biblical Tradition,* 59.

The reason for this is that apart from certain pre-Marcan complexes[17] the material used by Mark existed as isolated pericopes. Although these pericopes must have had introductions of some sort, they did not possess seams uniting them to one another. In order to join these pericopes together Mark had either to create the seams we find in his Gospel or rework the original introductions that introduced the isolated pericopes. There may have been occasions when the introductions to the isolated pericopes would have served as seams, but frequently this would not have been so.

One means then by which we can ascertain a Marcan redaction history is by the investigation of how Mark joined the various materials available to him. The cement he used to bind these materials together reveals something of his own particular theological emphasis. Since we now recognize that the Evangelists were not scissors and paste men but theologians, it is obvious that the investigation of the way the Evangelists cemented together the various isolated materials available to them must reveal something of their unique theological interests.[18]

The Marcan Insertions

Another means by which we can ascertain a Marcan redaction history is by the investigation of the Marcan insertions or *Zwischenbemerkungen*. Two insertions that have frequently been discussed in this regard are Mark 14:28 and 16: 7. Lohmeyer[19] has argued that these two insertions by Mark refer to the parousia rather than the resurrection, and Marxsen[20] has argued from them that Mark wrote his Gospel to urge his readers to flee to Galilee in order to await the imminent parousia. Other scholars have also recognized the importance of investigating the Marcan insertions.[21] It is quite evident that when the Evangelist

17. We mean here "pre-Mark's Gospel" complexes. It may be that Mark himself was the author of certain of these complexes.

18. For further discussion, see the author's "A Seam in Mark (1:21–22): A Redactional Investigation," pp. 69–96.

19. Lohmeyer, *Galiläa und Jerusalem*.

20. Marxsen, *Mark the Evangelist*, 75f.

21. See Best, *Temptation and the Passion*, 9; Schweizer, *Der Evangelium nach Markus*, 5; Frör, *Wege zur Schriftauslegung*, 254.

inserts a statement into some tradition he does so in order to comment upon or explain that tradition to his readers. The investigation of this comment will therefore reveal something of the Evangelist's particular theology.

The Marcan Summaries

In the Gospel of Mark there frequently appear statements that summarize Jesus' activity, message, or fame. These summaries are extremely important for the investigation of a Marcan redaction history. Various scholars have pointed out the importance of the summaries for the *redaktionsgeschichtlich* investigation of Mark.[22] It is almost certain that the summaries found in Mark did not circulate independently during the oral period. This is especially true with regard to such brief summaries as Mark 1:28, 39; 2:13; and 6:6b. Since these summaries are not part of a pericope, for they are seldom essential to any pericope, their brevity makes their independent existence highly questionable. Most probably therefore they were composed by the Evangelist.

It has been argued that these summaries often contain traditional material. This is certainly true with regard to the larger summaries such as Mark 1:14–15; 3:7–12; 6:53–56; 9:30–32; and 10:32–34. Yet, even if these summaries contain traditional material, they are still helpful for our investigation because Mark had to compose them. In other words, in these summaries Mark did not simply write down a traditional pericope. He personally composed these summaries and selected the particular material that he wanted to insert into them. The summaries are therefore especially important for our investigation because even if they contain traditional material Mark had to create or compose them. They did not exist before him. He has selected, according to his own particular interests, those pieces of tradition that were important to him. His selection of material here is far more important than his selection of the individual pericopes that he wished to include in his Gospel, because the latter did not require the amount of creative activity comparable to the creation of the various summaries out of diverse traditional material.

22. See Best, *Temptation and the Passion*, 64; Schweizer, *Das Evangelium nach Markus*, 5; Marxsen, "Redaktionsgeschichtliche Erklärung," 258.

The Marcan Creation of Pericopes

It has already become evident that certain parts of the Gospel of Mark are due to the creative activity of the Evangelist. This has been apparent in our discussion of the Marcan seams, insertions, and summaries. If we could demonstrate that Mark created certain pericopes, this would be extremely helpful in ascertaining a Marcan redaction history.[23] The question that faces us, however, is not whether Mark created certain pericopes appearing in his Gospel (perhaps he did and perhaps he did not) but whether we are able to demonstrate that such and such a pericope was in fact the creation of Mark. This is the rub! If we seek to prove that Mark created a certain pericope, we are faced with five possibilities: (1) it was historically true; (2) it has a historical basis but was reworked by Mark; (3) it was created by the community; (4) it was created by the community and reworked by Mark; and (5) it was created by Mark. Historical criticism may be able to separate the first possibility from the remaining four, but the separation of the fifth possibility from the third, and especially the second and fourth possibilities is extremely difficult and probably impossible. It seems best therefore to look elsewhere than in the creation of various pericopes by the Evangelist for a means for ascertaining a Marcan redaction history.

The Marcan Modification of the Material

Another means by which we can ascertain a Marcan redaction history is by observing how the Evangelist modified the traditions he received. We have already referred to the modification of certain traditions by the creation or reworking of certain seams, insertions, and summaries. Here we are not concerned with the modification of the tradition in these areas. We are concerned rather with the changes made by the Evangelist to the pericopes and sayings he received in order that he might stress his own particular point of view. We would distinguish between a Marcan insertion and a Marcan modification of the material. The former refers to an additional statement that the

23. Winter ("Markus xiv 53b, 55–64") seeks to do just this. He states (p. 263): "Kein Traditionselement, auch kein sekundäres, sondern schriftstellerische Absicht liegt der Erzählung in Mc. xiv 53b, 55–64 zugrunde."

Evangelist has inserted into the material, whereas the latter refers to the changing of the audience, the situation, or certain words in the tradition in order to make the tradition say what he wanted it to.

The great difficulty facing us is that we must first ascertain the pre-Marcan tradition, so that by comparing it with Mark we can determine the Marcan redaction. Thereupon we can investigate the redaction in order to ascertain the redaction history of the Evangelist. The difficulty of ascertaining the pre-Marcan tradition is not to be minimized. The "marcanizing" of the pericopes by the Evangelist makes our task more difficult because some of our guides such as the vocabulary and style are not absolute but only relative. In other words, a Marcan vocabulary and style here as well as in the investigation of the seams, insertions, and summaries do not assure us of a Marcan redaction but only of the *possibility* of such a redaction.[24] The situation is not entirely hopeless, however, because several additional means of detecting the Marcan modification of the tradition are available.

The Comparison of Mark with Matthew and Luke

A frequent method used to ascertain the Marcan modification of the tradition is to compare Mark with the other Synoptic Gospels.[25] By such a comparison it is hoped that we can ascertain the pre-Marcan tradition. This is a difficult procedure

24. Lambrecht in his *Die Redaktion der Markus-Apokalypse*, 89, rightly comments, "Die gleiche Ansicht wird mit Recht ferner vorbringen, dass das *Markinische* eines Textes nicht ipso facto auf eine 'creatio' oder auf eine 'unhistorische Wiedergabe' schliessen lässt. Es ist doch (noch einmal!) normal und natürlich, das bei der Niederlegung des Traditionsgutes Markus spontan seinen Eigenen Stil schreibt! Es kann ohne weiteres zugegeben werden, dass die oft hervorgehobene markinische Wortwahl und seine Stileigenheit allein diese Frage nicht entscheiden können."

25. Schreiber in his article, "Die Christologie des Markus-evangeliums," 154, states, "Wo Matthäus oder Lukas oder gar beide Evangelisten den Markustext in einem bestimmten Punkt, womöglich über das ganze Evangelium hin, ändern, liegt sehr wahrscheinlich eine theologische Aussage des Markus vor, die sie ablehnen. Dieser Grundsatz gilt besonders dann, wenn festgestellt werden kann, dass ihre eigene Theologie der des Markus in diesen Punkt widerspricht." See also Marxsen, *Mark the Evangelist*, 124, who states with regard to his investigation of the term εὐαγγέλιον, "If we can establish that the synoptic material as a whole is not aware of the term εὐαγγέλιον (except for passages where Mark gives it or which are dependent on Mark), that at least indicates that the evangelist quite probably introduced the term into the tradition."

because in general the changes made by Matthew and Luke to their Marcan source reveal primarily a Matthean and Lukan redaction history and not a Marcan one.[26] There are times, however, when an agreement between Matthew and Luke against Mark may point to an older form of the tradition than contained in Mark. It may be in such an instance that Mark has modified the tradition that he received and that Matthew and Luke agree against Mark because they both reject the Marcan modification in favor of the pre-Marcan tradition with which they were both familiar. An example of this may be Mark 14:62 and parallels. A difficulty presents itself here, however. Could it be that the tradition Mark used already contained this "modification" whereas the tradition with which both Matthew and Luke were familiar did not? If this is the case, we are dealing with different forms of the tradition and not a Marcan redaction history.[27]

It is not necessary to limit our investigation of the Marcan modifications to the Matthew–Luke agreements against Mark. There are times when an Evangelist apparently changes Mark because he was familiar with a tradition that is more primitive than the tradition found in Mark.[28] In such an instance he may witness to a pre-Marcan tradition and thus reveal the Marcan redaction. The account of the wicked husbandmen in Luke (and the Gospel of Thomas) is seen by Jeremias[29] as being more primitive than the account in Mark 12:1–11. If this is true, the differ-

26. Because of this Schreiber is not entirely correct. When the particular theological viewpoints of Matthew and Luke clash with Mark, their change of Mark reveals not so much a Marcan redaction history as a Matthean and Lukan one.

27. The greatest single weakness of Lohmeyer's work is that he does not sufficiently distinguish between the Galilean tradition allegedly used by Mark and the Evangelist's own particular emphasis. Because of this we must conclude that although Lohmeyer at times alludes to the *redaktionsgeschichtlich* interests of the Evangelist, he was primarily concerned with the second *Sitz im Leben* or the form-critical investigation of the tradition. (See Marxsen, *Mark the Evangelist*, 28 n. 38.) It could, of course, be argued that if Mark possessed a Galilean tradition and a Jerusalem tradition and chose the one over the other that this would reveal his own theological emphasis. (This Lohmeyer in fact did. See *Galiläa und Jerusalem*, 98.) It would be difficult if not impossible, however, to demonstrate that an Evangelist possessed both traditions and chose one over the other.

28. Jeremias, *Parables of Jesus*, 70f., even compares Mark with the Gospel of Thomas in order to arrive at the more primitive tradition.

29. Ibid.

ence between the account in Mark and the account in Luke may be due to the *redaktionsgeschichtlich* interests of the Evangelist.[30]

It would appear therefore that the comparison of Matthew and Luke with Mark is a valid method by which we can ascertain the Marcan modification of the tradition. We must, however, keep uppermost in our minds the following considerations: (1) the changes of the Marcan account by Matthew and Luke witness primarily to a Matthean and Lukan redaction criticism rather than a Marcan one; (2) the changes made by Matthew and Luke may witness to their favoring a different tradition rather than the tradition Mark used and, if this is true, we are dealing primarily with form-critical problems and not *redaktionsgeschichtlich* ones; and (3) the alleged modification should possess a typically Marcan vocabulary, style, and theme and should be in agreement with the general Marcan scheme.

The Investigation of "Misformed" Pericopes

According to form criticism there existed certain "rules" or "laws" that supervised the transmission of the Gospel pericopes during the oral period. These "laws" tended to give to the oral material a particular shape and form. Divergence from this pure form may be due to the modification of the pericopes by the Evangelist. If a pericope therefore contains material that would have been difficult to transmit during the oral period, this may be due to a Marcan modification of the pericope. An example of this is Mark 11:27–33. The anacoluthon of verse 32 would have been impossible to transmit orally. It is therefore probably due to the hand of Mark. It would seem therefore that when a pericope is sufficiently "misformed," so that it would not have been able to be repeated as such during the oral period, we can legitimately claim that this pericope has undergone modification by the hand of the Evangelist.

The Investigation of the Inconsistency
Between Mark's Account and What Actually Happened

One of the first attempts to ascertain a Marcan redaction criticism, the attempt by William Wrede, sought to do so by

---

30. Unfortunately Jeremias does not investigate the significance of the Marcan redaction here, but this is not his purpose. This is a good example of how some form critics, once they ascertain the Evangelists' redaction, set aside the redaction and investigate only the tradition.

demonstrating an inconsistency between what Mark records and what actually happened.[31] Yet if by critical historical investigation this can actually be demonstrated, what have we in fact proven? We have demonstrated that there is an inconsistency between the first and third *Sitze im Leben or* between the first and the second *Sitze im Leben*. Merely demonstrating an inconsistency would not, however, demonstrate that this inconsistency is due to the modification of the tradition by the Evangelist. It may very well be due to a pre-Marcan modification. On the other hand such a demonstration is helpful in raising the possibility that such an inconsistency is due to the Evangelist, and if we were to discover a "consistent" inconsistency that portrays a Marcan vocabulary, style, theme, and the like, then the Evangelist may very well be the cause of this inconsistency.[32]

The Marcan Selection of Material

Another way in which the Evangelist reveals his theological emphases is by means of his selection of material.[33] It must be admitted from the start that Mark need not have chosen every pericope in his Gospel because it contained his particular theology or point of view. He may have included some simply because they were well known. Others stood in complexes that would have required him to excise them if he wanted to exclude them from his Gospel, and Mark apparently was inclined to use these complexes as whole units, so that the pericopes in such units appear in Mark even if they do not necessarily contain his own particular point of view or even conflict with his scheme. It should not be surprising therefore if occasionally

31. *Das Messiasgeheimnis in den Evangelien*, 46f. and 15.

32. Another method sometimes used to ascertain a Marcan redaction history is to observe the way Mark used "Q". (So Nicolardot, *Les procédés de rédaction*, 215–16; Larfield, *Die Neutestamentlichen Evangelien*, 251f.; Bacon, *Gospel of Mark*, 156f.; Grant, *Gospels*, 87). It would appear quite certain, however, that Mark did not know "Q" (see Streeter, *Four Gospels*, 186–91; Feine et al., *Introduction to the New Testament*, 55; and Throckmorton, "Did Mark Know Q," 327) so that this method is not valid.

33. See Schreiber, "Die Christologie des Markus-evangeliums," 155; Grundmann, *Das Evangelium nach Markus*, 15; Best, *Temptation and the Passion*, 103–11; Frör, *Biblische Hermeneutik*, 246; Rohde, *Rediscovering the Teaching of the Evangelists*, 14; Johnson, *Theology of the Gospels*, 21; Vögtle, "Was Heisst 'Auslegung der Schrift'?" 53; Steinmetz, "Literaturbericht," 64.

we find in Mark material contradicting somewhat his own particular emphases.[34] Nevertheless in general the selection of material made by Mark must of necessity reveal something of his own particular theological interests.

The Marcan Omission of Material

If the selection of material reveals something of the Evangelist's theological emphases, we can expect that the Gospel traditions that he chose to omit from his Gospel will also reveal something of his particular theological emphases. There is, however, a major difficulty in the use of this means for ascertaining a Marcan redaction history. Whereas we know what Mark chose to include in his Gospel, we do not have any certain way of knowing what he chose to exclude. We simply do not know what sources and materials Mark possessed.[35] As a result it is more difficult to ascertain a Marcan redaction history from what we do not find in the Gospel of Mark. Nevertheless this method does give some hints as to areas of the tradition that Mark chose not to stress. An example of this is the few exorcisms recorded in Mark. In his work, *The Problem of History in Mark*, James M. Robinson sought to demonstrate that Mark desired to portray Jesus as a victor over satanic powers. If this were the intention of Mark, however, we might expect to find a greater number of exorcisms in Mark. The lack of such stories weakens Robinson's thesis. One cannot place an inordinate amount of weight on this argument, however, because we do not know how many exorcism stories were available to Mark.

34. The position of Mark 2:19–20 seems contrary to the general scheme. According to the Marcan scheme we would expect to read of this reference to Jesus' death after Mark 8:31f. The reason that it appears "out of place" in Mark is no doubt due to the fact that it was already found in the pre-Marcan complex of Mark 2:1–3:6.

35. Best, *Temptation and the Passion*, 103, sees this problem clearly. He states, "If we knew that Mark had a great amount of material about the teaching of Jesus, say a 'copy' of Q and only three exorcism accounts, and chose to omit most of the teaching and put in all three exorcisms, this would obviously lead us to conclude that for him exorcisms were most important. Equally had he at his disposal only the teaching of Jesus which he has inserted and a hundred exorcism stories from which he selected the present three then we would come to quite a different conclusion about the importance of the exorcisms for Mark. Unfortunately we are not in a position to draw either conclusion."

This is, of course, the great unknown that weakens any argument based upon the Marcan omission of material.

The Marcan Arrangement of the Material

It has been recognized by many scholars that the arrangement that Mark gave to his material is due in part to his own particular theological emphasis.[36] The investigation of the Marcan arrangement is of great importance in ascertaining a Marcan redaction history. We are not concerned here primarily with the question of literary style but of the theological emphasis that results from the arrangement of the material. We must be aware at the start that a theological purpose need not lie at the root of every Marcan arrangement. At times an arrangement may be due to topical or even geographical considerations. Furthermore to a certain extent there existed a pre-Marcan arrangement of certain material. The extent to which this is true is debated. Certainly, however, the work of John the Baptist, the baptism of Jesus, the call of the disciples, and perhaps the temptation were already associated before Mark with the beginning of Jesus' ministry. As for the Lord's Supper, Gethsemane, the betrayal, the trial, the crucifixion, and the resurrection, these events were already arranged before Mark at the end of Jesus' ministry because they had of necessity to come at the end. If the temporal designation that we find in Mark 9:2 was in the pre-Marcan tradition, then the transfiguration and the confession of Peter may also have been associated together before Mark.

C. H. Dodd sought to demonstrate that a pre-Marcan order of the Gospel events existed along the lines of Acts 10:37–41.[37] Dodd's thesis has been much criticized.[38] If, however, his thesis

36. See Nicolardot, *Les procédés de rédaction*, 216; Rohde, *Rediscovering the Teaching of the Evangelists*, 14; Vögtle, "Was Heisst 'Auslegung der Schrift'?" 53; Burkill, *Mysterious Revelation*, 5; Marxsen, "Redaktionsgeschichtliche Erklärung," 258; Schreiber, "Die Christologie des Markus-evangeliums," 155; Best, *Temptation and the Passion*, 112–33; Keck, "Introduction to Mark's Gospel," 369; Schweizer, *Das Evangelium nach Markus*, 5; Steinmetz, "Literaturbericht"; Perrin, *What Is Redaction Criticism?* 1; and Grundmann, *Das Evangelium nach Markus*, 15, who states, "Die Stellung einer Pericope im Kontext ist häufig der älteste Kommentar, der ihr gegeben wird."

37. "Framework of the Gospel Narrative," 396–400.

38. The most important criticism of Dodd's thesis is Nineham's "Order of Events in St. Mark's Gospel."

is correct, this would further limit the freedom of Mark in arranging his material. The existence of certain pre-Marcan complexes also limited the freedom of the Evangelist to place the pericopes found within them wherever he desired because they were already found in these complexes. The extent to which these complexes existed and the question of whether Mark himself composed any of them is difficult to answer. What is clear is that certain complexes did exist and that Mark did not therefore have a completely free hand in the arrangement of the material found in them.

Nevertheless much of the material available to Mark could be arranged in accordance with his own particular theological purposes. There are several means by which Mark reveals his own theological emphases.

The Arrangement of the Individual Pericopes

Mark was free to a certain extent to place the individual pericopes and sayings wherever he desired. An example of this is Mark 8:27–10:52. This concentration of teaching material was almost certainly not connected to the passion sayings before Mark.[39] The systematic arrangement of this material clearly indicates that Mark has collected this material and arranged it to make a theological point. Each instance of a passion saying reveals the following pattern:

Passion Saying	Disciples Err	Theme of Discipleship
Mark 8:31–32	Mark 8:33 (Peter errs)	Mark 8:34–9:1—Discipleship involves suffering like Christ[40]
Mark 9:30–32	Mark 9:34 (The Twelve err)	Mark 9:33–37—Discipleship involves serving like Christ[41]
Mark 10:32–34	Mark 10:35f. (James and John err)	Mark 10:42–45—Discipleship involves serving like Christ[42]

It seems clear that Mark has given to his materials a distinct arrangement. By this arrangement he seeks to stress that disciple-

39. See Riesenfeld, "Tradition und Redaktion," 160; Schweizer, *Das Evangelium nach Markus,* 124; and Grundmann, *Das Evangelium nach Markus,* 217.

40. Note verse 34—ἀράτω τὸν σταυρὸν αὐτοῦ—and verse 35—ὃς δ' ἂν ἀπολέσει τὴν ψυχὴν αὐτοῦ ἕνεκεν ἐμοῦ καὶ τοῦ εὐαγγελίου. . . .

41. Note verse 35—ἔσται πάντων ἔσχατος καὶ πάντων διάκονος.

42. Note verse 43—ἔσται ὑμῶν διάκονος; verse 44—ἔσται πάντων δοῦλος; and verse 45—ὁ υἱὸς τοῦ ἀνθρώπου οὐκ ἦλθεν διακονηθῆναι ἀλλὰ διακονῆσαι. . . .

ship involves following the Crucified One. Discipleship involves an *imitatio Christi*.

The Placing of One Pericope inside Another

There are a number of instances in Mark where we find one pericope inserted into the framework of another:

Mark 3:22–30	into	Mark 3:19b–21 and 31–35;
Mark 5:25–34	into	Mark 5:21–24 and 35–43;
Mark 6:14–29	into	Mark 6:6b–13 and 30f.;
Mark 11:15–19	into	Mark 11:12–14 and 20–25; and
Mark 14:3–9	into	Mark 14:1–2 and 10–11[43]

It is quite probable that a Marcan arrangement is witnessed to in several of these instances, for the frequency of occurrence argues against all of these being pre-Marcan. In order to ascertain a redaction history from such a "sandwich," we must first of all establish whether this "sandwich" is due to the hand of Mark. The question then must be raised as to whether both incidents took place at the same time or were located in the same place. If either of these two questions is answered in the affirmative, it is questionable if we can assert that there is any *redaktions-geschichtlich* significance in the arrangement. Another question that must then be raised is whether these two incidents were placed together simply because they deal with a similar theme. If this is true, the arrangement may be due primarily to topical rather than theological considerations. Finally it must be borne in mind that a Marcan redaction history can only be ascertained from such a "sandwich" if in some way the inserted pericope interprets or is interpreted by the pericope into which it has been inserted. A possible example of this is Mark 11:12–25. By this "sandwich" Mark may be interpreting the cleansing of the temple by means of the pericope about the cursing of the fig tree. By this arrangement the cleansing of the temple, which originally may have referred to a reformation (see v. 16), is now apparently portrayed as an act of judgment.[44]

43. Possibly Mark 14:55–65 into Mark 14:53–54 and 66–72 as well as Mark 15:16–20 into Mark 15:6–15 and 21–32 might also be considered examples of this "sandwiching."

44. It is quite possible that in our account the figs symbolize Israel (cf. Hos. 9:10; Jer. 24; 29:17) and the destruction of the fig tree symbolizes judgment

The Geographical Scheme of Mark

The uniqueness of the geographical scheme in Mark has been seen by many scholars as being due to a Marcan redactional emphasis.[45] Actually the Marcan scheme may be due to any of three reasons: (1) Mark never fully mastered his material and decided that only one short period of ministry in Jerusalem had in fact taken place. It is evident that Mark's own material contradicts this.[46] Jesus must have been in Jerusalem more than once, but Mark may not have known this.[47] (2) Since the tradition associated most of Jesus' teaching and healing ministry with Galilee and his passion with Jerusalem, Mark used the Galilee–Jerusalem scheme as a convenient literary device to group his material. (3) Mark decided to use the Galilee–Jerusalem scheme to stress a particular theological point. The geographical scheme found in Mark may be of great importance for our study and reveal a Marcan redaction history. This still has not been fully demonstrated, however, and the theological significance of this scheme is far from clear.

The Marcan Introduction

It is evident from the other three Gospels that the introductions to these Gospels are extremely helpful in revealing the theological purpose and emphasis that each writer brought

---

(cf. Hos. 2:12 and Isa. 34:4). See Robin, "Cursing of the Fig Tree," 276–81. By his "sandwiching" these two incidents, Mark causes the theme of judgment in the fig tree pericope to "rub off" on the cleansing pericope. Schweizer, *Das Evangelium nach Markus*, 130, rightly gives to this section of Mark the title, "Das Ende des Tempels Israels und der Aufbruch Gottes zu den Heiden." The cleansing of the temple is for Mark an act of judgment in which Jesus rejected Israel. The proximity of Mark 12:1–11, whose placement in the midst of a collection of controversy stories (Mark 11:27–33 and 12:13–37) is surely Marcan, also indicates that Mark seeks at this point in his Gospel to stress the divine judgment of Israel. For further discussion, see pp. 121–33.

45. See Lohmeyer, *Galiläa und Jerusalem*; Lightfoot, *Locality and Doctrine in the Gospels*; Marxsen, *Mark the Evangelist*, 54–116; Best, *Temptation and the Passion*, 174f.; Feine et al., *Introduction to the New Testament*, 65; Boobyer, "Galilee and Galileans," 334–48.

46. See Mark 10:46f.; 11:2f.; 14:3, 13f., 49; and 15:41.

47. Best, *Temptation and the Passion*, 112, raises this possibility. This question is intimately related to the question of whether Mark created the one-year cycle of Jesus' ministry or whether John created the three-year cycle. Or were there two traditions? These questions may be unanswerable.

with him in the writing of his Gospel. It is only reasonable to
expect the same to be true in the case of Mark. During the oral
period the various pericopes circulated independently and in
certain complexes. In writing his "life of Christ" Mark had to
begin somewhere. Where he would begin and how he would
begin had to be his decision. The introduction of his Gospel
must therefore reveal something of his purpose in writing.[48]
We shall only mention here two possible *redaktionsgeschichtlich*
emphases of the Evangelist contained in his introduction. Mark
apparently seeks to stress in his introduction that Jesus is the fulfillment of the Old Testament prophecies. He does this by the
two prophecies that introduce the Gospel and by his description
of the Baptist.[49] Mark also apparently seeks to stress that the
coming of the Christ inaugurated a new era in salvation history. The Marcan *Heilsgeschichte* is sufficiently developed that a
clear distinction is even made between the period of immi-
nence, that is, the coming of Elijah *redivivus*,[50] and the actual
appearance of the kingdom in the coming of Jesus,[51] for it is

48. Keck, "Introduction to Mark's Gospel," 352, laments that "almost never
does the introduction figure in discussions of Mark's purpose." He goes on to say
(p. 353) that "Mark assumed his contemporary readers (in contrast with modern scholars) did not have the whole of his work in mind when they began, and
that therefore the opening paragraph was his opportunity to orient them to
what he wanted to say and how he wanted to say it."

49. Note also the term πεπλήρωται in Mark 1:15. Marxsen, *Mark the Evangelist*,
42, and Suhl, *Die Funktion*, 131, deny this. Suhl maintains that Mark does not
portray the Baptist as the fulfiller of the Old Testament prophecies, but that
his coming is simply *Schriftgemäss*. But what is the difference? Robinson, *Problem of History in Mark*, 24, is certainly more correct when he states that "The fact
that the ministry of John is seen from the viewpoint of fulfillment is confirmed
by an analysis of the Marcan presentation of John. This presentation is characterized by a remarkable correlation of prophecy (vv. 2–3) and history (vv.
4–8)."

50. Cf. Mark 1:6 with 2 Kings 1:8 and Zech. 13:4 and Mark 9:11–13 with
Mal. 3:1 and 4:5.

51. The term ἐγγίζειν, which appears in the Marcan summary of 1:14–15, can
mean both "to come near" and "to arrive." What is crucial for our investigation
is not what Jesus may have meant by this term but what *Mark* meant by it.
Mark sees the Baptist as the coming Elijah who is to prepare people for the
kingdom. With his coming the kingdom is near. With the coming of the Christ
the kingdom is not merely "near," for it was already "near" in the coming of the
Baptist. For Mark the coming of the Christ means that the kingdom has arrived.
This is evident by the fulfillment of the Old Testament prophecies concerning the coming of the "new age"; the presence of a new teaching (see Mark
1:21–22 and 27b, which are a Marcan seam and insertion); the defeat of hostile

only after the Baptist disappears from the scene (see Mark 1:14) that Jesus proclaims the new age (Mark 1:15). It is evident therefore that the investigation of the Marcan introduction will be an important means for ascertaining a Marcan redaction history.

The Marcan Conclusion

Even as the introduction of a work is important for ascertaining the author's purpose in writing so also is the conclusion of that work. The purpose for which an author writes is usually revealed in some way by the way the work ends. This is certainly true in the case of John (John 20:31),[52] Matthew (Matt. 28:19–20), and Luke (Luke 24:49).[53] We should be able to assume a priori that this is also true in the case of Mark. With Mark, however, we encounter a major problem. The basic problem is the classic question of where the Gospel of Mark originally ended. Since the work of Lightfoot on this question,[54] the view that Mark originally ended at Mark 16:8 has gained support.[55] There are, however, several reasons for still maintaining that the original ending of Mark is lost.[56] Because of the confusion as to the ending of Mark, it would appear that rather than clarifying for us the *redaktionsgeschichtlich* emphases of the Evangelist, our present conclusion to the Gospel of Mark still remains an enigma and offers little assistance in the investigation of a Marcan redaction history.

powers (see Mark 1:27b); the forgiveness of sins (see Mark 2:1–12, esp. v. 10; and Mark 1:4–5); and so on.

52. This is true regardless of whether the Gospel of John originally ended at chapter 20 or 21.

53. In the case of Luke the "conclusion" serves as an "introduction" to his next work.

54. Lightfoot devoted the first two chapters of his work to this question.

55. See Feine et al., *Introduction to the New Testament*, 72, for a list of some of the scholars who take this position.

56. Briefly some of these are: (1) although Lightfoot has found examples in which a Greek sentence ended in γάρ, there is no example of any work ever having ended in this manner. (2) Metzger in his *Text of the New Testament*, 228f., has pointed out that the term φοβεῖσθαι is never used absolutely in Mark except in this instance, if the Gospel originally ended at Mark 16:8. (3) Since Mark 14:28 and 16:7 point to a future resurrection appearance of the risen Christ in Galilee and no such appearance is recorded in our present form of the Gospel, the Gospel must have originally contained such an account that unfortunately is now lost.

The Marcan Vocabulary[57]

The religious language that a person uses often helps reveal something of that individual's particular theological emphasis and stress. A sermon by a minister of existentialistic conviction would be characterized by a specific vocabulary; a sermon by a minister whose main concern lay in the area of social action would be characterized by another; and a sermon by a minister of fundamentalistic persuasion would be characterized by still another. To be sure much that they would say would involve similar terms and phrases, but again and again certain specific words and phrases would arise that would betray their own particular emphasis. Matthew reveals something of his own particular theological emphasis by his frequent use of such terms as πληροῦν, ῥηθέν, and γέγραπται. Mark does likewise by his frequent use of such terms as διδάσκειν—διδάσκαλος—διδαχή, κηρύσσειν εὐαγγέλιον, ἐξουσία, δύναμις—δύνασθαι, θαμβεῖσθαι—θαυμάζειν—ἐκπλήσσεσθαι, δεῖ, παραδίδοναι, ἀκολουθεῖν, πίστις—πιστεύειν, λόγος, and σώζειν. These terms furthermore often appear in the seams, insertions, and summaries. What their significance is for understanding a Marcan redaction history is, of course, beyond the limits of this chapter. What is important for us here is to note that the investigation of the vocabulary itself will be a useful means for ascertaining a Marcan redaction history.

The Marcan Christological Titles

Closely related to the investigation of the Marcan vocabulary is the investigation of the Marcan Christological titles. The importance of such an investigation is evident, because the theology of Mark, like the theology of the entire New Testament, is Christocentric. It would seem therefore that the titles that Mark gave to Jesus would be of utmost importance in understanding what the Evangelist thought, believed, and desired to stress concerning the "pioneer and perfector of our faith." When we observe the freedom with which Matthew and

57. We are not concerned here with the investigation of the vocabulary in order to ascertain whether a seam or insertion is Marcan. We are concerned here with what the vocabulary that Mark uses reveals as to his theological interests.

Luke alter the titles Mark gave to Jesus,[58] it would appear that Mark also probably changed the titles he found in his sources. This being so, the titles used of Jesus both in the pericopes and in the seams will reveal the Christological preference of Mark, and this preference will be a theological preference and not merely an aesthetic one. The investigation of the Christological titles used by Mark will therefore be a helpful means for ascertaining a Marcan redaction history.

Conclusion

In concluding our brief discussion of the various means for ascertaining a Marcan redaction history it must be pointed out that not all the means mentioned are of equal value. Some of them, such as the investigation of the creation of pericopes, the omission of material, and the conclusion are of little, if any, value. Other means, such as the investigation of the seams, the insertions, and summaries, the modification of the material, the selection of material, the arrangement of the material, the introduction, the vocabulary, and the Christological titles, are of great value.[59] The pursuit of a Marcan redaction history is a difficult task, but it is not an impossible one. In the past errors have been made because a proper methodology was not followed. By using a proper methodology, such as we have outlined above, it is hoped that some of these errors may be avoided in the future.

58. See Best, *Temptation and the Passion*, 160–61. For a discussion of the alteration of the title "Son of man" in the Gospel tradition, see Jeremias, "Die älteste Schicht," 159–72.

59. In certain instances these means overlap, for the investigation of the Marcan introduction will involve the investigation of the seams, insertions, summaries, modification, and arrangement found in the introduction.

4

A Seam in
Mark (1:21–22)
A Redactional Investigation

With the publication of Hans Conzelmann's *Die Mitte der Zeit* and Willi Marxsen's *Der Evangelist Markus* in the mid-1950s, the study of the Gospels experienced a shift in interest. The former interest in the form-critical investigation of the second *Sitz im Leben* was displaced[1] by the *redaktionsgeschichtlich* investigation of what Marxsen called the third *Sitz im Leben*.[2] Whereas form-critical scholarship once thought of the Evangelists primarily as "scissors and paste men" or *Sammler*, the Evangelists are today recognized as individual theologians possessing their own unique theological views, insights, and emphases. As a result recent scholarship has concentrated its efforts on the investigation of the particular theological interests of the individual Gospel writers. What is the Evangelist's particular purpose in recording the various Gospel traditions found in his work? What does the Evangelist's editing of his sources reveal about

1. Karnetzki, "Die Galiläische Redaktion im Markus-evangelium," 238, states, "Sie ist heute die Zeit der redaktionsgeschichtlichen Untersuchungen." See also Suhl, *Die Funktion*, 9.
2. Marxsen, *Der Evangelist Markus*, 12.

the situation in which and for which he wrote his Gospel? These are the kinds of questions that scholarship is now interested in investigating.

The purpose of this chapter is to investigate one of the means by which we can ascertain the *redaktionsgeschichtlich* interests of the first Evangelist. It has been generally recognized by scholars that one of the most useful means by which we can ascertain the unique theological interests of Mark is the investigation of the Marcan seams.[3] The importance of the Marcan seams in the investigation of a Marcan *Redaktionsgeschichte* is evident, for apart from certain pre-Marcan complexes[4] the materials used by the Evangelist existed as isolated pericopes. Although these pericopes possessed some sort of an introduction, they did not possess seams uniting them one to another. In order for Mark to bring together the various materials, both oral and written, available to him, he had either to create the seams we find in his Gospel or rework the original introductions found in his material. At times the existing introductions to the materials would have served this purpose, but frequently this would not have been so. As a result Mark had to rework the existing introductions or create seams to bind the various materials together. Undoubtedly the Evangelist in so doing would reveal something of his own particular theological interests and the situation in which and for which he was writing. Using the language of the form critics, we seek by the investigation of the Marcan seams to ascertain what particular theological interests impregnated the "paste" by which this "scissors and paste man" joined together the materials available to him.

Ascertaining the Marcan Seams

The question must be raised at this point as to how we shall be able to ascertain a Marcan seam. How can we distinguish between the pre-Marcan tradition and the Marcan redaction in a potential seam? Unfortunately there is no single test that can answer this question. There are, however, a number of

3. Lohmeyer, *Galiläa und Jerusalem*, 26; Lightfoot, *Locality and Doctrine in the Gospels*, 112; Marxsen, *Der Evangelist Markus*, 12, 34; Best, *Temptation and the Passion*, ix, 63, 71; Schweizer, *Das Evangelium nach Markus*, 4–5; Grundmann, *Die Geschichte Jesu Christi*, 15; Koch, *Was Ist Formgeschichte?* 63.

4. We mean here "pre-Mark's Gospel" complexes. It may very well be that Mark himself was the author of these complexes.

"canons" that will help indicate whether a verse is a Marcan seam or the extent to which a potential Marcan seam possesses Marcan or pre-Marcan material. These "canons" will frequently also be of help in the investigation of the Marcan insertions and summaries. By applying these "canons" to a particular verse, we shall be able to arrive at the probability of a verse being a Marcan seam or the extent to which it is Marcan. As in all historical science we shall have to content ourselves with less than mathematical precision.

Is the vocabulary Marcan? In an article on the Synoptic Gospels Kendrick Grobel has stated

> If the view of the Formgeschichtler that the greatest "author-activity" of the synoptic writers took place in the connecting (or separating) verses at the beginning of pericopes is correct, then those introductory verses, as a class, may be expected to show a higher frequency of words and phrases characteristic of the respective evangelist than the traditionally crystallized bodies of the pericopes themselves.[5]

Since the Evangelist has "marcanized" the material that he received from the tradition by retelling it in his own words and in his own style, we would expect to find for the most part a similarity between the vocabulary of the pericopes and the seams. Nevertheless the presupposition of the *Formgeschichtler*, as Grobel put it, is a sound one. Grobel tested this presupposition in the following way.

> He took the seven peculiarities of vocabulary listed by Hawkins[6] as being most distinctive for Mark[7] and investigated the frequency in which they appeared in the seams and in the pericopes. Grobel considered 97 of the 651 verses found in Mark as Markan "seams."[8] Of the 96 instances that these distinctive terms

5. "Idiosyncracies of the Synoptists," 405.
6. *Horae Synopticae*, 10–15.
7. These are ἐκθαμβέομαι, ἔρχομαι (historic present), εὐθέως or εὐθύς, ὅ ἐστιν, περιβλέπομαι, πολλά (adverb), and συνζητέω.
8. Grobel arrived at this figure in the following way. He observed that in the Huck Synopsis Mark consists of 102 divisions. Eliminating the 3 divisions that contain only one verse (actually there are 4—Mark 1:39; 11:11; 15:1, 21), he arrived at 99 pericopes. Since some of these lacked any introduction and some introductions possessed 2 verses, he arrived at 97 verses out of the 651 verses contained in the Gospel that he called seams. There are several criti-

appear in Mark they are found 37 times in the "seams." This
means that although the "seams" make up only 15% of the
gospel, 38% of all these Markan peculiarities appear in these
"seams." Whatever may be the criticism of Grobel's methodology,
it seems to this writer that he has demonstrated that the Markan
seams possess a more uniquely Markan vocabulary than the pericopes.[9]

Grobel's study involved terms that are *unique* to the Gospel of
Mark. The question of the Marcan character of the vocabulary
of the potential Marcan seams, however, need not be limited to
that which is *uniquely* Marcan. Of course if the vocabulary of a
potential seam is uniquely Marcan, then this argues fairly
forcibly in favor of this verse being a Marcan seam. We can
also ask ourselves the question, however, whether the vocabulary of a potential seam is *characteristically* Marcan. Here we are
seeking to ascertain whether the verse in question contains a
vocabulary in common with the rest of the Gospel. In other
words we are seeking to determine whether the vocabulary in a
potential seam possesses a typically Marcan character.

It would be helpful in the *redaktionsgeschichtlich* investigation of Mark if the Evangelist had used certain terms *only in*
his seams. This would make it much simpler to ascertain his
redaction. Unfortunately Mark did not do so. No single term
or phrase is found only in the Marcan seams. Some terms, however, that frequently appear in the seams and thus often witness
to a Marcan redaction are εὐθύς, πάλιν, εἰς οἶκον, ἔρχεσθαι,
ἄρχειν, εἰσέρχεσθαι, ἐλθών, ἰδών, ἀκούσας, ἀκολουθεῖν, ἐξουσία,
κηρύσσειν, εὐαγγέλιον, διδάσκειν, ἐξέρχεσθαι, πολλά (adverb),
and συνάγειν.[10] These are favorite terms of the Evangelist, and
their appearance in certain verses often witnesses to these verses
being Marcan seams.

---

cisms that can be raised as to Grobel's methodology, but in general it seems
acceptable, although it would be possible to "refine" the method.

9. Grobel, "Idiosyncracies of the Synoptists," 410, concludes that "The sta-
tistical study strongly corroborates the view of the Formgeschichtler that the
greatest author-activity of the synoptic writers took place in the connecting
(or separating) verses that introduce the originally separate pericopes."

10. Hawkins' work, although dated, still possesses valuable information
concerning the Marcan vocabulary and style. See also Bultmann, *History of the
Synoptic Tradition*, 339–40, for additional terms that Mark frequently uses in
his seams.

The presence of a characteristically Marcan vocabulary in these potential seams, however, does not guarantee that these verses are Marcan. Since Mark rewrote the traditions and put them into his own words, we would expect that these verses would in general contain a characteristically Marcan vocabulary whether they were Marcan or pre-Marcan.[11] Actually this "canon" is more helpful in a negative way. Whereas a Marcan vocabulary may witness to a Marcan redaction, a non-Marcan vocabulary in a potential seam witnesses strongly in favor of this verse being non-Marcan or traditional. A single *hapax*, of course, does not determine that a verse is pre-Marcan, for Mark did not consciously decide that every word he used in his seams would be used more than once. An example of this is Mark 10:1c. The reference to Jesus' teaching according to his custom is almost certainly Marcan despite the fact that εἰώθει is a *hapax*. There are also times when the setting of a scene would require the use of certain terms not found elsewhere. An example of this is Mark 13:1f. The vocabulary here is unique, but what else could it be? The scene is unique.

The test of whether the vocabulary of a potential seam is characteristically Marcan is a limited tool in seeking to ascertain the Marcan redaction. It is actually more helpful in a negative way in determining if a verse is non-Marcan. Nevertheless this is a useful tool for ascertaining a Marcan redaction because it can provide support to other arguments that a particular verse is a Marcan seam. It cannot usually bear the burden of proof, although in a few instances such as the Marcan insertion of Mark 13:10 the argument from the Marcan character of the vocabulary is quite weighty. A uniquely Marcan vocabulary then argues in favor of a potential seam being Marcan; a non-Marcan vocabulary argues against such a verse being Marcan; and a characteristically Marcan vocabulary argues *mildly* in favor of such a verse being Marcan. The latter at best, however,

11. Lambrecht, *Die Redaktion der Markus-Apokalypse*, 89, rightly comments, "Die gleiche Ansicht wird mit Recht ferner vorbringen, daß das *Markinische* eines Textes nicht ipso facto auf eine 'creatio' oder auf eine 'unhistorische Wiedergabe' schließen läßt. Es ist doch (noch einmal!) normal und natürlich, daß bei der Niederlegung des Traditionsgutes Markus spontan seinen eigenen Stil schreibt! Es kann ohne weiteres zugegeben werden, daß die oft hervorgehobene markinische Wortwahl und seine Stileigenheit allein diese Frage nicht entscheiden können."

can only add its support to other arguments. It cannot bear
the burden of proof.

Is the style Marcan? There exist several surveys of the Marcan literary style,[12] so that the Marcan simplicity of style is well
known. We would expect that in the Marcan seams the Marcan
literary characteristics would appear in higher proportion than
in the traditional material. Unfortunately whereas the Marcan
peculiarities of style have been compared with their parallels
in Matthew and Luke[13] no such attempt has been made to compare the Marcan peculiarities of style in the Marcan seams with
the pericopes in the same way Grobel has done in the area of
vocabulary. Using Grobel's method let us investigate one of
the common stylistic features of Mark.

> One of the characteristics of Mark is that he frequently uses
> the verb ἄρχειν with an infinitive. This construction appears 26
> times in Mark. Examining the same 97 seams Grobel used, we
> find this construction 9 times. This means that of all the instances
> that we find this construction in Mark 34.5% of them appear
> in the 15% of the gospel which Grobel considered as seams.
> Actually the percentage would be higher if we included other
> instances in which this construction occurs and which are clearly
> Markan redactions. We cannot include Mc 1 45; 6 7, 34b, 55; and
> 8 31, however, because they do not qualify as seams according to
> Grobel's method.

It is apparent from this example that we can expect that the
Marcan stylistic characteristics will occur more frequently in
the seams than in the pericopes.

Other stylistic characteristics of Mark are the frequent use
of the periphrastic,[14] the genitive absolute,[15] the impersonal

---

12. Zerwick, *Untersuchungen zum Markus-Stil*; Doudna, *Greek of the Gospel of
Mark*; Turner, "Marcan Usage"; Taylor, *Gospel According to St. Mark*, 57f.; Hart-
mann, *Der Aufbau des Markusevangeliums*. For an excellent discussion of the
use of the participle, periphrastic, and the genitive absolute and an excellent bibliography, see Hartman, *Testimonia Linguae*.

13. Ibid., pp. 15f.

14. Turner, "Marcan Usage," 349–51, lists the following twenty-four
instances: Mark 1:6, 13, 22, 33, 39; 2:6, 18; 4:38; 5:5, 11; 6:52; 9:4; 10:22, 32, 32b;
14:4, 40, 49, 54; 15:7, 26, 40, 43, 46.

15. Argyle, "Genitive Absolute in Biblical Greek," 285, states that there are
thirty instances of the genitive absolute in Mark. Hartman, *Testimonium Linguae*,
22, indicates that there are at least thirty-seven. In a rapid reading of Mark the

plural,[16] the double negative,[17] the historic present, parataxis, asyndeton, the conjunctive participle with adjuncts at the beginning of a sentence,[18] anacoluthon, pleonasm, and the tendency to use θέλειν as an auxillary verb.[19]

This means for ascertaining whether a verse is a Marcan seam is more helpful in a negative way. The absence of a Marcan style or the presence of features decidedly non-Marcan argues strongly that such a verse is pre-Marcan in origin. An example of this is the Greek period found in Mark 5:25–27. Nowhere else in Mark do we find such a period, and the style here is in sharp contrast to the Evangelist's fondness for parataxis. We can therefore conclude with a fair amount of certainty that these verses are pre-Marcan in origin. On the other hand if a verse does exhibit a Marcan style then we have only a supporting argument that this verse is a Marcan seam. As in the case of the argument from vocabulary, this argument cannot stand alone. It cannot prove by itself that a verse is a Marcan seam.[20] It can, however, lend support to other arguments that a particular verse is a Marcan seam.

Does the verse contain a Marcan theme? Rudolf Bultmann has argued that form criticism moves in a circle.[21] This is quite apparent when we seek to discern the Marcan redaction by

---

present writer came across thirty-four. These are Mark *1:32*; 4:17, *35*; *5:2*, 18, *21*, 35; *6:2*, 21, 22, 35, 47, *54*; *8:1*; *9:9*, 28; *10:17*, *46*; 11:11, *12*, *27*; *13:1*, 3; *14:3* (two), *17*, 18, *22*, *43*, 66; *15:33*, 42; *16:1*, 2. We find twenty-one instances (these are in italics) of the genitive absolute in the seams that Grobel listed. If we use the figure that Hartman gives (thirty-seven) this means that 57 percent of the genitive absolutes found in Mark are contained in the 15 percent of Mark that Grobel listed as seams. Certainly the use of the genitive absolute is a Marcan stylistic characteristic.

16. Turner, "Marcan Usage," 378f., lists twenty-one instances of the impersonal plural in Mark. These are Mark 1:21, 22, 29, 30, 32, 45; 2:2, 3, 18; 3:1, 2, 31, 32; 5:14, 35; 6:14, 33, 42, 43, 53, 54; 7:31, 32; 8:22; 10:1, 2, 13, 49; 13:9, 11; and 14:12. He also lists as possibilities Mark 3:21 and 14:1. The majority of these appear in what are probable Marcan redactions.

17. We find the following double negatives in Mark: Mark 1:44; 2:2; 3:20, 27; 5:3, 37; 6:5; 7:12; 9:8; 11:14; 12:14; 14:25, 60, 61; 15:4, 5; 16:8. We could add to these the nine instances of οὐ μή that occur in Mark.

18. See Hartman, *Testimonium Linguae*, 15f.

19. Turner, "Marcan Usage," 355, lists some twenty-five instances.

20. See note 11.

21. Bultmann, *History of the Synoptic Tradition*, 5.

means of this question, for we must deduce the Marcan themes by discerning the Marcan redaction and we must discern the Marcan redaction by deducing the Marcan themes. This method possesses certain dangers, but it is a legitimate and necessary method.[22] Once we determine that Mark seeks to stress the teaching activity of Jesus[23] and the secrecy motif,[24] then it will be quite likely that when these themes appear in certain potential seams, insertions, and summaries these verses are indeed Marcan seams, insertions, and summaries.

Again it must be pointed out that this is not a conclusive "canon." If a verse contains a Marcan theme or emphasis this does not prove that this verse is a Marcan seam, for it is quite possible that the traditions Mark used also contained, although to a lesser extent, this same theme.[25] If we assume that every time we come across a Marcan theme this verse is therefore a

22. The criticism of the form critics by Gerhardsson, *Memory and Manuscript*, 10, is therefore not justified in this regard.

23. We find this theme stressed in the following potential seams: Mark 1:21–22; 2:2 (Jesus speaks the word); 3:14 (the disciples are called by Jesus to preach); 6:2, 12 (the disciples are sent to preach); 30 (the disciples report what they taught); 7:14 (Jesus speaks to the crowd); 8:31, 34 (Jesus speaks to the crowds and the disciples); 9:31; 12:1 (Jesus speaks in parables); 35, 38a; 13:1 (Jesus the Teacher speaks to the disciples). It is found in the following potential Marcan insertions: Mark 6:34; 11:17a, 18, and in the following potential Marcan summaries: Mark 1:14–15 (Jesus comes preaching), 39 (Jesus preaches); 2:13; 4:1–2, 10–12 (indirectly), 33–34 (indirectly); 6:6b; 10:1 (teaching is Jesus' *custom*); 32 (indirectly). Certainly not every one of these references is due to the hand of Mark, but it is undeniable that Mark frequently seeks to portray Jesus as a teacher. The frequency that Jesus is called διδάσκαλος (twelve times) and ῥαββί (four times) also supports this view.

24. We find this theme in the following verses that are possible Marcan seams: Mark 5:43; 7:17, 24, 36–37; 8:26, 30; 9:9, 30. Two possible Marcan insertions that contain this theme are Mark 1:44 and 3:23a. It is also found in the following summaries that may be Marcan: Mark 1:34b; 3:12; 4:10–12, 33–34. We are not arguing here that all these references are due to the hand of Mark. We are simply arguing that the frequency with which the messianic secret occurs in verses that are possible Marcan redactions is too great to deny that the messianic secret is a Marcan motif and theme.

25. The messianic secret is an example of this. Wrede argued that the secrecy motif was already contained in part in the sources that Mark used. This has been further demonstrated in the following works: Burkill, "Hidden Son of Man,"189–213; Schweizer, "Zur Frage des Messiasgeheimnisses bei Markus," 1–8; and Sjöberg, *Der Verborgene Menschensohn*. For an unsuccessful attempt to deny that the secrecy motif was at least in part pre-Marcan, see Strecker, "Zur Messiasgeheimnistheorie im Markusevangelium," 96.

Marcan redaction, we are saying in effect that this theme is a de novo creation of the Evangelist. This would be to err. Nevertheless the fact that a verse contains a Marcan theme does argue in favor of the possibility of that verse being a Marcan seam.

Do we find in the verse an unnecessary redundancy? There are certain verses in which the Evangelist has apparently inserted a phrase to express his own point of view where this phrase is redundant and unnecessary. We find an example of this in Mark 12:38. The loose sayings that Mark placed in his Gospel frequently begin with καὶ ἔλεγεν αὐτοῖς.[26] The phrase ἐν τῇ διδαχῇ αὐτοῦ is therefore quite redundant and probably is a Marcan redaction. Some other examples of this are: Mark 11:17 (the expression καὶ ἐδίδασκεν is clearly redundant and unnecessary and its omission by Matthew and Luke proves this); 12:35 (the participle διδάσκων is clearly redundant when added to ἀποκριθεὶς . . . ἔλεγεν); and 9:31[27] (the verb ἐδίδασκεν is clearly unnecessary with καὶ ἔλεγεν αὐτοῖς).

Is the verse essential to the pericope? This "canon" is equally helpful in the investigation of potential insertions and summaries. An example of the latter is Mark 1:28. This summary is unnecessary to the pericope because the previous verse provides an excellent conclusion to the account. Furthermore it breaks the continuity between verses 23 and 29. Another example is Mark 2:13b. In this verse the description of Jesus' teaching the crowds is clearly unessential with regard to what follows and may even stand in contradiction to it. What is essential to the pericope is that Jesus passed by and saw Levi. The presence of the crowd in verse 13b is not part of the original pericope, because the people in verse 15 are certainly not the crowd referred to in verse 13b.

We must be cautious in our use of this "canon," however, because the fact that a potential seam can be omitted from a pericope is not proof in itself that this potential seam is a Marcan creation. Almost every pericope contains some traditional material that could be omitted. As in the methods we have

26. Some examples of this are Mark 4:13, 21, 24, 26, 30, 35; 9:1, 19, 29; 10:39.

27. This redundancy witnesses to a Marcan redaction no matter what view we take as to whether Mark 9:30–32 is traditional or Marcan. For the view that these verses are Marcan in the fullest sense of the meaning, see Strecker, "Die Leidens- und Auferstehungsvoraussagen im Markusevangelium," 31.

already mentioned, this "canon" cannot stand alone. It cannot bear the entire weight of demonstrating that a verse is a Marcan seam.

On the other hand the fact that a verse is essential to a pericope argues strongly in favor of this verse being pre-Marcan. An example of this is Mark 2:1–2. Whereas verse 1 may witness to some editorial work on the part of the Evangelist, verse 2 (excluding the last five words) is essential to the pericope. Apart from the description of the crowd, verse 3 and the following pericope make no sense. The fact that a verse is essential to the pericope therefore argues strongly in favor of this verse being part of the pre-Marcan tradition.[28] On the other hand the fact that a verse can be omitted from the pericope argues *mildly* in favor of it being a possible Marcan redaction, but it is by no means a conclusive argument.

Does the verse conflict with the pericope? If a verse stands in conflict with the pericope it introduces, it is probable that this verse is a Marcan seam. A few examples of this can be mentioned. In Mark 3:20 we read καὶ ἔρχεται εἰς οἶκον. This stands in seeming conflict with what we read in verse 21f., for there Jesus is not in a house but outside. Apparently Mark has composed this seam as an introduction to the following pericope even though it does not fit.[29] It is possible that this conflict existed during the oral period, but it is more likely that the conflict is due to the redaction of Mark, for with the constant repetition of this pericope during the oral period this inconsistency would probably have been omitted. Another example is Mark 8:22. We read here of Jesus' entrance into Bethsaida. Bethsaida was a city (πόλις). Yet in the pericope we read of a village (κώμη). It is quite possible therefore that Mark has introduced this pericope with a localization that does not fit.[30] We can also mention here Mark 2:13–14, where the introduction in verse 13 seems to conflict with the account in verse 14 and fol-

28. This does not eliminate the possibility that the verse in question could have been reworked by the Evangelist.

29. The expressions ἐν οἴκῳ, εἰς οἶκον, ἐν οἰκίᾳ, and εἰς οἰκίαν frequently occur in Marcan redactions. See Mark 2:1, 15; 3:20; 7:17, 24; 8:26; 10:10; and 14:3.

30. Taylor, *Gospel According to St. Mark*, 370, argues that κώμη may be correct, however, if the older fishing village is meant.

lowing. We have discussed this verse above[31] and need not discuss it again.

> In the examples that we have just mentioned other arguments for thinking that these verses are Markan seams could also be listed, but it is not our purpose here to demonstrate that these verses are Markan seams. We seek only to demonstrate that when a verse conflicts with the pericope it introduces this conflict argues in favor of this verse being a Markan seam.[32]

Does the verse conflict with the general Marcan scheme or pattern? If we answer this question in the affirmative, this argues in favor of the verses being pre-Marcan. Hegermann in an important article[33] has sought to demonstrate that some of the localizations found in Mark 4–8 are pre-Marcan because they contradict the general Marcan scheme for this section of the Gospel. It is not our purpose here to attempt to prove or disprove Hegermann's thesis. We again simply seek to point out that if such a conflict does exist it is more likely to have resulted from a conflict between the traditional localization of the pericope and the Marcan scheme than from Mark having created this localization in conflict with his own scheme.

A well-known example of this is Mark 2:18–20. In this pericope we have a clear conflict with the general Marcan scheme in which Jesus speaks of his death only after the experience of Caesarea Philippi (see Mark 8:31f.). Almost certainly Mark 2:18–20 is a piece of the tradition that has been bound in the pre-Marcan complex of Mark 2:1–3:6. This conflict with the Marcan scheme argues against these verses being a Marcan creation. It is true that in this instance we are dealing with a pericope and not a potential seam, but the principle is the same. When a verse conflicts with the general Marcan scheme, this circumstance argues against this verse being a Marcan creation. In the case of a potential seam it argues against the verse being a Marcan seam.

31. See above page 77.
32. The present writer recognizes that the pre-Marcan tradition need not have been perfectly consistent. Some of the inconsistency between certain "seams" and the tradition may therefore be pre-Marcan, but it is more probable that such an inconsistency stems from the editorial work of the Evangelist.
33. "Bethsaida und Gennesar," 130–40.

Are there any Semiticisms in the verse? If we were to discover that a potential Marcan seam contained a Semitism, this might tend to indicate that this verse was pre-Marcan in origin. There are, however, some seemingly insurmountable problems in seeking to demonstrate that a verse is pre-Marcan because it contains a Semitism. One of the problems is the difficulty of demonstrating that a phrase or construction in Greek is a Semitism. We know from the papyri that koine Greek had absorbed many Semitisms even as the English language has absorbed certain French, Spanish, German, Latin, and Hebrew terms, phrases, and constructions. We are also more aware today of how great an influence the Greek Old Testament exerted upon the early church. On occasion the writers of the New Testament may have consciously or unconsciously modeled their style after the LXX, so that the Semitic style of the LXX may be the cause of certain Semitisms found in the New Testament.[34] Perhaps the greatest problem, however, when we seek to demonstrate that an expression or phrase is a Semitism is the fact that the majority of these alleged Semitisms are acceptable Greek and are found many times in the papyri. As a result we must frequently argue that an expression is a Semitism because it appears more frequently in the New Testament than in the koine, but whereas we may argue that the frequent appearance of a construction is a Semitism, it is difficult to demonstrate that any one particular occurrence is a Semitism. Another major difficulty in attempting to demonstrate that a verse is pre-Marcan because it contains a Semitism involves the question of the authorship of the Gospel of Mark.

It is not our purpose in this article to investigate this question. We raise the issue here, however, because if the writer of this gospel is the John Mark of Acts 12 12, then a semitism could very well have entered into a seam because of the Semitic background of the author.[35] It would appear therefore that this means

34. We shall not discuss the problem of differentiating between a "Hebrasim" and an "Aramaism."

Nigel Turner has even argued that the influence of the LXX upon the writers of the New Testament was so great that the Greek of the New Testament is a truly unique Greek and must be recognized as such. See *Grammar of New Testament Greek*, 3:4.

35. It is generally agreed that the use of ἄρχειν with an infinitive is a Semitism. (See Taylor, *Gospel According to St. Mark*, 63, for a list of scholars who

of testing whether a verse is Markan or pre-Markan will only be valid if we conclude that the author of this gospel was a Greek. This, too, however, is confronted with the problem that due to the influence of the LXX even a Greek might have constructed seams containing semitisms.

It appears in the light of our discussion that the attempt to demonstrate that a verse is pre-Marcan because it contains a Semitism is of dubious value because of: (1) the difficulty in demonstrating that any particular phrase or construction is Semitic and (2) the fact that even a Greek Christian could have consciously or unconsciously patterned his Gospel after the LXX, which contains many Semitisms. One need only observe how frequently the language of the King James Version of the Bible enters into the conversation and writings of Christians today to see the validity of this last objection.

Does the verse appear in a pre-Marcan complex? The question of whether Mark 5:24b is a Marcan seam will be determined to a great extent by the question of whether Mark 4:25–5:43 existed as a pre-Marcan complex[36] and by the question of whether these two accounts were already "sandwiched" together before Mark wrote his Gospel. If Mark were the first to join Mark 5:21–24a, 35–43 and Mark 5:24b–34 into this "sandwich," then Mark no doubt composed this verse in order to join the two pericopes. If the two incidents were already joined, however, then the original compiler must have composed this verse or a verse very much like it, because such a seam was necessary to unite these two pericopes.

If it could be concluded that Mark took over the pre-Marcan complexes without much change or modification this

---

maintain this. See also Doudna, *Greek of the Gospel of Mark*, 111f.) This construction, however, appears frequently in the Marcan seams. (See Mark 1:45; 4:1; 5:20; 6:2, 34, 55; 8:31; 10:28, 32; 12:1; 13:5. All of these may not be Marcan seams, but the majority probably are.) The frequent use of this construction in the Marcan seams may be due to the influence of the LXX or it may be due to the writer having come from a Semitic background.

36. Some of the reasons for thinking that Mark 4:35–5:43 was a pre-Marcan complex are: the geographical designations in 4:35; 5:1 and 21 tie this passage together; the fact that this section is a collection of four miracle stories; the fact that all four miracle stories are portrayed as taking place within twenty-four hours; the interweaving of Mark 5:21–24a, 35–43 and 5:24b–34 appears to be pre-Marcan.

would indicate that we should treat the various seams, insertions, and summaries found in these complexes as being for
the most part traditional. When one investigates these complexes, however, it is evident that the Evangelist felt quite free
to modify them in order to stress his own particular theological
emphasis. In the first complex (Mark 1:21–39 or 45)[37] we see the
hand of the Evangelist quite clearly in Mark 1:21–23a, 27, 28,
34c, and 39 and in the second complex (Mark 2:1–3:6)[38] we
see his hand in Mark 2:1, 13, 15c, and 3:6. It is apparent then
that Mark felt quite free to modify these complexes and to add
comments and summaries to them in order to emphasize his
own particular theology.

The question of evaluating a seam in the pre-Marcan complexes raises an important issue. Since the pericopes in these
complexes were already joined before Mark wrote his Gospel,
the Evangelist did not need to join the various traditions. As
a result Mark did not need to create seams. In other words
whereas in the case of the individual pericopes, Mark needed to
create seams or rework the original introductions and conclusions in order to join the isolated pericopes, in the complexes
these pericopes were already so joined. As a result the Evangelist did not have to create any seams or adapt the introductions and conclusions of the pericopes to join the various
materials available. Unless we conclude that the Evangelist
would have purposely rejected every traditional seam in these
complexes, the probability of a verse in such a complex being a

37. Some of the reasons for thinking that Mark 1:21–39 was a pre-Marcan
complex are: all the events in this section reportedly take place in one twenty-
four-hour period; all the events take place in one city or region (cf. vv. 23, 29,
33, 38; cf. also the door in v. 32, which refers to the house of v. 29); the four
incidents involve three healings (vv. 21–27, 29–31, and 32–34) and a concluding incident, so that it may have been a complex of healings. If we conclude
that Mark 1:40–45 was originally part of this complex, then we can add another
healing story to the complex, but some of the other arguments we have stated
will not apply.

38. Some of the reasons for thinking that Mark 2:1–3:6 was a pre-Marcan
complex are: the passage consists of five consecutive pronouncement stories, so
that it appears as if it were a collection; there is a gradual crescendo of opposi-
tion in the complex; the reference to the death of Jesus is too early in the Marcan scheme (cf. Mark 8:31), so that the fasting pericope was probably already
bound to the surrounding material before Mark wrote his Gospel. For a still
valuable discussion of this section of Mark, see Albertz, *Die synoptischen Streitgespräche*, 5f.

Marcan seam will therefore be somewhat less than elsewhere. Nevertheless each potential Marcan seam in a pre-Marcan complex must be investigated individually before any conclusions are drawn.[39]

There exist several other "canons" for ascertaining whether a potential seam is Marcan or traditional. One such "canon" is "Do we find in the verse a description of a Palestinian *Sitz im Leben?*" David Daube[40] has sought to demonstrate that Mark 1:21–22 and 27 are not so much an editorial redaction by the Evangelist as a piece of tradition stemming from the first *Sitz im Leben*. He has argued that the term "scribes" must be understood not as "learned theologians" but as "elementary teachers." The scribes are to be understood as standing in contrast to the more superior "rabbis." These scribes lacked the authority (*reshuth* or ἐξουσία) to lay down a new rule (*halakha hadhasha*). The amazement of the people in Mark 1:22 therefore refers to a historical situation in which the people in the synagogue were amazed over the fact that Jesus taught not as the scribes but as an authoritative rabbi who possessed authority (*reshuth*). They wondered at "Jesus's delivering 'a new *horaya* to all appearances founded on authority.'"[41] Daube even argues that authoritative rabbis were expected to possess familiarity with and power over the world of spirits,[42] so that the exorcism in this account would be in keeping with his thesis that Jesus possessed *reshuth*.

We shall not evaluate Daube's thesis here, for we shall discuss it again when we investigate Mark 1:21–22.[43] What is important for us here is to note that if it can be demonstrated that a potential seam reveals a Palestinian *Sitz im Leben*, in a manner such as Daube argues, then this will argue against this potential seam being Marcan in origin. This "canon" unfortunately will be of

39. Best, *Temptation and the Passion*, 71, therefore errs when he argues that "The section ii. 1–iii. 6 is generally held to have come to Mark as a unit, a complex of conflict stories. It can not then include much editorial work apart from its beginning and end." We might expect less editorial work on the part of the Evangelist in a complex than in other parts of his Gospel, but Mark was not as limited with respect to these complexes as Best suggests. The various insertions and summaries of the Evangelist in the pre-Marcan complexes prove this.

40. "ἐξουσία in Mark I 22 and 27," 45–59, and *New Testament and Rabbinic Judaism*, 205–23.

41. *New Testament and Rabbinic Judaism*, 213.

42. See Billerbeck, *Kommentar zum Neuen Testament*, 4:527f.

43. See below p. 89.

limited value, however, because it is extremely difficult to demonstrate that a particular verse demands a Palestinian *Sitz im
Leben*. We can also ask if a Palestinian *Sitz im Leben* could not
have entered into a seam through the hand of the Evangelist. If
the writer of Mark were John Mark whose home was Jerusalem,
this is entirely possible.

Another possible "canon" is suggested by Georg Strecker. He
has suggested that when we find statements of "strikingly concrete character"[44] in Mark these are pre-Marcan. He assumes a
priori that the redaction of the Evangelist will be general in
nature. In the same article Strecker also argues that all summaries in the Gospel are to be considered as stemming from
the hand of the Evangelist.[45] Yet some of these summaries are
quite specific and concrete.[46] Furthermore in his own article
he violates this "canon" for he considers Mark 10:33–34 as the
work of the Evangelist, and yet this saying is certainly quite
specific and concrete. Whereas there may be some value in
assuming that the Marcan redactions will tend to be general
in nature and that specific and concrete statements and descriptions tend to be pre-Marcan in origin, this "canon" is too vague
to be of much help in our investigation.

Having listed some of the various means by which we can
ascertain whether a verse witnesses to a Marcan redaction, let us
now investigate a potential seam that may reveal a *redaktionsgeschichtlich* emphasis on the part of the Evangelist in order to
see how the investigation of the seams in Mark will be of help
in ascertaining a Marcan *Redaktionsgeschichte*.

The Investigation of Mark 1:21–22

As in the case of most of the Marcan geographical designations, our potential seam does not conclude the preceding pericope (Mark 1:16–20) but introduces the subsequent pericope
(Mark 1:23–27) and complex (Mark 1:21–39 or 45).[47] Using the
various guides that we have discussed above, let us investigate

44. "Passion- and Resurrection Predictions," 422.
45. Ibid., 423.
46. Cf. Mark 3:7–12 and 6:53–56.
47. Whereas Mark 1:21 may serve as an introduction to either the pericope
or the complex, it is evident that Mark 1:22 introduces the pericope. (Cf. Mark
1:22 with 27b, which is part of the pericope.)

these verses in order to ascertain the extent of the Marcan redaction, if there is any, in this potential seam.

Is the vocabulary Marcan?

In the verses under discussion we find the following terms: εἰσπορεύεσθαι—this term is found 8 times in Mark: καὶ εὐθύς—the adverb εὐθύς is used forty times in the gospel and frequently is found in Markan seams introducing the various pericopes; σάββατα—the plural is found 6 times in Mark, and in Mc 2 23.24 and 3 2 it refers, as here, to a single sabbath day; διδάσκειν—this verb is found 17 times in Mark and is a favorite term of the evangelist for describing Jesus' activity;[48] ἐκπλήσσεσθαι—this verb is found 5 times in Mark, and of the other 4 instances Mc 6 2 7 37 and 11 18 may very well be either Markan seams or insertions; ἐξουσία—this term is used 10 times by the evangelist and is of great importance for understanding the "redaktionsgeschichtlich" interests of the evangelist; διδαχή—this term is used 5 times in Mark and like the verb is a favorite way of Mark describing the activity of Jesus; γραμματεῖς—this term is used 21 times in Mark; Καφαρναούμ—this term is used 3 times in Mark; συναγωγή—this term is found 8 times in Mark; εἰσέρχεσθαι—this term, assuming that it should be read, appears 30 times in Mark.

It is apparent that these two verses contain no terms unusual for Mark that would argue in favor of their being traditional. On the other hand there are several terms that the Evangelist frequently uses and that are of special interest to him. It is quite clear therefore that this potential seam exhibits a characteristically and almost uniquely Marcan vocabulary.

Is the style Marcan? We find in these two verses some typically Marcan stylistic features. These include parataxis, the impersonal plural, the historic present, the imperfect paraphrastic, and the use of γάρ to introduce an explanatory comment. With regard to the latter it appears that there are many occasions where the Evangelist has sought to add to the traditional material an explanatory comment for his Gentile readers.[49] He frequently does this by means of a γάρ clause. Some

48. This verb is usually used absolutely as we find it here. Mark 6:34b is an exception.

49. The frequent explanatory notes, which are clearly meant to explain Hebrew terms and customs to non-Jews, destroys Marxsen's thesis that Mark was

examples of this may be: Mark 1:16, 22; 2:15; 3:10; 5:8, 28, 42; 6:14, 17, 18, 20, 31, 48, 52; 7:3; 9:6 (2), 31; 11:13, 18 (2), 32; 12:12; 14:2, 56; 15:10; 16:4 and 8 (2).

Do these verses contain a Marcan theme? We have already pointed out that Mark seeks to stress Jesus' activity as a teacher.[50] We find this emphasis in the potential seam under discussion along with two other themes that Mark seeks to emphasize. These are the amazement created by Jesus' activity[51] and the authority that Jesus possessed.[52] There are present therefore in this potential seam at least three Marcan themes.

Do we find in these verses an unnecessary redundancy? Although these verses may appear at first to contain a redundancy because of the threefold reference to Jesus' teaching, on closer examination it is evident that each time a new thought is introduced. As a result we do not find in these verses an unnecessary redundancy. The question is not so much whether there is a redundancy in these verses but whether these verses are themselves redundant, that is, whether this potential seam is essential to the pericope.

Are these verses essential to the pericope? Because of the twofold reference to the synagogue in verses 23 and 29, it would appear that the localization of this incident in the synagogue is pre-Marcan. If this is so, the question must be raised as to whether Jesus' teaching in the synagogue is a necessary introduction to the pericope. After all if Jesus was portrayed as being in a synagogue, would not the tradition have portrayed him as teaching? What else would he have been there for? To listen? It is evident that the tradition did portray Jesus as teaching in the synagogue (cf. Mark 6:2f. and Luke 4:16f.). Following this line of thought it would seem that something like verse 21 at least was necessarily part of the pericope. Yet this line of argument comes to nought over the fact that in Mark 3:1–5 we have a similar healing in a synagogue and no mention is made of Jesus' teaching. The healing story is simply introduced by "And Jesus

---

writing to the Jewish Christians in Jerusalem and its environs in order for them to flee to Galilee to await the parousia. Some of these explanatory notes for Gentile readers are Mark 3:17, 22; 5:41; 7:3–4, 11; 9:43; 10:46; 14:12, 36; 15:22, 34, 42.

50. See note 23.

51. See Mark 1:22, 27; 5:20; 6:2, 6; 7:37; 10:24, 26, 32; 11:18; 15:5, 44.

52. See Mark 1:22, 27; 2:10; 3:15; 6:7; 11:28, 29, 33; 13:34.

entered again into the synagogue." As a result we cannot argue that a statement about Jesus teaching is necessary for the pericope simply because the setting of the pericope was the synagogue.

On the other hand some introduction to the pericope must have existed. Some scholars argue that verses 23–27 are a self-contained miracle story and possess all that is necessary for such a story.[53] Even if this is so, however, this would not prove that Mark 1:21–22 was not attached to the story. We could omit verse 27b–d ("so that they questioned among themselves, saying, 'What is this? A new teaching! With authority he commands even the unclean spirits, and they obey him'") without making the story senseless, that is, they are unnecessary to the pericope, but apart from the expression "a new teaching with authority" there is general agreement that the last part of verse 27 is pre-Marcan. Yet the question must be raised as to whether verses 23–27 are really a self-contained miracle story. The beginning of the story with verse 23 appears to be too abrupt. In every other miracle story there is a more elaborate introduction than simply "There was a man in the synagogue who cried out. . . . " One would expect at least something like "Once when Jesus entered into a synagogue. . . ." Something like Mark 3:1a ("Again he entered the synagogue . . .") must have introduced the pericope, for a miracle story usually begins by someone coming to Jesus (Mark 1:40f.; 5:21f., 25f.; 10:46f.; Matt. 9:27f.; Luke 7:11f.), someone being brought to Jesus (Mark 2:1f.; 7:32f.; 8:22f.), or Jesus arriving somewhere (Mark 1:29f.; 5:1f.; 9:14f.). Nowhere do we find that Jesus is simply there when something happens. It seems therefore that verses 23–27 are not a self-contained miracle story, but that something like Mark 1:21b or Mark 3:1a[54] originally introduced the pericope.

Do these verses conflict with the pericope? Whereas in the potential seam the teaching of Jesus is emphasized, we do not find any mention of Jesus teaching in the pericope itself apart from the statement "a new teaching with authority" found in verse 27, which itself is probably a Marcan addition to the tradition. It should also be noted that we do not usually find that a traditional healing story occurs in a context of teaching. Mark

53. So Burkill, *Mysterious Revelation*, 72–73.
54. Burkill (ibid., 33) introduces this miracle story with this kind of an introduction.

2:2b ("and he was preaching the word to them") appears at
first to be an exception to this, but upon closer examination
it appears that the reference to Jesus teaching (actually "preaching the word") in this healing story may be an insertion by the
Evangelist. The original healing story may not have contained
this reference to teaching, for a reference to Jesus teaching in
this healing story appears somewhat unnecessary. In Mark 10:1
we find that Mark has in a similar manner introduced a pronouncement story in the context of Jesus' teaching, and this,
too, is unique. It is customary to introduce a pronouncement
story by a healing (Mark 3:1f. and 22f.), controversial conduct
on the part of Jesus (Mark 2:1f., 15f., 18f., 23f.; 7:1f.), an incident
(Mark 3:31f.; 9:38f.; 10:13f., 17f.), or without any introduction
(Mark 11:27f., 12:13f., 18f., 28f.). Nowhere else does a description of Jesus teaching introduce such a story.

It would appear that the description of Jesus teaching,
although it does not necessarily conflict with the pericope,
does appear to be out of place.[55] This does not prove conclusively that the teaching emphasis in the verses under consideration is a Marcan redaction, but it does support the view that
the pericope did not originally have the present emphasis on
Jesus' teaching activity.

Do these verses conflict with the general Marcan scheme or pattern?
No such conflict is apparent in these verses.

Are there any Semitisms in these verses? There does not appear
to be any Semitisms in these verses, so that we cannot attempt
to demonstrate that these verses are pre-Marcan by this means.

Do these verses appear in a pre-Marcan complex? We have stated
above[56] that we think that Mark 1:21–39 (or 45) existed as a
pre-Marcan complex. If this pericope existed in such a complex, would not this introductory pericope have had a more
elaborate introduction than simply "There was a man . . ."?
One would expect that the introductory pericope in a complex
would have possessed an introduction at least as elaborate as
those in the middle of the complex.[57] Furthermore the theme of

55. Knigge in his "Meaning of Mark," 55, goes even further. He argues that
verses 21, 22, and 27 ("a new teaching with authority") are Marcan because
they *contradict* the miracle theme of the pericope.

56. See note 37.

57. Cf. the introductions found in verses 29, 32, 35, and 40 (if vv. 40–45
are part of the complex).

this complex is "a day in the life of Jesus." One would expect that the complex would therefore begin with a description of Jesus' activity. It is *his* actions that the complex seeks to emphasize. Yet if the pericope begins at verse 23, we find that the chronological pattern is broken and that it is not Jesus we encounter first in the complex but a man with an unclean spirit. The fact that this pericope stands in a pre-Marcan complex argues for a more extensive introduction than simply verse 23a. We would expect that the pre-Marcan compiler who smoothly joined the various pericopes to form this complex would also have introduced the complex with something more than verse 23a. Of course, if Mark himself were the compiler of this complex, then all the editorial work would be his.

Do we find in these verses a description of a Palestinian Sitz im Leben? We have already described the attempt by Daube to demonstrate that verses 21 and 22 and the phrase "a new teaching with authority" in verse 27 reflect a Palestinian *Sitz im Leben* and that these verses were not only part of the pre-Marcan tradition but part of the first *Sitz im Leben*,[58] so that we need not give a recapitulation of his thesis. If the thesis of Daube is correct, we would have to conclude that verse 22 and the expression "a new teaching with authority" were always part of the tradition and thus not a Marcan redaction. There are a number of reasons, however, why we cannot accept Daube's thesis. For one, Daube's thesis demands that the term "scribes" originally meant "inferior teachers in contrast to the rabbis."[59] Yet in the church certainly it was never thought that the teaching of Jesus possessed an authority "greater than the inferior teachers (the scribes) and (almost?) as good as the rabbis." From the first time that this story was told it was assumed that the teaching of Jesus possessed an authority such as no rabbi or prophet ever possessed. It could, of course, be true that the original incident was later misunderstood and reinterpreted by the church, but to what extent can we say that the "scribes" and "rabbis" were so clearly differentiated? Daube acknowledges that in the New Testament the term "scribe" refers not to an inferior teacher but to a learned man. This means that only in the first *Sitz im*

---

58. See above p. 83.

59. The present writer does not deny that the term "scribes" can have a meaning such as Daube maintains. (See Gerhardsson, *Memory and Manuscript*, 57.) What he denies is that it must or that it usually did.

Leben could this term possibly mean "inferior teacher." We must assume according to Daube's thesis that the account in Mark is literally correct and that Jesus was specifically compared to the inferior scribal teachers and not the learned rabbis. It might be possible, if the rest of Daube's thesis were convincing, to accept this definition of "scribes," but as it stands this term cannot by itself be interpreted to mean "inferior teachers."[60]

Daube also argues that the authority spoken of in verses 22 and 27 is a specific and technical term for *reshuth,* which is the authority to lay down binding decisions concerning legal matters. Yet in the pericope—and we must remember that Daube is arguing for the pre-Marcan origin (actually the historicity) of the pericope—this authority is attributed to Jesus not because of the binding decision he lays down, for none is even mentioned, but because of his power over the demon. Daube refers to the fact that the rabbis were expected to possess familiarity with and power over the world of spirits,[61] but what is secondary with regard to the authority of the rabbis, that is, power over the demons, is primary with regard to the authority of Jesus in our pericope, and what is primary with regard to the authority of the rabbis, that is, power to lay down binding decisions, is not even mentioned. It appears therefore that Daube's attempt to find a Palestinian *Sitz im Leben* in these verses is not successful.

Now that we have investigated these verses, what can we conclude as to the probability of these verses being a Marcan seam? In our investigation we discovered that both the vocabulary and the style argue in favor of these verses being a Marcan redaction. We also discovered that the emphasis on Jesus' teaching, on Jesus' authority, and on the amazement that Jesus' actions produce are Marcan themes, so that this argues in favor of Mark 1:21–22 being a Marcan seam. We also discovered that the teaching emphasis found in these verses is not essential to the pericope and that, although this emphasis does not necessarily conflict with the pericope, it stands in conflict with the usual way of introducing a healing story in the second *Sitz im Leben.* The only limiting fact that we discovered is that since the pericope is contained in a pre-Marcan complex it must have

60. Daube, *New Testament and Rabbinic Judaism,* 211, acknowledges this.
61. Daube is correct in this. See note 42.

been introduced by at least a statement such as verse 2:1b or Mark 3:1a. In the light of all this it would appear that the Marcan redaction consists of verse 22,[62] the καὶ εὐθύς in verse 23, and the διδαχὴ καινὴ κατ᾽ ἐξουσίαν in verse 27.[63] It may very well be that the emphasis on teaching in verse 21 and the geographical localization are also due to Mark, but this is less certain.

Ascertaining the Marcan redaction, however, is only part of our task. *Redaktionsgeschichtlich* investigation differs from form-critical investigation in that having ascertained the redaction it now concentrates its energies upon the investigation of the theological significance of the redaction, whereas form criticism lays aside the redaction in order to investigate the pericope. With regard to the Marcan redaction in these verses we find that the Evangelist has stressed that Jesus taught and that his teaching possessed a unique authority. Why did Jesus' teaching possess this authority? Whereas the authority of the scribes was wholly derivative, stemming from the collected opinions of their predecessors, was the authority of Jesus direct and independent of such quotations or the opinions of the rabbis?[64] This is true with regard to the Gospel of Matthew, where we find the frequent, "Ye have heard it said but I say . . . ," but we do not find any trace of this in Mark. Is it because Jesus taught "in terms of real-life situations without appealing to the written word"?[65] We do not find any trace of this in our passage. Or is it because the audience was amazed that Jesus performed his exorcisms without any magical incantations?[66] Again noth-

---

62. Best, *Temptation and the Passion,* 68, argues that Mark would not have referred to the scribes as the enemies of Jesus because in a Hellenistic environment such a reference would be meaningless. The term "scribes" appears in Mark twenty-one times, however, and Mark, like any reader of the Gospels today, thought readily of the scribes when he thought of the opponents of Jesus. The fact that they are mentioned in Mark 8:31 and 10:33 (regardless of whether these verses are traditional, Marcan summaries, or Marcan creations) shows that Mark must have thought of the scribes as enemies of Jesus. It would have been natural therefore for him to refer to them in Mark 1:22.

63. This is essentially the same view as that of Pesch, "Wirkens Jesu in Kapharnaum," 117f. See also Bultmann, *History of the Synoptic Tradition,* 209; Schweizer, *Das Evangelium nach Markus,* 26–27; and Sundwall, *Die Zusammensetzung des Markusevangeliums,* 9.

64. So Nineham, *Gospel of St. Mark,* 74.

65. So Lindars, *New Testament Apologetic,* 30.

66. So Taylor, *Gospel According to St. Mark,* 176. See Josephus, *Antiquities* 8.2.5 for an example of such an incantation.

ing like this is said or implied by Mark. All such attempts err in seeking to explain from out of the first *Sitz im Leben* a description of Jesus whose origin took place in the third *Sitz im Leben*. Since we have seen that the stress on Jesus' teaching with authority is due to the hand of Mark, we must be concerned with why the Evangelist thought the teaching of Jesus possessed authority.

From the Marcan insertion in verse 27 and from the fact that Mark has introduced a pericope of an exorcism by means of a description of Jesus' teaching authority, it is evident that for Mark these two activities are intimately related.[67] The exorcisms of Jesus witness to the authority of his teaching. Since Jesus possesses authority over the demons, it is therefore evident that his teaching must also possess authority. Mark sees this exorcism as a "seal" of Jesus' authority as a teacher.[68] It is important to note that Mark by his redaction emphasizes Jesus' teaching at the expense of his exorcising. Whereas originally the pericope portrayed Jesus primarily as a thaumaturge, Mark by his redaction has made the central emphasis of the pericope fall upon Jesus' activity as a teacher. The exorcism that was once the key thought of the pericope now serves primarily as a verification of Jesus' teaching authority. It would appear therefore that Best is correct in his criticism of J. M. Robinson's thesis.[69] For Mark, Jesus is primarily a teacher and not an exorcist![70]

There is another possible redactional emphasis in this seam, which is related to the emphasis on Jesus' teaching authority. It was expected that the messianic age would bring with it a new teaching[71] as well as the defeat of the evil pow-

67. Best, *Temptation and the Passion*, 68–69, is therefore not exactly correct when he argues that in Mark 1:21–22 Mark pictures Jesus above all as a teacher. His exorcisms, Best maintains, come later. Yet Mark 1:21–22 serves as an introduction to Mark 1:23f., and it is evident from verse 27 that Jesus' authority as a teacher comes partly at least from his ability to cast out demons.

68. Schweizer, *Das Evangelium nach Markus*, 27, correctly states, "Das Wunder ist das Vollmachtszeichen für Jesu Lehre." Although Daube's thesis must be rejected, he is correct in seeing that the authority of a rabbi and his ability to exorcise demons are related. See John 3:2.

69. See his *Problem of History in Mark*.

70. See Schweizer, "Anmerkungen zur Theologie des Markus," 39, for a similar view.

71. See The Targum on Isa. 12:3; 1 Enoch 5:8; 48:1; 49:1f.; 91:10; 2 Bar. 44:14; Sibylline Orcles 3.757; 1 Macc. 4:46; 14:41. For a detailed survey of the rabbinic literature, see Billerbeck, *Kommentar zum Neuen Testament*, 4:1f. A

ers.[72] In this the first pericope after the summary, excluding the call of the four fishermen to discipleship, Mark emphasizes the "newness" of Jesus' teaching. It may be therefore that Mark by his redaction also sought to stress that Jesus, the Messiah, brought to the "new age" a new teaching.[73]

Ἰησοῦς Διδάσκαλος in Mark

It has been customary to claim a greater interest in the teaching of Jesus for Matthew than for Mark.[74] The reason for this is obvious. Matthew contains a great deal more teaching material than does Mark. Yet in two instances[75] where Mark has the title "Teacher" Matthew has changed it to "Lord," and in three instances[76] where Mark has "Teacher" Matthew omits it. Furthermore Matthew eliminates the verb διδάσκειν nine times[77] from the parallel account in Mark, and once he changes it.[78] In all Matthew uses the term διδάσκαλος in his Gospel twelve times as compared to twelve times for Mark. He uses διδάσκειν fourteen times as compared to seventeen times for Mark, and he uses διδαχή three compared to five times for Mark. In the light of the fact that Matthew contains over 58 percent more material than Mark[79] it would appear that Mark as well as Matthew portrays Jesus as a teacher. Matthew seeks to do so primarily by listing the sayings and teachings of Jesus. Mark seeks to do so primarily by referring to Jesus' teaching activity and by calling him "teacher."

---

detailed discussion of this question is also found in Davies, *Sermon on the Mount,* 109f., and *Torah.*

72. See note 42.

73. The use of the term καινός is significant, for "Καινός is the epitome of the wholly different and miraculous thing which is brought by the time of salvation" (*TDNT,* 3:449).

Davies, *Sermon on the Mount,* 100, 190, maintains that Matthew saw the messianic connotation in the expression "new teaching" and so in Matt. 7:28 omits the term "new" in order to temper the language.

74. So Bultmann, *History of the Synoptic Tradition,* 356.

75. Mark 4:38–Matt. 8:25; Mark 9:17–Matt. 17:15.

76. Mark 10:20–Matt. 19:20; Mark 10:35–Matt. 20:20; Mark 13:1–Matt. 24:1.

77. See Mark 2:13; 4:1, 2; 6:34; 9:31; 10:1; 11:17; 12:14, 35 and parallels.

78. Mark 8:31–Matt. 16:21.

79. This figure was obtained by observing that in the Nestle Greek text Matthew consists of eighty-four pages and Mark of fifty-three pages.

The great emphasis Mark places upon Jesus as a teacher raises the question, "If Mark sought to portray Jesus as a teacher, why do we not find a great deal more of Jesus' teachings in his Gospel?" Martin Dibelius recognized this problem and argued that the transmission of the sayings of Jesus and the transmission of his deeds and actions proceeded in different ways.[80] As a result until the time of Mark the sayings of Jesus were never combined with the narrative accounts of Jesus' deeds, so that it was natural for Mark to seek to keep the two separate. Whatever the value of such a view with regard to the individual narratives, it is of no value when the Gospel as a whole is taken into consideration. Mark clearly sees no inconsistency in including a parable collection (Mark 4:1f.), teachings on greatness (Mark 9:33f.), teachings on temptation (Mark 9:42f.), and an eschatological discourse (Mark 13:1f.) in his Gospel. Bultmann[81] agrees with Dibelius. Since Mark sought to unite *"the Hellenistic kerygma about Christ"* with the *"tradition of the story of Jesus,"*[82] the question is not why Mark omitted so much of the sayings of Jesus but why he included any at all. Bultmann can only say this, however, because he does not fully recognize the *redaktionsgeschichtlich* emphasis of Mark upon Jesus' teaching. Best also recognizes the problem created by the meager amount of teaching material found in Mark in the light of the Marcan emphasis upon Jesus' teaching. He concludes that possibly Mark may not have possessed any more of the teachings of Jesus than he included in his Gospel.[83] But is this likely? It is difficult for this writer to believe that Mark possessed no more of the teachings of Jesus than found in Mark. This is especially difficult to believe if the writer of this Gospel was John Mark, who was a friend of Peter, Paul, and Barnabas, and whose

80. In his *From Tradition to Gospel,* Dibelius states that *"the handing down of the actual words of Jesus depends upon a law different from that which governed the gathering together of Mark's material."* On p. 264 he states that it is with Mark that we begin the process of putting together the words of Jesus with the deeds of Jesus. From the pre-Marcan complex found in Mark 2:1–3:6, however, it would appear that before Mark wrote his Gospel the union of narrative material and sayings had already taken place. See Mark 2:19–22.

81. Bultmann, *History of the Synoptic Tradition,* 347.

82. Ibid.

83. Best, *Temptation and the Passion,* 103.

home was the meeting place of the early church (Acts 12:12). At one time Burnett Hillman Streeter thought that Mark may have written his Gospel as an introduction for "Q,"[84] but this is extremely unlikely because the differences between Mark and "Q" in the material they report in common (the baptismal accounts, Mark 4:21–25, and Mark 4:20–32) indicates that Mark did not know "Q." W. D. Davies has argued that Mark was written in reaction to the overemphasis "Q" placed on the teachings of Jesus.[85] Two things, however, mitigate against this. First, it is doubtful that Mark knew Q.[86] Second, the great emphasis Mark gives to the teaching activity of Jesus contradicts the view that Mark is seeking to minimize the teachings of Jesus. Eduard Schweizer has sought to explain this problem by stating that Mark sought to guard against the possibility of seeking to understand Jesus in terms of what can be ascertained and recorded in history.[87] The attempt to keep kerygmatic theology from the "heresy" of historicism may be a goal of the twentieth-century existentialist, but it certainly was not that of Mark. If Mark sought to avoid the heresy of historicism, why did he insert so many geographical and temporal designations into his Gospel? Why not leave them timeless and placeless pieces of kerygma? Perhaps the best explanation so far has been put forth by Friedrich Normann.[88] Normann gives two reasons for this emphasis upon Jesus teaching as found in Mark. First, it corresponds to the historical situation of the first *Sitz im Leben*. Jesus was a teacher and Mark was well aware of this. Second, Mark sought to give support to the catechetical practice of the early church by demonstrating that Jesus frequently taught his disciples. Unfortunately no explanation has been put forth of yet that is entirely convincing. The question still remains "Why does Mark seek to portray Jesus as a teacher and yet include so little of his teachings in the Gospel?"

84. *Four Gospels*, 187.
85. *Paul and Rabbinic Judaism*, 142.
86. See Streeter, *Four Gospels*, 186–91; Taylor, *Gospel According to St. Mark*, 87; and Throckmorton, "Did Mark Know Q," 327. For the opposing view, see Brown, "Mark as Witness," 44.
87. "Anmerkungen zur Theologie des Markus," 44–45.
88. *Christos Didaskalos*, 18.

Conclusion

The importance of the Marcan seams in *redaktionsgeschichtlich* investigation is clearly evident from the above investigation. From the Marcan seam of Mark 1:21–22 we have learned that Mark seeks to portray to his readers a picture of Jesus as a teacher. For Mark, Jesus is far more a teacher than an exorcist. We have also mentioned briefly that by stressing the "newness" of Jesus' teaching Mark may be seeking to demonstrate to his readers that Jesus' coming was the inauguration of a new age. Besides these two *redaktionsgeschichtlich* emphases we have alluded to two others found in this seam. Mark seeks to stress the authority of Jesus. In our seam Jesus possesses authority over demons. His teaching also possesses a unique authority. According to Mark 2:10 Jesus possesses authority to forgive sins, and in Mark 11:28f. we find that he possesses authority to cleanse the temple. A second emphasis we alluded to is the amazement that Jesus' actions cause. It is quite evident from our investigation of this seam that the writer of the second Gospel is no mere "scissors and paste man." His purpose in writing his Gospel is not merely to record the Gospel traditions but to give a theological interpretation of those traditions.

5

The Transfiguration in Mark (9:2–8)

A Misplaced Resurrection Account?

Since the turn of the century[1] the thesis that the transfiguration was originally a resurrection account has gained a number of adherents.[2] Some scholars have gone so far as to claim

---

1. According to Baltensweiler (*Die Verklärung Jesu*, 91) the first to espouse this view was Wellhausen (*Das Evangelium Marci*, 71). Blinzler (*Die neutestamentlichen Berichte*, 116 n. 90) and Schmithals ("Der Markusschluss," 384 n. 11) have pointed out that G. Volkmar had earlier suggested this.

2. Besides G. Volkmar and J. Wellhausen, Blinzler (*Die neutestamentlichen Berichte*, 116 nn. 90, 120) lists as advocates of this view the following: H. von Soden, B. W. Bacon, P. Wendland, G. Wohlenberg, H. Stocks, and J. Kreyenbühl. Schmithals ("Der Markusschluss," 384 n. 13) adds the following: R. Bultmann, W. Bousset, E. Klostermann, G. Bertram, K. G. Goetz, M. Goguel, M. S. Enslin, O. J. F. Seitz, C. E. Carlston, P. Vielhauer, H. Koester, and J. M. Robinson. In addition to these we can also add Loisy, *Les évangiles synoptiques*, 2:39–40; Montefiore, *Synoptic Gospels*, 1:204; Käsemann, "Wunder im NT"; Betz, "Jesus as Divine Man," 120; Weeden, *Mark*, 118–26; Beare, "Concerning Jesus of Nazareth," 59; McCurley, "'And after Six Days,'" 79; Schmithals, "Der Markusschluss," 385, 394; and perhaps Thrall, "Elijah and Moses," 305–17, especially 310.

that this is now the majority view today,[3] and others state dog-
matically that the burden of proof lies upon those who deny
this thesis.[4] In several recent works on Mark the thesis that
Mark has purposely transferred the story of the transfiguration,
which was originally a pre-Marcan resurrection account, into the
lifetime of the historical Jesus forms the basis for a particular
view of why Mark wrote his Gospel. Theodore J. Weeden,[5] for
instance, argues that the pre-Marcan version of the transfiguration account was originally a resurrection account that
belonged to the tradition of Mark's opponents and that this
account was the cornerstone of their Christological position.
Mark, by predating the transfiguration in the ministry of Jesus
and making it a prefigurement of the parousia, has shifted the
time of the exaltation from the time of the resurrection (and
thus the present time of the church) to the time of the parousia.

The purpose of this chapter is to investigate critically the
arguments that have been set forth in support of the theory
that the transfiguration was originally a resurrection account
and to posit some arguments in favor of the view that in the
pre-Marcan tradition the transfiguration referred to an event
within the lifetime of the historical Jesus. In particular, we shall
seek to establish that Mark did not transform a resurrection
account into our present account of the transfiguration.

The Transfiguration—A Pre-Marcan Resurrection Account

Terminological Considerations

Several arguments have been adduced to the effect that certain terms contained in the transfiguration account are best
explained if the account originally referred to a resurrection
appearance. The use of the term ὤφθη (there appeared) in Mark
9:4 indicates to some that this account was originally a resurrection account, for this term is "used almost as a technical

---

3. Klostermann (*Das Markusevangelium*, 86) states: "Die meisten modernen
Erklärer nahmen . . . mit Recht an, dass es sich eigentlich um eine Auferstehungsgeschichte handelt." Blinzler (*Die neutestamentlichen Berichte*, 118) rightly
criticizes him for this statement.

4. Carlston ("Transfiguration and Resurrection," 235) states: "In short, the
'misplaced resurrection account' can be disproved as the correct explanation of
the Transfiguration only if objections to the more primitive form—appearance
directly from heaven—can be shown to be insuperable."

5. *Mark*, 123–34; also see McCurley, "'And after Six Days,'" 79; and
Schmithals, "Der Markusschluss," 385.

word in the description of resurrection appearances."[6] This argument can be quickly dismissed, however, for ὤφθη is not used in the account to describe Jesus at all. It is not Jesus who ὤφθη, but Elijah with Moses. On the other hand, if we claim that originally ὤφθη referred to Jesus in the pericope and that Mark by his redaction modified the tradition so that its original sense was lost, we encounter two problems. First, we encounter the difficulty that the term occurs too late in the pericope to refer to an appearance of the risen Lord, for Jesus has been present all along and has already been transfigured. Mark would not only have had to change the subject of ὤφθη but also the location of the term. Furthermore, we no longer can claim then that ὤφθη is a *terminus technicus* for the resurrection in the mind of Mark. This would create a great problem for Weeden's thesis, for elsewhere he argues strongly that Mark's careful use of ὄψεσθε (you will see) in Mark 16:7, which is a Marcan insertion, implies that he has the parousia in mind for if he had meant the resurrection he would have used ὤφθη.[7]

It has also been argued that the presence of a cloud in the account would be more appropriate in a resurrection context, for the cloud is an appropriate vehicle for ascension.[8] Acts 1:9 and Revelation 11:12 are given as examples. Yet are we to assume from Acts 1:9 that νεφέλη (cloud) is a kind of *terminus technicus* for the resurrection–ascension of Jesus? In the transfiguration it must be noted that the cloud comes upon αὐτοῖς (them), not Jesus alone. The αὐτοῖς must refer here to Jesus, Elijah, and Moses, or to all present.[9] It is not an ascension-cloud at all, for when it disappears Jesus remains behind whereas Elijah (cf. 2 Kings 2:1–2) and Moses have ascended. Actually, the presence of the cloud in the account does not refer to Jesus or the glory of Jesus but is a sign for the presence of God.[10] The presence of the cloud, moreover, cannot refer to the parousia, since the term occurs in the singular, not the plural,[11] and whereas the

---

6. Weeden, *Mark*, 119.

7. Ibid., 111–12.

8. Ibid., 120.

9. The αὐτούς in Luke 9:34 seems to indicate this.

10. So Horstmann (*Studien*, 99) and Baltensweiler (*Die Verklärung Jesu*, 85 n. 87).

11. Horstmann, *Studien*, 99. The Son of man is usually portrayed as coming on the *clouds* of heaven. See Matt. 24:30; 26:64; Mark 13:26; 14:62; 1 Thess. 4:17; Rev. 1:17. Luke 21:27 is the only exception.

Son of man at the parousia comes with the *clouds* of heaven, in this account the *cloud* goes away and the Son of man remains.[12] The presence of the cloud in the transfiguration account is, therefore, not to be associated with either the ascension or the parousia but most probably with the presence of God.[13] A cloud in the account in no way proves that originally the account stood as a resurrection story.

The reference to a high mountain in this account is also seen by some as an indication that the transfiguration was originally a resurrection account. Rudolf Bultmann has suggested that the mountain in the account is essentially the same mountain referred to in Matthew 28:16,[14] and C. E. Carlston argues that in only two other instances in the New Testament do we find mention of a ὄρος ὑψηλὸν (high mountain), and in both of these (Matt. 4:8 and Rev. 21:10) the place designated is a place of "epiphany and supernatural encounter."[15] Does an "epiphany and supernatural encounter," however, require that the incident in question be a resurrection? Certainly not, for neither Matthew 4:8 nor Revelation 21:10 refers to a resurrection. As to the ὄρος (mountain) in this account, it is true that a mountain figures in one resurrection account, but we also read of a mountain in Matthew 5:1–2 and Mark 3:13–19 (see also Matt. 14:23). The presence of a mountain or a high mountain, therefore, does not affect in any way whether an account was a resurrection or nonresurrection account.

Although the term δόξα (glory) does not appear as a descriptive term for Jesus in the Marcan and Matthean accounts (it does appear in Luke 9:32), it is evident that in these accounts we are dealing with a "glorified" Jesus. Yet the glory of Jesus present at the transfiguration is a glory frequently associated in the New Testament with the resurrected Lord (Acts 7:55; 9:3; 22:6, 9, 11; 26:13; 1 Cor. 15:8, 40; 1 Pet. 1:11, 21; Heb. 2:9; 1 Tim.

12. We shall not enter at this time into the question of whether Jesus spoke of the Son of man or used this title of himself. We will only assume that before Mark was written the early church identified Jesus as the Son of man.

13. Baltensweiler (*Die Verklärung Jesu,* 93) points out that the cloud serves "bei der Himmelfahrt und bei der Parusie deutlich als Gefährt, in der Verklärungsgeschichte dagegen 'überschattet' sie die Gestalten."

14. *History of the Synoptic Tradition,* 259. See Baltensweiler (*Die Verklärung Jesu,* 57–59) for the view that the "high mountain" in the account ties the transfiguration with the temptation account.

15. Carlston, "Transfiguration and Resurrection," 237.

3:16).[16] It is also pointed out that the glorification of clothes in apocalyptic literature is a distinctive characteristic of the exalted state of a heavenly being.[17] As a result, it is argued, the transfiguration must originally have been a resurrection pericope that spoke of the δόξα of the risen Christ. Because of the importance of this point, we shall put off our discussion of this matter until later.[18]

Still another terminological consideration that has led some scholars into thinking that the transfiguration was originally a resurrection story is the temporal designation with which the account begins. It is argued that the few explicit datings we find in the synoptic accounts very often have to do with the resurrection.[19] Various views have been posited as to what the "after six days" refers.[20] Recently, F. R. McCurley has argued that "after six days" is a common Semitic literary pattern that dramatically prepares for the climactic event of the seventh day.[21] Assuming that the temporal designation is pre-Marcan, he argues that originally this designation stood within the peri-

16. Ibid., 235; cf. Boobyer (*Transfiguration Story*, 24–25) and Thrall ("Elijah and Moses," 310), who states: "The tradition which we know to be earlier than Mark, and with which we may legitimately conjecture that he was acquainted, implies that Jesus appeared to his followers after the Resurrection in precisely the state of glory in which he is pictured in the Transfiguration scene." As Boobyer himself points out, the risen Christ who appeared to Paul possessed a glorious heavenly body, and Paul regards his own experience as of the same order as those of Peter and James and all the apostles.

17. Cf. 1 Enoch 62:15–16; 2 Enoch 22:8; Rev. 4:4; 7:9. Robinson ("On the *Gattung*,"116) points out that "in gnostic Gospels, cast normally in the framework of resurrection appearances, a luminous apparition comparable to the transfiguration is the rule."

18. See below, pp. 108–10.

19. Carlston, "Transfiguration and Resurrection," 236; cf. also Baltensweiler, *Die Verklärung Jesu,* 92.

20. Carlston ("Transfiguration and Resurrection," 236) lists the following: the six days of Moses on Mount Sinai (Exod. 24:16); the six days of the week leading up to the Sabbath; the six days between the Day of Atonement and the Feast of Tabernacles; the seven days of the Feast of Tabernacles; a hexaemeron of teaching such as found in John 1:19–2:11; and the traditional six-day interval between the first and second initiation in the mysteries.

21. "'And after Six Days,'" 67–81. The attempt by McCurley to transpose the temporal designation from the beginning of the account into the middle has no support from the text itself. Furthermore, it is unnecessary. If the temporal phrase, "and 'after six days' (Mark 9:2), is thus equivalent to the expression, 'and on the seventh day'" (p. 81), and if this is a literary device that points to a climactic action on the seventh day, does not a transfiguration six days after

cope and referred to a six-day period of waiting and preparation on the mountain after which the risen Lord experienced his
ascension.[22] That the temporal designation in Mark 9:2 is pre-
Marcan can be assumed[23] and that it is connected with some
event in the pre-Marcan tradition is evident, but McCurley's
attempt to place the designation within the pericope finds no
support in the text at all. Not only does it find no support in the
text, but it is also opposed by the text. In contrast to McCurley's
reconstruction of the text, does not the present connection of
the transfiguration with the events at Caesarea Philippi found
in Mark, Matthew, and Luke deserve a priori consideration?
Certainly the transfiguration provides a perfect climax to the
events at Caesarea Philippi. It must also be noted that there
are several explicit datings in the synoptic accounts that have
nothing to do with the resurrection,[24] so that the presence of a
temporal designation does not require that the account must
have been a resurrection account. Moreover, the reference to
"after six days" would be most unusual for a resurrection appearance since the temporal designations associated in the tradition with the resurrection are "after three days," "on the first
day," and "during forty days."

Form-Critical Considerations

It has been argued by several scholars that the similarity
between the transfiguration and various resurrection accounts
indicates that originally the transfiguration must have been a
resurrection account. Both occur on the same day, the Sabbath;[25] the dress and glory of the angels in the resurrection
accounts are paralleled by Jesus' metamorphosis in the transfiguration account; the sonship of Jesus is mentioned in both

---

the confession at Caesarea Philippi seem more climactic than an ascension
after six days on a mountain?

22. Ibid., 79, 81.

23. Bultmann, *History of the Synoptic Tradition*, 243; Baltensweiler, *Die Verklärung Jesu*, 46; Horstmann, *Studien*, 100; McCurley, "'And after Six Days,'" 81;
Schmidt, *Der Rahmen*, 222.

24. Mark 1:32, 35; 11:12, 20; 14:1, 12; 15:1.

25. Thrall's argument ("Elijah and Moses," 311) that "'after six days' implies
'on the seventh day,' and Mark takes pains to point out that it was on the Sabbath that the Resurrection itself took place" is beside the point. We are not
interested here with any possible Marcan redaction, but with what the "after six
days" would have meant in the pre-Marcan tradition.

and the divine sonship of Jesus is usually associated with the resurrection (cf. Acts 13:33; Rom. 1:4);[26] and only in the transfiguration and the resurrection is a miracle performed on Jesus rather than by him.[27]

Later in this chapter we shall see that a stronger case can be made for the dissimilarity of the transfiguration and the accounts of the resurrection appearances,[28] but at this point we shall simply look critically at the alleged similarities. With regard to the day of the resurrection it is very difficult to conceive of anyone in the early church assuming that a resurrection appearance "after six days" would refer to a Sabbath-day resurrection.[29] One need not be guilty of historicizing, if one asks the question, "Six days after what?" A resurrection appearance "after six days" would have been dated, in the mind of the early church, from the crucifixion. This is evident from the parallel expression "after three days." "After six days," therefore, would not imply that Jesus rose on the Sabbath, but six days after the crucifixion. If the account referred to a Sabbath-day resurrection, we would expect μετὰ τὴν ἕμκτεν ἡμέραν (after the sixth day) rather than μετὰ ἑξ ἡμέρας (after six days).

With regard to the similarity of dress between the angels at the resurrection and Jesus at the transfiguration, it must be noted that any such similarity is outweighed far more by the dissimilarity between the appearance of Jesus in the resurrection accounts and in the transfiguration account. As for the claim that Jesus' sonship is primarily associated with the resurrection, this is debatable. The Gospel tradition assumed that the historical Jesus was no less the Son of God than the risen Lord,[30] and it should be noted that at the baptism there is a divine voice affirming Jesus' sonship just as at the transfiguration. The final argument mentioned is that only in the transfiguration and the resurrection accounts is a miracle worked on Jesus

26. Ibid. Thrall's article is somewhat confusing in that one is never sure as to what *Sitz im Leben* she is referring.

27. Carlston, "Transfiguration and Resurrection," 234.

28. See below, pp. 113–16.

29. So Thrall, "Elijah and Moses," 311.

30. Cf. Mark 3:11; 5:7; 12:6; 13:32; 14:61–62; 15:39; Matt. 2:15; 4:3, 6; 14:33; 16:16; 27:40, 43; Luke 1:35; 4:41. That much of the above is redactional is, of course, true. Nevertheless, it is evident that the early church associated divine sonship with the historical Jesus.

rather than by him. This is simply not true. Certainly the baptism accounts portray a miracle being worked on Jesus before the resurrection and the similarities between the baptism and the transfiguration are far closer than those between the transfiguration and any resurrection account.

Redactional Considerations

A number of scholars have attempted on the basis of the Marcan redaction of this passage to demonstrate that the transfiguration and the events of Caesarea Philippi were not connected in the pre-Marcan tradition and that the Marcan redaction indicates that originally the transfiguration was a resurrection account. K. G. Goetz has argued that Mark 9:2–10 breaks the sequence of Mark 9:1 and 9:11–12.[31] As a result, he claims that the transfiguration was not connected originally to Peter's confession. It is far from certain, however, that Mark 9:11–12 was originally connected with Mark 9:1. On the contrary, a good case could be made for assuming that the saying about Elijah (Mark 9:11–12) was originally connected to the transfiguration account, in which Elijah plays so prominent a part. Yet even if Goetz's thesis is granted, it proves at most that the transfiguration account was not connected to the events of Caesarea Philippi or Mark 9:11–12 in the pre-Marcan tradition. It in no way follows that the transfiguration must therefore have been a resurrection account in the pre-Marcan tradition.

It has also been argued that in Mark the transfiguration clearly serves the purpose of confirming Peter's confession and ratifying Jesus' prediction of his suffering and resurrection;[32] and since the passion sayings are primarily a Marcan redaction,[33] the arrangement of the transfiguration after Peter's confession and the passion prediction serves Mark's purpose well. There is no denying that in its present position the transfiguration serves the Marcan redactional aim well. It would be most surprising if it did not. Yet this does not prove that before this these two accounts were not connected, and even if they were

31. Goetz, *Petrus*, 78; Bultmann, *History of the Synoptic Tradition,* 124; Klostermann, *Das Markusevangelium,* 98; Horstmann, *Studien,* 72. For the view that Mark 9:11–13 fits better with the transfiguration account, see Schmidt, *Der Rahmen,* 226; Taylor, *Gospel According to St. Mark,* 393–94.

32. Carlston, "Transfiguration and Resurrection," 240.

33. Schreiber, "Die Christologie des Markusevangeliums," 154–83.

not connected, this does not prove that the transfiguration lay before Mark as a resurrection account.

According to W. Schmithals Mark 9:9–10, which is clearly Marcan, indicates that Mark is explaining to his readers that the reason the transfiguration was known to them as a resurrection account was due to the fact that the disciples were forbidden to talk about the incident until after the resurrection. Since the disciples faithfully kept Jesus' word on this matter, the account was subsequently misunderstood.[34] Schmithals' hypothesis is interesting and unique, but it labors under insurmountable objections. Can one take the Marcan secrecy motif in Mark 9:9–10 and interpret it uniquely in this one instance, as Schmithals does? It must be remembered that this is not the only command to silence in Mark. Are we to assume that Mark 1:21–28, 32–34, 40–45; 3:7–12; 5:35–43; 7:31–37; and 8:27–30 are all to be understood as resurrection accounts in the Marcan tradition because there is present in each a command to secrecy? A more important and basic objection, however, is the fact that this explanation is based upon too many unproven assumptions. For one it assumes that the transfiguration was a pre-Marcan resurrection account. Second, it assumes that Mark's readers knew it as such an account. Third, it assumes that the secrecy motif would have been interpreted by his readers to mean "since this incident was not to be spoken of until after the resurrection, it was subsequently understood as a resurrection account." Finally, it assumes that Mark believed that his readers who only knew of this account as a resurrection account would immediately give up their understanding of the account and accept this new interpretation. Any one of these assumptions is doubtful, but to assume all four is most unlikely. Essentially, Schmithals' argument is not a proof of his assumption that the transfiguration was a pre-Marcan resurrection account but an interpretation of what Mark was doing based upon that assumption.[35]

Although a great deal has been written on the subject, there still does not exist any consensus on the extent of the Marcan

---

34. "Der Markusschluss," 394–95.

35. This writer believes that an even better case could be made out, if one wanted, for assuming that Mark created the transfiguration account and that Mark 9:9–10 is an attempt to explain why his readers had never heard of the story before.

redaction of the passage and thus of the pre-Marcan form of the tradition. Many scholars are agreed that verse 6 is Marcan;[36] McCurley includes verse 5;[37] and M. Horstmann includes the ἀκούετε αὐτοῦ (listen to him) of verse 7.[38] As to the original form of the account, various theories of partition have been proposed, but here too there has been no consensus.[39]

Historical Considerations

One argument presented by Carlston in favor of the transfiguration having been originally a resurrection account is that if such an incident took place in the lifetime of Jesus the subsequent behavior of the disciples would be inexplicable. If Peter, James, and John were present at a "transfiguration," could they later have denied their Lord?[40] At this point we must remember, however, that our primary task is a limited one, that is, to demonstrate that the transfiguration was not a pre-Marcan resurrection account that the Evangelist transformed into an event in the ministry of Jesus. Whatever may be the value of Carlston's argument with regard to the first *Sitz im Leben* (the period of the historical Jesus), it possesses no value for the account in the second (the period of the early church). Certainly in the

36. Bultmann, *History of the Synoptic Tradition*, 261; Thrall, "Elijah and Moses," 308; Weeden, *Mark*, 121; Horstmann, *Studien*, 81; Baltensweiler, *Die Verklärung Jesu*, 31; McCurley, "'And after Six Days,'" 77; Hahn, *Titles of Jesus*, 300.

37. "'And after Six Days,'" 77.

38. *Studien*, 89.

39. Lohmeyer ("Die Verklärung Jesu," 186–215) initially argued that verses 2, 3, and 6 are secondary, but later (*Das Evangelium des Markus*, 174 n. 7) changed his opinion in favor of the unity of the account. Müller ("Die Verklärung Jesu," 57) argues that the present account consists of two stories: verses 2c–6 + 8 and verses 2a–b + 7 + (9). Horstmann's conclusion (*Studien*, 80) seems a reasonable minimum: "Die vorliegende Perikope gliedert sich in drei Teile: 1. Verklärung Jesu auf dem Berg und die Erscheinung von Elias und Moses, 2. Vorschlag des Petrus, Hütten zu bauen, 3. Wolke und Wolkenstimme. Dadurch, dass die Wolkenstimme einerseits die notwendige Korrektur des Petrus darstellt und anderseits deutend zurückgreift auf das Verklärungsgeschehen, ist eine Geschlossenheit der Erzählung gegeben."

40. He states ("Transfiguration and Resurrection," 233) that "fewer facts in the subsequent history of the disciples are more certain than Peter's denial and the 'cowardice' of all three disciples at the crucifixion; yet it seems *a priori* unlikely that such conduct would follow an experience of this kind, and it is *a posteriori* evident that doubt and fear were banished for these disciples by the Resurrection, not the Transfiguration."

second *Sitz im Leben* the account could have made sense even as the account in Mark made sense to Matthew and Luke and to many readers after them. If Matthew–Mark–Luke could accept the transfiguration as an event in the life of Jesus, why should we imagine that the pre-Marcan tradition could not? Furthermore, if for the sake of argument we assume the historicity of the account, would it have been impossible for Peter to deny his Lord after such an experience?

What concerns us in this chapter, however, is the fact that whatever the historical difficulties and the kind of event, if any, that gave rise to the account, there is no reason why the form of the story in the second *Sitz im Leben* could not be substantially the same as the form in which we find it in Mark.

Parallels to the Synoptic Accounts of the Transfiguration

According to some scholars[41] the account of the transfiguration in the Apocalypse of Peter, especially in the Ethiopic version, is not only independent of the synoptic accounts but more original despite its later date, and in this work the transfiguration is clearly a resurrection-ascension account. Two of the reasons given for the originality of the account in the Apocalypse of Peter are that the story is more of a unit in it than in the Synoptics and that at times it appears that only Peter is present. The first of these arguments is based upon a subjective judgment[42] and, even if granted, would prove nothing. As for the second argument, we must remember that the account is found in the Apocalypse of *Peter,* and the reason for his prominence is self-evident. There are serious objections, however, to the view that the Apocalypse of Peter contains an independent and more original account of the transfiguration that portrayed the event as a resurrection-ascension account. The *terminus a quo* for the account is ca. A.D. 100 since the writer in chapter 3 has probably used 4 Ezra 5:33. If the parable of the fig tree in chapter 2 refers to Bar Cochba, then we must date the account ca. A.D. 135.[43] That the Apocalypse of Peter could witness to an independent, more authentic oral tradition than Mark, even though written

41. E. g., Goetz, *Petrus,* 81–82.
42. Sanders (*Synoptic Tradition,* 272) summarizes his conclusions by saying *"dogmatic statements that a certain characteristic proves a certain passage to be earlier than another are never justified."*
43. Hennecke, *New Testament Apocrypha,* 2:664.

between thirty-five and seventy years later, is hypothetically possible but not very likely. It would appear that any of the following possibilities would seem more probable: (1) the writer knew of and used one or more of the Synoptic Gospels and changed the account to suit his purpose; (2) the writer did not possess any written copy of the Synoptic Gospel(s) but knew of the tradition originating from them and knowingly/unknowingly changed them;[44] (3) the writer knew of an oral tradition that was corrupt and unknowingly used it. We should also note that the resurrection is not mentioned in the Apocalypse of Peter. The work begins with a scene from Mark 13 and its parallels, where Jesus is seated with his disciples on the Mount of Olives. The teaching found on his lips comes from the "historical Jesus"[45] rather than the risen Lord. After the account of the transfiguration (chaps. 15–16), the seventeenth and final chapter speaks of an ascension. To assume that the writer knew of the transfiguration as a resurrection account encounters the difficulty that no mention is made of the resurrection anywhere in the work.[46] Even if we grant that the whole scene of the Apocalypse of Peter must be a resurrection appearance, since it ends with the ascension, we must acknowledge that the material incorporated into this "resurrection appearance" comes from the ministry of the historical Jesus. If the sayings of chapters 1 and following have all been transformed from sayings of the historical Jesus to sayings of the risen Christ by the author of the Apocalypse of Peter, it is not unlikely that he has done the same with regard to the transfiguration account.

It is frequently argued that in 2 Peter 1 we have an account that came to the writer independently of the Synoptics,[47] in which the transfiguration was likewise understood by him to be a resurrection account.[48] The reason generally given for this

44. So Bultmann, *History of the Synoptic Tradition,* 259 n. 2.

45. Much of chapter 1 comes from Matthew 24 and chapter 2 from Luke 13.

46. Boobyer (*Transfiguration Story,* 14) states that "to speak of it [the transfiguration] as a resurrection and ascension story as though they were one and the same thing is a mistake which obscures a significant point."

47. Schmithals, "Der Markusschluss," 396; cf. Blinzler, *Die neutestamentlichen Berichte,* 72. In contrast, see Horstmann, *Studien,* 88–89; Schelkle, *Die Petrusbriefe,* 198 n. 3.

48. Bertram, "Die Himmelfahrt Jesu," 189–90; Bultmann, *History of the Synoptic Tradition,* 259; Robinson, "On the *Gattung,*" 117; Weeden, *Mark,* 120–21; Schmithals, "Der Markusschluss," 395–97.

view is that the expression "honor and glory" can only refer to the resurrection or exaltation. Although it can be debated whether the account in 2 Peter 1:16–18 is independent of the Synoptics, the basic issue narrows down to two questions: Can "honor and glory" refer only to a resurrection appearance?[49] Does the account in 2 Peter necessitate our understanding it as a resurrection account? It should be noted that these words are not in any way technical terms for the resurrection. On the contrary, τιμή (honor) is never used in any resurrection account[50] and δόξα has closer associations with the parousia than with the resurrection.[51] Mark, however, has no problem in associating "glory" with an event in the ministry of Jesus, for he introduces the transfiguration account with a reference to seeing the kingdom come in "power,"[52] and Luke expressly states that Moses and Elijah appeared "in glory" and that Peter and those with him saw "his glory," so that these two writers see no difficulty in attributing "glory" to an event in the ministry of Jesus. There is, therefore, no reason why δόξα cannot refer to an event in the earthly life of Jesus, for Luke in his redaction explicitly does so. Furthermore, John 1:14 (cf. 1 Cor. 2:8) also refers to the δόξα of the earthly Jesus. To say that the reference to "honor and glory" in 2 Peter 1 requires that we understand this passage as referring to a resurrection account is incorrect. Yet even if 2 Peter 1:16–18 could be interpreted as a resurrection account, can we say that the evidence is such that it must be? The answer to this question is clearly in the negative. Yet again, even assuming for the sake of argument that we have in 2 Peter

49. Schmithals (ibid., 396) seeks to argue that the receiving of "glory and honor" follows the voice from heaven (which occurred at the resurrection) and is prospective only. The difficulty with this is that all the participles in verses 16–18 are aorists (ὄντες does not count since there is no aorist form) and it is best to see γενηθέντες (became), λαβών (received), ἐνεχθείσης (borne), and ἐνεχθεῖσαν (borne) as referring to the same event.

50. In Heb. 2:7, 9; 3:3 (cf. 1:8, 13; 4:14–16; 8:1); also in Rev. 5:12 it is not the risen Christ in fellowship with his disciples who receives "honor" but the ascended Christ who sits at God's right hand.

51. Boobyer (*Transfiguration Story*, 44) states: "There is no instance of *timē* standing alone with reference to Christ's resurrection or exultation; and *doxa* is still less favorable for Bultmann's point—it has stronger parousia associations than uses in connection with the resurrection and exultation." Cf. also Thrall, "Elijah and Moses," 309.

52. Cf. Mark 8:38, where the parallel is to see the Son of man come in "glory" with his holy angels.

1:16–18 a resurrection account, must we then assume that this stems from an early more authentic tradition than that found in the Synoptics? Again we must answer in the negative.[53]

There is an additional argument against interpreting 2 Peter 1:16–18 as a reference to the resurrection. It is clear from 2 Peter 2:19 and 3:15–16 that the opponents in this epistle claimed the support of the apostle Paul and his teaching. Why does the author cite the transfiguration to emphasize the authority of Peter? If the transfiguration were a resurrection acccount, the opponents could boast that Paul, too, had seen the risen Lord but since the transfiguration was not a resurrection acccount they could not make such a claim and the superiority of the Petrine authority was consequently demonstrated. Within the epistle, therefore, 2 Peter 1:16–18 supports the position of the author best, if it refers to an event in the life of Jesus in which Paul did not share rather than to a resurrection appearance.

A Priori Assumptions

Two final arguments in favor of the thesis that the transfiguration is a misplaced resurrection acccount need to be mentioned. The first is the argument that such an event does not harmonize with what we know about the earthly ministry of Jesus and of the naturalistic laws that govern all existence.[54] This argument, however, is irrelevant to the discussion. We must keep in mind that we are not concerned here with the question of the historicity of the account. During the second *Sitz im Leben* the transfiguration would have harmonized with what the early church "knew" of the earthly ministry of Jesus and of the "divine" laws that govern all existence. If because of naturalistic presuppositions one denies the historicity of the account, a de novo creation of the account or a "mythologizing" of an incident in the life of Jesus could have been placed as easily within the ministry of Jesus as elsewhere.

The second argument, which is probably more subconscious than conscious, is that it is easier to place the origin of such an

53. We should note carefully the switch from "I" to "we" in 2 Pet. 1:16–18. Certainly the writer did not understand this tradition as referring to the resurrection appearance to Peter.

54. Ramsay (*Glory of God*, 104–5) states: "In some of the expositions of this theory the strongest reason for it was simply an *a priori* feeling that an event of this sort is incongruous with the earthly ministry of Jesus." Cf. also Carlston, "Transfiguration and Resurrection," 234.

event as the transfiguration under the appellation of "resurrection appearance" because here we are dealing with *Geschichte* and not "history," and so in the minds of some it is easier somehow to explain the origin of the transfiguration account out of this context than out of the ministry of Jesus.[55] Again, this argument misses the mark, for whereas we may see Jesus' ministry as "history" and his resurrection as *Geschichte* and thus feel more comfortable with placing an account like the transfiguration with the resurrection tradition, the early church had no such difficulty. For the ministry of Jesus was messianic and *geschichtlich*.

Such arguments may cause an individual to deny the historicity of the event portrayed in the transfiguration account, but they have no value in deciding whether Mark found the account as a resurrection account or not. Furthermore, it has no value in deciding whether the original form of the account placed it within the ministry of Jesus or with the resurrection appearances.

In concluding this analysis of the arguments that the transfiguration was originally a pre-Marcan resurrection account, one becomes impressed not so much by the force of the arguments marshalled in support of this thesis but by their weakness.[56] On the other hand, as one analyzes the arguments in favor of the traditional view, it will become even more surprising that so many scholars have espoused the view that originally the transfiguration was a pre-Marcan resurrection account.

The Transfiguration—A Pre-Marcan Account of the Glorification of the Historical Jesus

Terminological Considerations

If one seeks to understand the transfiguration as a misplaced resurrection account, one encounters certain terms and phrases

55. Ibid.; cf. Haenchen, *Der Weg Jesu*, 310.

56. Baltensweiler (*Die Verklärung Jesu*, 95) states: "Es zeigt sich also, dass die Theorie, die in der Verklärungsgeschichte eine später vorausdatierte Auferstehungsgeschichte oder eine Christophanie sehen will, in keiner Weise befriedigen kann. Es ist unbegreiflich, dass sie überhaupt so viele Anhänger und Vertreter finden konnte. Denn sie findet im Text keinen eindeutigen Anhaltspunkt; im Gegenteil, ihre Vertreter sind gezwungen, eindeutige Aussage umzubiegen oder gar einfach zu eliminieren. Es gibt in der Tat keine andere Hypothese, die so wenig geeignet ist, gerade die für die Verklärungsgeschichte typischen Züge zu erklären, als die Theorie einer ursprünglichen Auferstehungsgeschichte."

that appear incongruent with a resurrection account. In verse 5 Jesus is addressed as ῥαββί (Rabbi). Certainly the use of this term in the account is best explained in a nonresurrection context, for one would expect in a resurrection context a term such as κύριε. Matthew and Luke had difficulties even in the present context and changed the term to κύριε (Lord) and ἐπιστάτα (Master), respectively. Any attempt to attribute the term ῥαββί or the verse to a Marcan redaction encounters the difficulty that ῥαββί is not a Marcan term, for it is found in only two other instances in Mark (11:21; 14:45; cf. 10:51). If the term is pre-Marcan and integral to the account, it is most difficult to conceive of the account as a resurrection appearance of the risen "Rabbi."[57]

Another difficulty are the words ἀκούετε αὐτοῦ in verse 7. If these words are integral to the account, this would argue against the account being a resurrection scene, for what need is there for a voice from heaven telling the disciples to "hear the risen Lord"? In fact, what need would there be of a voice at all?[58] The resurrection itself was sufficient to declare Jesus' sonship (cf. Rom. 1:3–4). It is not surprising, therefore, that we do not read in any explicit resurrection account of a voice from heaven,[59] but if there were such a voice one would expect something like "be witnesses" or "believe in him!"[60] It is possible, however, that this is a redactional addition to the account.[61] The main argument for this is that the expression draws our attention to Mark 8:31–32, and the union of the transfiguration and Mark 8:31–32 is probably Marcan. Yet even if it be granted that ἀκούετε αὐτοῦ is Marcan, this would demonstrate only that Mark is emphasizing that the transfiguration should be interpreted in the light of the events of Caesarea Philippi. It does not demonstrate that the transfiguration was originally a pre-Marcan resurrection account; it does not even prove that

57. So Lane, *Gospel of Mark*, 316.
58. Schelke (*Die Petrusbriefe*, 198 n. 3) states: "Eine Himmelstimme bei einer Auferstehungsvision wäre ganz singulär."
59. Schweizer, *Good News*, 180; Dodd, "Appearances of the Risen Christ," 25.
60. Blinzler (*Die neutestamentlichen Berichte*, 125) points this out: "Die Himmelstimme V. 7 fordert: 'Hört ihn!' Wenn Jesus tatsächlich jetzt die Erde verlassen sollte, wären diese Worte doch ganz unpassend. Sinnvoll wäre vielleicht: 'Glaubt an ihn!' oder "Hört auf das, was er euch gesagt hat!'" Cf. also Müller, "Die Verklärung Jesu," 60.
61. Horstmann, *Studien*, 89.

the transfiguration was not originally connected to the Caesarea Philippi account.

Form-Critical Considerations

C. H. Dodd has argued that in form the transfiguration contrasts with the general type of resurrection accounts in almost every particular. He then lists the following contrasts:[62]

(i) Whereas R [general type of postresurrection narrative] invariably starts with the disciples "orphaned" of the Lord and records a reunion, in T [the transfiguration] they are together throughout. If the Evangelists were making use of a form of tradition which began with a separation, it would have been easy enough to contrive a setting for it (cf. Jn. 6:15–16, Mk. 6:45).

(ii) In R, a word of Jesus always has a significant place, either as greeting, or as reproach, or as command, or as any two or all three of these. In T, He is silent throughout.

(iii) In T, a voice from heaven proclaims the status and dignity of Christ. There is no voice from heaven in R. Only in Rev. 1:10–11 is there a voice (apparently) from heaven, drawing the seer's attention to the vision which he is to see. In the accounts of the appearance to Paul the voice from heaven is that of Christ Himself.

(iv) In T, Christ is accompanied by Moses and Elijah; in fact the "appearance" (*ōphthē autois!*) is that of the two personages of antiquity and not of Christ Himself (who is there all alone). In R, Christ always appears alone (never accompanied, e.g., by the angels who figure as heralds of the resurrection).[63]

(v) In T, Christ is seen by His disciples clothed in visible glory. This trait is conspicuously absent from R in the Gospels. Only in Rev. 1:16 is He described as "shining like the sun in his power", and this, as we have seen, stands quite apart from the Gospel tradition. Its absence is perhaps the more remarkable because a dazzling light provides the visible form in which Christ appeared to Paul according to Acts; and since Paul himself includes his own experience in the list of appearances of the risen Lord, there may well have been a temptation to colour other forms of R accordingly. If so, the evangelists have resisted the temptation.[64]

62. "Appearances of the Risen Christ," 25; cf. also Cranfield, *Gospel According to St. Mark*, 293.

63. Schweizer (*Good News*, 180) and Baltensweiler (*Die Verklärung Jesu*, 94) also point out that no Easter story tells of any heavenly companions. See also Schniewind, *Das Evangelium nach Markus*, 116.

64. See also Schweizer, *Good News*, 180; and Baltensweiler, *Die Verklärung Jesu*, 93–94. The latter states: "In keinem Auferstehungsbericht erscheint Jesus

With regard to the latter point it can be argued that the risen Christ does possess certain supernatural features. He can vanish (Luke 24:31), appear mysteriously (Luke 24:36), and go through closed doors (John 20:19). He is even mistaken for someone else (Luke 24:13–14; John 20:11–12), but it must be pointed out that in such instances the risen Christ is always mistaken for another *man* (John 20:15; Luke 24:16)! There is, on the other hand, a sharp contrast between the appearance of the risen Christ and the angels. Carlston sees this point and argues that in the vision of Stephen (Acts 7:55), the conversion of Paul, and in the account in the Apocalypse of Peter the risen Christ appears in glory.[65] We have already discussed the latter account and need only point out that in chapters 1–14 there is every indication that the "risen" Christ possesses no glory. It is only in the story of the transfiguration that he possesses glory. As for the account of Stephen, the Christ who is seen in glory is the risen Christ who has already ascended to heaven (Acts 1:9–11) and stands at the right hand of God (Acts 7:55). Certainly, this is not a general type of resurrection account. It should furthermore be noted that the δόξα in Acts 7:55 is associated with God and not Jesus! The conversion of Paul is likewise not to be considered a general type of resurrection account.[66] The fact remains that the "glory" of the transfigured Jesus is a strong argument against rather than for the view that the transfiguration is a misplaced resurrection account.

Another strong argument in favor of the traditional view is the reference to the presence of Peter, James, and John at the transfiguration. No resurrection story speaks of Jesus being with these three disciples, whereas on several occasions they are present with Jesus during his ministry (Mark 5:35–43; 14:32–42; cf. 1:16–20, 29; 13:3). It has been argued that originally the

---

in einem in überirdisches Weiss verwandelten Kleid oder in seiner Doxa. Der Auferstandene hat noch keine 'Herrlichkeit' (Joh 20, 17), nur die Erhöhte (1 Tim. 3, 16). . . . Interessant ist, dass in der Emmausgeschichte der Auferstandene den beiden Jüngen darlegt, dass 'Christus dies leiden musste und dann in seiner 'Herrlichkeit' eingehen (Lk. 24, 26). Er selbst wird von den Jüngern gerade nicht an seiner Herrlichkeit, sondern am Brechen des Brotes erkannt (V. 35)."

65. Carlston, "Transfiguration and Resurrection," 235.

66. Baltensweiler (*Die Verklärung Jesu*, 93) points out that Acts 9:3 does not refer to the risen Christ but to the "light from heaven."

account spoke only of Peter.[67] Support for this is sought in the fact that Peter is the only one of the disciples who speaks and because the Apocalypse of Peter hints that Peter alone was present. Yet in Mark 14:32–42, although the three disciples were all present, Peter alone is singled out. As the spokesman of the disciples it is not illogical that he would speak on behalf of the three. As for the Apocalypse of Peter, it needs to be pointed out that in the account Jesus climbs the "holy" mountain with his *disciples*, and "we" could not look at their faces, "we" prayed, "we" saw, "we" marvelled, he showed "us." It is true that Peter is the main character and is the speaker but what else would one expect in the Apocalypse of Peter? What is significant in the account is not that Peter is the spokesman but that other disciples are mentioned as being present during the transfiguration. It should also be noted in this regard that the writer of 2 Peter carefully changes from "I" in 2 Peter 1:12–15 to "we" in 2 Peter 1:16–18. Does this suggest that in the tradition available to him Peter was not alone in the account? In the Marcan account we should observe carefully the use of αὐτούς (them), μόνους (by themselves), αὐτῶν (them)—verse 2; αὐτοῖς (to them)—verse 4; ἡμᾶς (us or we), ποιήσωμεν (let us make)—verse 5; ἔκφοβοι γὰρ ἐγένοντο (for they were exceedingly afraid)—verse 6; ἀκούετε αὐτοῦ (you listen)—verse 7; περιβλεψάμενοι (they looking around), εἶδον (they saw), ἑαυτῶν (them)—verse 8. This tends to indicate that James and John were integral parts of the pre-Marcan account. There does not appear to be, therefore, any exegetical ground for the view that originally the transfiguration account spoke only of Peter. Such a conclusion is drawn from a priori considerations alone.

If the above is correct and the pericope originally referred to Peter–James–John, then we must acknowledge that the earliest list of resurrection appearances,[68] found in 1 Corinthians 15:3–4, knows of no resurrection appearance to Peter–James–John, and such an appearance almost certainly would not have remained unknown to Paul. Furthermore, we possess no known resurrection account that refers to an appearance of

---

67. Goetz, *Petrus*, 77; Bultmann, *History of the Synoptic Tradition*, 260; Müller, "Die Verklärung Jesu," 61. For the view that the presence of James and John is pre-Marcan, see Horstmann (*Studien*, 83–85).

68. Bode (*First Easter Morning*, 103) maintains that the tradition that Paul is quoting here may have been formulated by the end of the 30s.

the risen Christ to these three disciples. The presence of Peter–James–John in the transfiguration account, therefore, argues strongly against the account having been originally a resurrection account. After contrasting the transfiguration and the resurrection accounts, Dodd concludes:

> To set over against these points of difference I cannot find a single point of resemblance. If the theory of a displaced post-resurrection appearance is to be evoked for the understanding of this difficult *pericope*, it must be without any support from form-criticism, and indeed in the teeth of the presumption which formal analysis establishes.[69]

Carlston, however, has argued that the uniqueness of the transfiguration account makes it sui generis and that comparison with the resurrection accounts is invalid.[70] This may or may not be true, but Dodd's analysis has clearly demonstrated that any comparison of the transfiguration and the resurrection accounts indicates that they are more unlike than like each other! As a result, we can conclude that form-critical considerations do not support the view that the transfiguration is a misplaced resurrection account but, if anything, argue against this view.

Historical Considerations

At this point it may be profitable to look at some aspects of the account that are obstacles to believing that originally the transfiguration was a resurrection account. The first involves the words of Peter in verse 5: ποιήσωμεν τρεῖς σκηνάς, σοὶ μίαν καὶ Μωϋσεῖ μίαν καὶ Ἡλίᾳ μίαν ("let us make three booths, one for you and one for Moses and one for Elijah"). This statement is unexplainable if this were a resurrection story, for placing

---

69. "Appearances of the Risen Christ," 25. Cf. also Ramsay (*Glory of God*, 117–18), who states: "There is so little resemblance between the details of the Transfiguration and the circumstances of the Resurrection appearances that it is hard to see how any of the evangelists can have thought of the former as a preparation for the latter. If the transfigured Christ is akin to the description in the Epistles of the glorified state of Christ and the Christians, there is no real correspondence with the descriptions of His appearances to the apostles and the women."

70. He states ("Transfiguration and Resurrection," 234): "It is consequently not form-critical pedantry to insist that in function and type this story fits with other resurrection appearances."

the historical Jesus on the same level as Moses and Elijah is conceivable, but would any resurrection story place the risen Lord on the same level as Moses and Elijah? Surely not! Bultmann and others have seen this difficulty and as a result argue that originally verse 7 followed verse 4.[71] Yet it has already been pointed out that the term ῥαββί in verse 5 argues in favor of this verse being pre-Marcan. Furthermore, if verse 6a and b or both are Marcan explanatory comments, this would also suggest that verse 5 is pre-Marcan, because such explanatory comments usually follow some statement in the tradition that the Evangelist is seeking to explain rather than his own redaction.[72]

A second historical problem in seeking to understand the account as a pre-Marcan resurrection story has to do with the transfiguration itself. There are indications that the risen Christ was awaiting transformation or glory (John 20:17; cf. also John 7:39; 12:16; 16:14; 17:1, 5; Acts 3:13; Heb. 5:5), but this glorification was permanent whereas that of the transfiguration was temporary according to the present form of the story. This would mean that after the resurrection Jesus was glorified temporarily and then later permanently glorified, but whereas it is possible to understand Jesus being temporarily transfigured only to lose this glory, it is difficult to see how the tradition would do the same with the risen Christ. Of course, it can be argued that originally in the pre-Marcan account the risen Christ did not lose this glory but immediately ascended into heaven.[73] All such reconstructions of the text, however, are based less on form-critical and historical grounds than upon a priori assumptions.[74]

71. Bultmann, *History of the Synoptic Tradition,* 260–61.
72. Cf. Mark 1:16, 22; 2:15; 3:21; 5:8, 28, 42; 6:14, 18, 20, 31, 48, 52; 7:3; 10:22; 11:13, 18, 32; 14:2, 40, 56; 15:10; 16:8.
73. Note here, however, that in the Luke 24:50–51 and Acts 1:9–11 accounts of the ascension the risen Christ does not ascend in glorified form.
74. The only support for such a reconstruction is the form of the account in the Apocalypse of Peter. Yet the account in this work exhibits characteristics that argue for it being less original than the Marcan account. Note the following secondary characteristics: in chapter 15 the mount of transfiguration is referred to as the "holy mountain"; there is greater detail in the description of the two messengers (e.g., their hair looks like a rainbow); in chapter 16 Jesus is described as "God Jesus Christ"; Jesus is addressed as "Lord" rather than "Rabbi"; Peter asks where Abraham, Isaac, and Jacob are; they are shown a garden full of trees; there is a reference to the blessedness of the persecuted. Boobyer (*Transfiguration Story,* 13–14), therefore, is certainly correct when he says, "Are not the

The Witness of Matthew and Luke

One point usually overlooked in the discussion is the agreement of Matthew and Luke with Mark in portraying the transfiguration account as an event in the life of Jesus. Generally, such agreement is minimized by stating that since these Gospels are interdependent we possess only the single witness of their Marcan source. Yet unless we were to assume that Matthew and Luke never knew of the transfiguration account before they read it in Mark, we must see in their use of Mark corroborative testimony that they agree with Mark that the transfiguration is not a resurrection account but a story about the historical Jesus.

On the other hand, there are certain agreements between Matthew and Luke that may indicate that they knew another tradition independent of Mark that they have incorporated into their accounts.[75] The unique contribution of the Lukan account (Luke 9:31–33a) has led some scholars to believe that Luke used a non-Marcan tradition at this point.[76] If Matthew and/or Luke knew and used independent traditions to supplement their Marcan source, then their agreement with Mark is even more impressive testimony to the pre-Marcan form of the story being an incident in the ministry of Jesus. In this regard it need only be pointed out that if the Lukan addition is an independent tradition that was connected to the transfiguration account, the transfiguration could not have been a resurrec-

---

removal of abruptness and explanations of details more often signs of the secondary nature of a piece of tradition—especially when they mean the expansion of a story in the direction of what is fanciful, as undoubtedly is the case with the Apocalypse of Peter version of this story?"

75. Note the following Matthew–Luke agreements: ἰδοὺ (behold, Matt. 17:3 and Luke 9:30); the order Moses and Elijah (Matt. 17:3 and Luke 9:30); the reference to the face of Jesus (Matt. 17:2 and Luke 9:29); changing ῥαββί to κύριε (Lord, Matt. 17:5) and ἐπιστάτα (Master, Luke 9:33); referring to Peter speaking (Matt. 17:5 and Luke 9:34); λέγουσα (says, Matt. 17:5 and Luke 9:35). See Manson, *Teaching of Jesus*, 32, for the view that this account was also in Q. For the view that Matthew and Luke did not possess an additional source besides Mark, see Streeter, *Four Gospels*, 315–16.

76. So Taylor, *Behind the Third Gospel*, 89; Blinzler, *Die neutestamentlichen Berichte*, 42–44, 57–62. Cf. also Fuller (*Foundations of New Testament Christology*, 172) who states: "The Lucan account of the transfiguration contains notable deviations from Mark, which are such as to suggest not merely editorial modification but the preservation of valuable independent tradition."

tion account for the addition speaks of Jesus' exodus, which he was about to fulfill in Jerusalem. On the other hand, if this addition was a loose piece of tradition that Luke attached to the account, this intensifies Luke's corroboration of Mark's account as an incident in the life of Jesus. If the addition is traditional, however, it is quite likely that it was associated with the transfiguration since nowhere else do Moses and Elijah ever appear to Jesus.

Conclusion

In light of the evidence presented above the present writer is surprised at the number of scholars who have advanced the view that the transfiguration account was originally a resurrection story and the more recent view that it was Mark who out of redactional considerations changed it into its present form. The evidence in favor of the traditional view is weighty, indeed, and the criticism of the thesis of a misplaced resurrection account by J. Blinzler, H. Baltensweiler, C. H. Dodd, and G. H. Boobyer have in the mind of this writer never been answered. The arguments presented in this chapter do not claim to be definitive, but it is hoped that they will appear to be sufficiently weighty so as to make scholars pause before they so quickly reject the traditional view.

6

The Cleansing of the Temple in Mark (11:15–19)
Reformation or Judgment?

The differences between the Synoptic Gospels and the Gospel of John are well known. Despite these differences, however, all four Gospels share several incidents. One of these is the cleansing of the temple. The purpose of this chapter is to investigate this incident as it is recorded in Mark 11. We shall not concern ourselves with the historical question. We shall seek rather to investigate the particular interpretation that Mark gave to this incident. How did the Evangelist interpret this incident? Did he understand it primarily as an attempt by Jesus to purify the temple worship, as an act of reformation? Did he interpret it as an act of judgment by which Jesus condemned the worship of Israel? Or did he hold some other interpretation?

The Cleansing of the Temple in the Pre-Marcan Tradition

In order to ascertain the particular theological interpretation that the second Evangelist gave to the account of the cleansing, we must first of all determine the pre-Marcan tradition of this incident. Once we know this, we can then compare the Marcan account with it and observe how the Evangelist modified, arranged, and introduced the pericope. It is through the investigation of the Marcan redaction that we shall be able to discern the theological interpretation that the Evangelist gave to this incident.[1] To do this, however, we must first determine the state and form of the pericope during the oral period.

The question of the dating of the temple cleansing is a classical problem. According to John 2:13–22 the incident took place early in Jesus' ministry. According to the synoptic tradition, however, the incident took place during the last week of Jesus' life. Scholars are divided as to which account is chronologically correct.[2] Fortunately for our study, the time of the event in the life of Jesus is not of major importance, for we are not concerned with the historical question but with the theological interpretation that the Evangelist gave to this incident. The setting of this incident in Mark at the end of Jesus' life does not contain any theological significance for us, because the incident could not have been placed earlier in Jesus' ministry due to the particular geographical and chronological arrangement that the Evangelist superimposed upon his Gospel. Since Jesus does not enter Jerusalem until Mark 11:1, the cleansing cannot take place until that point. What the theological significance of this geographical and chronological scheme may be for understanding the *redaktionsgeschichtlich* emphasis of the Evangelist is beyond the limits of this chapter.[3] It will, however, be of little significance if Mark was ignorant of any previous visits of Jesus to Jerusalem.[4] For us the relative merits of the Johannine or the Marcan datings

1. For a discussion of the various strata of the Gospel tradition and a definition of the term *Redaktionsgeschichte*, see the author's article, "What Is Redaction Criticism?" pp. 21–34

2. See Taylor, *Gospel According to St. Mark*, 461–62, for a listing of the views of various scholars on this matter.

3. Some of the scholars who see great theological significance in the geographical arrangement in Mark are Lohmeyer, *Galiläa und Jerusalem;* Lightfoot, *Locality and Doctrine in the Gospels;* Boobyer, "Galilee and Galileans"; Marxsen, *Der Evangelist Markus,* 54–116; Best, *Temptation and the Passion,* 174f. For an opposing view, see Burkill, *Mysterious Revelation,* 252–57.

4. Best, *Temptation and the Passion,* 112, raises this possibility.

are a question of the first rather than the third *Sitz im Leben* and thus do not concern us.

On the other hand the relationship between the pericope of the cleansing and the pericope of the cursing of the fig tree is extremely important, and in this regard the Johannine account is most helpful. The account of the cleansing as it is found in the fourth Gospel raises serious doubts as to whether the cleansing and the cursing pericopes were joined before the writing of the second Gospel, for the account in John 2:13f. is totally independent of any account of a cursing. This seems to indicate that there was no vital connection between these two pericopes during the oral period.[5] This view is supported by another consideration. In John 2:18f. we discover that the pericope of the cleansing of the temple is immediately followed by the question of Jesus' authority. In the Marcan account, if we remove the account of the cursing of the fig tree and its appended sayings, we find that the cleansing is also followed by an account in which the authority of Jesus is questioned. In John 2:18 Jesus is specifically asked for a sign to demonstrate his authority for cleansing the temple. In Mark 11:27 he is simply asked by what authority he does these things.[6] It is quite probable therefore that in the pre-Marcan tradition the cleansing of the temple and the question of the authority by which Jesus performed

5. Since John most probably did not know Mark (Sanders, *Gospel According to St. John*, 8; Morris, *Studies in the Fourth Gospel*, 61; Martyn, *History and Theology in the Fourth Gospel*, xx; Brown, *Gospel According to John I–XII*, 120; Dodd, *Historical Tradition in the Fourth Gospel*, 161; Schnackenburg, *Gospel According to St. John*, 33), this means that the fourth Gospel is either an independent witness to the same tradition that Mark is recounting or a witness to another tradition somewhat different from that of Mark. The possibility of two independent traditions, one of which associated the cursing with the cleansing, cannot be ruled out. On the other hand since the sandwich that places the two pericopes together is clearly a Marcan literary device, it seems more probable that John and Mark used the same tradition and that the association of these two events is Marcan. See Buse, "Cleansing of the Temple," 24, who states: "The explanation of the most complicated series of facts seems to be that both John and Mark were dependent upon an earlier account of the Temple Cleansing and that the influence of this earlier account led Matthew and Luke to make the same corrections in the Marcan story."

6. The ταῦτα in Mark 11:28 clearly refers to the cleansing of the temple, because the nearest incident providing a reason for this question is the cleansing. See Taylor, *Gospel According to St. Mark*, 469–70, 160. For an opposing view, see Schmidt, *Der Rahmen*, 294.

this act were integrally related.[7] If this is so, then we have further support for the view that the pre-Marcan tradition did not connect the cleansing and the cursing. It is also frequently argued that the Marcan account of the cursing of the fig tree is a modification by the early church of the parable found in Luke 13:6–9.[8] If this is so, then we have additional support for the view that originally the cleansing and the cursing were unrelated in the pre-Marcan tradition. Finally, it must be mentioned that some scholars maintain that the regal entry, the cleansing of the temple, and the subsequent question of Jesus' authority form a unit.[9] There is much to commend this view, for the cleansing of the temple may also be a messianic event.[10] If this is true, then the fig tree pericope does seem to be an intrusion into a collection of messianic pericopes; the regal entry, the cleansing, and the question of Jesus' authority to act in this "messianic" fashion.

In the light of our discussion above, it appears quite probable that originally there existed no vital connection between the pericope of the cleansing and that of the cursing of the fig tree. If we furthermore believe that originally the Gospel traditions circulated during the oral period as isolated pericopes, we can maintain that the burden of proof really lies upon anyone who argues for an original connection between these two incidents, and such a connection would be most difficult to demonstrate. Yet even if for the sake of argument we assume that the two incidents were connected in the pre-Marcan tradition, the particular arrangement or sandwich that we find in the Gospel is

7. See Bultmann, *History of the Synoptic Tradition*, 218; Taylor, *Gospel According to St. Mark*, 468; Best, *Temptation and the Passion*, 85; Jeremias, *Eucharistic Words of Jesus*, 91; Nineham, *Gospel of St. Mark*, 298. For the view that these two events were not originally connected, see Goguel, *Life of Jesus*, 416–17; Schmidt, *Der Rahmen*, 294.

8. This is the view of Brun, *Segen und Fluch*, 75f.; Klostermann, *Das Markusevangelium*, 116; Knox, *Sources of the Synoptic Gospels*, 1:80f.; Rawlinson, *Gospel According to St. Mark*, 154; Loisy, *Les évangiles synoptiques*, 2:284f.; Johnson, *Gospel According to St. Mark*, 154; Bundy, *Jesus and the First Three Gospels*, 425.

9. See Jeremias, *Eucharistic Words of Jesus*, 91; Nineham, *Gospel of St. Mark*, 298.

10. Jeremias, *Jesus als Weltvollender*, 35f. points out that the renewal of the temple was a sign of the end time. See also Gärtner, *Temple and the Community*, 105, who states, "One aspect of the work of the Messiah in the last days was believed to be the renewal of the temple."

clearly due to the hand of the Evangelist, for this is a peculiarity of his style.[11] By sandwiching these two accounts the Evangelist brings them into a much closer relationship than before, and we shall see shortly that in so doing the theme of the cursing pericope "rubs off" on the account of the cleansing.

A second matter that must be discussed at this point is the question of whether Mark 11:21–25 was originally part of the cursing pericope. Were these sayings part of the pericope during the pre-Marcan period, or were they appended to the account by the Evangelist? If the latter is true, then these sayings may be of assistance in helping us to ascertain how the Evangelist interpreted the two incidents under discussion. The sayings found in Mark 11:22–23 appear as a doublet in the first Gospel. We find them in Matthew 17:20 (and Luke 17:6) and in the Matthean parallel to our Marcan passage (Matt. 21:21). This doublet can be explained in several ways. It may be that in the oral period these sayings were contained in both the "Q" tradition and in the pre-Marcan tradition of the cursing of the fig tree. The sayings then would be a pre-Marcan appendage.[12] Support for this view comes from the fact that verse 21 would make a rather abrupt ending to the account. One expects some interpretative comment after the incident other than simply Peter's remark that the fig tree had withered. Furthermore Mark is less inclined than the other Evangelists to add the sayings of Jesus to his Gospel. Yet this is not the only instance in Mark of sayings appended to a pericope. We find possible examples in Mark 2:21–22, 27–28; 3:28–29; and 10:11–12, but here too we cannot be certain whether Mark appended these sayings or whether the tradition before Mark did so. On the other hand several scholars think that the sayings in Mark 11:22–25 were originally independent of the cursing pericope and that Mark appended them.[13] Certainty is impossible, so that we shall have

11. Cf. Mark 3:22–30 into 3:19b–21 and 31–35; Mark 5:25–34 into 5:21–24 and 35–43; Mark 6:14–29 into Mark 6:6b–13 and 30f.; Mark 14:3–9 into Mark 14:1–2 and 10–11; and possibly Mark 14:55–65 into Mark 14:53–54 and 66–72 as well as Mark 15:16–20 into Mark 15:6–15 and 21–32.

12. So Schweizer, *Das Evangelium nach Markus*, 132; Burkill, *Mysterious Revelation*, 198; cf. also Burkill, "Strain on the Secret," 38 n. 21.

13. So Best, *Temptation and the Passion*, 83; Nineham, *Gospel of St. Mark*, 298–300; Münderlein, "Die Verfluchung des Feigenbaumes," 89; Haenchen, *Der Weg Jesu*, 391; and probably Bultmann, *History of the Synoptic Tradition*, 25.

to discuss later how our understanding of the Marcan theological interpretation of the cleansing will be affected by either
possibility.

   With regard to the account of the cleansing itself, it should be
noted that if the regal entry, the cleansing, and the pericope
dealing with the authority of Jesus were originally a unit, then
much of verses 11 and 15 must be a duplication due to the hand
of the Evangelist. This view receives additional support from
the presence of such Marcan literary characteristics as the genitive absolute in verse 11;[14] the geographical designations;[15] and
certain typically Marcan terms.[16] Much of verses 18–19 also witnesses to the hand of the Evangelist because Mark frequently
introduces his own explanatory comments with a γάρ;[17] the
temporal designation in verse 19 ties the entire passage together
chronologically (cf. vv. 11, 12, and 20) and this scheme must
be due to the final editor; and certain words in these verses are
favorite Marcan terms.[18] Verse 16 is unique to Mark. If it is due
to his hand, then this will be of great importance for us because
it would indicate that at least in part the Evangelist interpreted
the cleansing of the temple as a reformation, for what is spoken in this verse is clearly a purification and not a condemnation
of the temple. On the other hand the incident may very well
be pre-Marcan or even historical.[19] The remark itself would seem
to be more relevant to a Palestinian *Sitz im Leben*[20] than a Hel-

   14. In a rapid reading of Mark the author came across thirty-four instances
of the genitive absolute. These are: Mark *1:32;* 4:17, *35;* *5:2,* 18, *21,* 35; *6:2,*
21, 22, *35, 47, 54;* *8:1;* *9:9,* 28; *10:17,* *46;* *11:11,* 12, 27; *13:1,* 3; *14:3* (two), *17,*
18, *22, 43, 66;* *15:33,* 42; *16:1,* 2. The majority of these (those italicized) give
strong evidence of being Markan, because they frequently introduce a new
pericope and often supply the temporal designation that ties the larger context together.

   15. Bultmann, *History of the Synoptic Tradition,* 242.

   16. See Jeremias, *Eucharistic Words of Jesus,* 91.

   17. Cf. Mark 1:16, 22; 2:15; 3:10, 21; 5:8, 28, 42; 6:14, 18, 20, 31, 48, 50, 52;
7:3; 9:6, 31; 11:13, 18, 32; 12:12; 14:2, 56; 15:10; 16:8. Many of these are
undoubtedly due to the hand of the Evangelist.

   18. The following see Mark 11:18–19 as Marcan: Nineham, *Gospel of St.
Mark,* 302–3; Bultmann, *History of the Synoptic Tradition,* 36; Taylor, *Gospel
According to St. Mark,* 461; Jeremias, *Eucharistic Words of Jesus,* 91.

   19. See Johnson, *Gospel According to St. Mark,* 190, for the view that Jesus
was enforcing a rule of the Mishnah. The rule itself is found in Berakoth 9.5. See
also Josephus, *Against Apion* 2.8.

   20. Bundy, *Jesus and the First Three Gospels,* 427.

lenistic one, because the temptation to use the temple as a short cut would be better understood by those who knew the construction and arrangement of the temple. For the Greek readers to whom Mark addressed his Gospel[21] such a remark would be less significant, for they would probably have been unaware of such a temptation. The omission of verse 16 by Matthew and Luke does not prove that this verse was composed by Mark. It more probably reveals that Matthew and Luke because of their own interests did not deem it important enough to include in their Gospels. As for the verb ἐδίδασκεν in verse 17, this is almost certainly due to the hand of the Evangelist, because it is a favorite term of his for describing the activity of Jesus, and it is clearly redundant here with ἔλεγεν. It has often been pointed out that Mark alone includes the words "for all nations" in verse 17. This may reveal his concern for a Gentile mission,[22] but it is probably safer not to read too much into this because these words are found in the Old Testament passage that Mark is quoting.

In summarizing our investigation of the pre-Marcan tradition we can now conclude the following: in the pre-Marcan stage of the tradition the accounts of the temple cleansing and the cursing of the fig tree were independent of each other; the original sequence in the pre-Marcan tradition may very well have been Mark 11:1-10, 15-17, 27b-33; the sandwiching of Mark 11:15-17 into Mark 11:12-14 and 20-25 is definitely Marcan; the sayings found at the end of the account of the cursing may have been pre-Marcan; verse 16 is most probably pre-Marcan; and the pre-Marcan form of the cleansing account probably consisted of Mark 11:15b-17 and possibly something like Mark 11:18a.

The Marcan Interpretation of the Cleansing

In seeking to ascertain the particular Marcan interpretation of the cleansing of the temple we must investigate the significance of his sandwiching this event into the fig tree pericope. There are several clear instances of such sandwiching in Mark. One of these is Mark 5:25-34 into Mark 5:21-24 and 35-43.

21. From the many explanatory comments on Aramaic terms and Jewish customs (see the references in note 17) it is evident that Mark is writing to Gentiles.

22. Cf. Mark 12:1-12; 13:10.

Assuming that this sandwich is due to the Evangelist, what is its significance? It is probable that the Evangelist has placed these two events together because they are closely related in theme. Both deal with a similar action on the part of Jesus. Both are healing miracles. Both therefore deal with a similar theme—Jesus' healing of the sick. Another Marcan sandwich is Mark 6:14–29 into Mark 6:6b–13 and 30f. Most scholars do not see any particular theological significance in this arrangement, and this is probably correct.[23] Mark apparently composed this sandwich in order to provide a period of time for the ministry of the disciples to take place.[24] A third example of this kind of a sandwich is Mark 14:3–9 into Mark 14:1–2 and 10–11. Ernest Best has argued that by this arrangement Mark has sought to stress that it is "as Messiah, the Anointed, that Jesus willingly goes to his death."[25] B. Gärtner argues that Mark by this sandwich has sought to explain the betrayal of Judas, for it was at his anointing when Jesus again spoke of his death that Judas became disillusioned and sought to betray Jesus.[26] Exactly what the significance of this sandwich may be is not entirely clear. What is clear is that by sandwiching these two events the Evangelist has intimately brought these two separate incidents together and that they are in some way related in his mind. Other examples of this type of sandwiching in Mark could be mentioned,[27] but from the three examples just given it is clear that frequently in sandwiching two incidents the Evangelist seeks to bring together two closely related passages or to interpret one incident by the other. It is quite likely that this is what he had in mind when he brought together and sandwiched the accounts of the cleansing of the temple and the cursing of the fig tree.

Since the Evangelist has purposely sandwiched these two pericopes, we must seek to understand the significance of the

23. Best, *Temptation and the Passion*, 76, argues that Mark seeks to portray by means of this sandwich that the final end of the forerunner foreshadowed the death of Jesus. This is not revealed, however, by the sandwich, for the sending out of the disciples has nothing to do with either the death of the Baptist or of Jesus.

24. So Nineham, *Gospel of St. Mark*, 172; Schweizer, *Das Evangelium nach Markus*, 74; and Feine et al., *Introduction to the New Testament*, 64.

25. Best, *Temptation and the Passion*, 90.

26. *Die rätselhaften Termini Nazoräer und Iskariot*, 53.

27. See note 11.

cursing of the fig tree if we are to understand the Evangelist's theological interpretation of the cleansing. Fortunately it is not necessary to address the question of whether Jesus could have cursed a fig tree or the question of when this incident took place,[28] for we are not concerned in this study with the question of the historicity of the event. We are concerned rather with what Mark must have thought of this incident in the tradition and how he interpreted it. Contrary to P. Carrington[29] Mark certainly must have understood the account as an actual cursing of an unfruitful fig tree. The explanatory comment found in verse 13c is, to say the least, confusing. Rather than explaining why Jesus cursed the fig tree it seems to make the cursing all the more confusing. Why curse a tree for not bearing fruit out of season?[30] It is not certain whether the comment is Marcan[31] or pre-Marcan.[32] The fact that Mark frequently introduces his explanatory comments with a γάρ[33] may favor the view that the comment is Marcan. But why would Mark add such a confusing comment? One possible reason is to heighten the symbolic significance of Jesus' action. Mark by his comment is telling his readers, "Now since it was not the season for figs we must understand that what Jesus was in fact doing was to act out a parable." G. Münderlein has argued that the incident is an acted parable on the part of Jesus.[34] This is quite possible because there was precedent in the Old Testament for such acted para-

28. For the view that this incident originally took place in the autumn during the Feast of Tabernacles, see Manson, "Cleansing of the Temple," 281; Smith, "No Time for Figs," 315–27; McKelvey, *New Temple,* 58.

29. *According to Mark,* 240.

30. Hiers , "'Not the Season for Figs,'" 395, seeks to explain this as follows: "Jesus expected to find fruit on the fig tree because he was expecting the messianic age to begin; for in the messianic age, figs—together with all other products of nature—would always be in season." If the comment is Marcan, then Hiers' explanation must be rejected because he is seeking to explain from the first *Sitz im Leben* a comment that originated in the third *Sitz im Leben.*

31. The following think that the comment is Marcan: Carrington, *According to Mark,* 237; Nineham, *Gospel of St. Mark,* 303; Taylor, *Gospel According to St. Mark,* 460; Burkill, *Mysterious Revelation,* 198 n. 19.

32. The following think that the comment is pre-Marcan: Robin, "Cursing of the Fig Tree," 280; Münderlein, "Die Verfluchung des Feigenbaumes," 99, 103; Bartsch, "Die 'Verfluchung' des Feigenbaumes," 258.

33. See note 17.

34. Münderlein, "Die Verfluchung des Feigenbaumes," 94; Zahn, *Das Evangelium des Matthäus,* 623; cf. also Robin, "Cursing of the Fig Tree."

bles.[35] Regardless of the intention of Jesus in this action, it would appear quite probable that the Evangelist understood it as such. This view receives support from the fact that figs frequently symbolize Israel in the Old Testament (cf. Hos. 9:10; Jer. 8:13; 24; 29:17; Joel 1:7; Mic. 7:1–6; Ezek. 17:24) and the destruction of the fig tree symbolizes judgment (Hos. 2:12; Isa. 34:4).[36] For Mark, as for many of his readers during the centuries, the cursing of the fig tree was probably understood as an act of judgment by which Jesus condemned a fig tree for being unfruitful. Probably Mark also understood it as an acted parable in which Jesus found Israel wanting of the fruits of righteousness and godliness and condemned her.

By sandwiching the cleansing of the temple between the account of the cursing the Evangelist brings the two incidents intimately together. Since they were originally independent and since Mark interrupts the original sequence of the pre-Marcan tradition, which had the question of Jesus' authority following immediately after the cleansing, this intimate association must be due to the fact that the Evangelist sees these two events as related in meaning. There is a similarity in theme. In seeing a similarity between these events the Evangelist thereby reveals that he interprets the incident of the cleansing as being similar to the incident of the cursing. Jesus' actions in these two incidents resemble each other. The judgment of the fig tree resembles the cleansing of the temple and vice versa. The cleansing therefore is not thought of by Mark as an act of reformation on the part of Jesus. On the contrary whereas the cleansing of the temple may have originally been thought of as an act of reformation (note v. 16), in Mark it is understood as an act of judgment. Jesus has rejected Israel. She has been weighed in the balances and found wanting. The kingdom will be given over to the Gentiles. Mark interprets the cleansing by means of the cursing.[37]

35. Cf. Jer. 13:1f.; 18:1–20; 19:1f.; 27:2; 28:10f.; Hos. 1:1–3; 2 Chron. 18:10; 1 Kings 11:29f.; 2 Kings 13:14f.; Isa. 8:1f.; Ezek. 4:1f.; 12:1f.; 24:1f. Cf. also Apoc. 10:8–11; 11:1f.
36. See Robin, "Cursing of the Fig Tree," 279.
37. Schweizer, *Das Evangelium nach Markus*, 5, states, "So wird die Tempelreinigung durch die Verfluchung des Feigenbaumes, die für Mark das Jerusalem und seinem Tempel drohende Gericht symbolisiert, eingerahmt." Cf. Best, *Temptation and the Passion*, 83: "It [the cursing of the fig tree] has been presumably placed here in order to imply the judgement of God over the Tem-

This interpretation finds additional support from the other materials that Mark has arranged in this part of his Gospel. In Mark 12:1–12 we find the parable of the vineyard and the tenants. Whatever may have been the original form of the parable, in its present state the parable clearly is an allegory in which Israel (the tenants) has been found wanting and is judged.[38] It is quite probable that the Evangelist is responsible for placing the parable at this point in his Gospel.[39] Clearly the theme of judgment, as well as the Gentile mission (cf. Mark 11:17 and 12:10–12), is contained within the parable. Mark has placed the parable at this point to reinforce and further clarify the similar theme as it is found in the accounts of the cleansing and the cursing.[40] If verse 9b ("He will come and destroy the tenants, and give the vineyard to others") is due to the hand of the Evangelist,[41] then it is all the more evident that the Evangelist is seeking in this section of his Gospel to emphasize the divine judgment that has come upon Israel as well as the universalism that results. As for the following complex,[42] it may be that the Evangelist has placed it at this point in order to

---

ple, the city, or Israel—there are many leaves, but no fruit." Cf. also Schlatter, *Die Evangelien nach Markus und Lukas*, 116; Nineham, *Gospel of St. Mark*, 298; Johnson, *Gospel According to St. Mark*, 188; Schiwy, *Weg ins Neue Testament*, 1:248; Münderlein, "Die Verfluchung des Feigenbaumes," 103; Robin, "Cursing of the Fig Tree," 280; Burkill, "Anti-Semitism in St. Mark's Gospel," 37; Farrer, *Study in St. Mark*, 161; Grundmann, *Das Evangelium nach Markus*, 230; Doeve, "Purification du Temple et Desséchement du Figuier"; McKelvey, *New Temple*, 65.

38. Concerning this parable Jeremias, *Parables of Jesus*, 70, states that "The vineyard is clearly Israel, the tenants are Israel's rulers and leaders, the owner of the vineyard is God, the messengers are the prophets, the son is Christ, the punishment of the husbandmen symbolizes the ruin of Israel, the 'other people' (Matt. 21:43) are the Gentile Church." For the view that the vineyard represents the temple and the tenants represents the priests, see Lohmeyer, *Lord of the Temple*, 44.

39. See Schweizer, *Das Evangelium nach Markus*, 137.

40. Cf. McKelvey, *New Temple*, 63, who states that "The parable of the disinheritance and destruction of the unfaithful and wicked husbandmen is probably to be included in the Marcan interpretation of the cleansing since it immediately follows the question on authority, and continues the judgment theme implied by the use of Jer. 7:11 at the cleansing."

41. Haenchen, *Der Weg Jesus*, 399.

42. For the view that this is a pre-Marcan complex originating in the Palestinian milieu, see Daube, "Four Types of Questions," 45–48, and *New Testament and Rabbinic Judaism*, 158f.

illustrate the rejection of the son spoken of in the previous parable. In Mark 13:1f. we also find another section that deals with the theme of judgment. It is around the destruction of Jerusalem and specifically the temple that the entire eschatological discourse rotates. This is evident from the way the Evangelist introduces the chapter.

When we bring together the results of our investigation we discover the following: the cleansing of the temple is purposely sandwiched into a pericope dealing with the judgment that comes upon an unfruitful tree; verse 13c may be a Marcan insertion stressing that the cursing of the fig tree is an acted parable; immediately following the pericope on Jesus' authority, which was connected to the cleansing periocope in the pre-Marcan tradition, the Evangelist has placed the parable of the vineyard and the tenants that portrays the judgment of God upon Israel; Mark 12:9b may be a Marcan insertion and clearly speaks of the judgment that must fall upon the evil tenants of the parable; and the little apocalypse is built around the destruction and judgment that are coming upon Israel as represented by the temple. From this it appears quite probable that the cleansing of the temple is seen by the Evangelist as a judgment and condemnation of Israel rather than as a reformation of the temple worship.

Conclusion

Two possible objections can be raised at this point concerning the interpretation just given. The first is why the Evangelist, if he understood the cleansing of the temple as a judgment, did not simply say so. Why did he not simply insert something such as "thus Jesus rejected both Israel and her worship"?[43] One of the dangers of redaction criticism is that the exegete may become too ingenuous in uncovering subtle allusions that the Evangelist himself was not aware of or ever had. The objection therefore is a valid one. In reply it can be said that perhaps in this instance the Evangelist did not think that an

43. Cf. Mark 7:19d. Schmid, *Gospel According to Mark*, 207, rejects the symbolic interpretation of the cursing of the fig tree on the part of Mark because the Evangelist did not add such a comment to the pericope. It is interesting to note that Schmid, *Gospel According to Mark*, 210, interprets the cleansing as a reformation.

explanatory remark was necessary. Throughout the centuries, even before redaction criticism became a truly scientific discipline, scholars have interpreted the cleansing of the temple as an act of judgment, at least in part, because of its association with the cursing of the fig tree.[44] This interpretation is therefore far from being ingenuous. A second objection that can be raised is that if Mark appended the sayings found in Mark 11:22–25 to the fig tree pericope then does not this indicate that the Evangelist interpreted the cursing of the fig tree primarily as an example for prayer? Does not this Marcan addition to the pericope indicate that the real understanding of the Evangelist is that our prayers will be answered even as Jesus' cursing of the fig tree was? This objection is also weighty and may be correct in part. For the Evangelist the cursing of the fig tree and the subsequent withering of the tree may be an example for prayer. But why must we limit the Evangelist to only one understanding of the incident? The cursing of the fig tree probably could have served both as an example for faithful prayer as well as an acted parable portraying the divine judgment and rejection of Israel.[45] On the other hand if the appended sayings were part of the pre-Marcan tradition, then this objection is greatly weakened.

Having observed the Marcan redaction of the cleansing pericope and its contextual materials, it is our conclusion that the cleansing of the temple has undergone a change in emphasis at the hands of the second Evangelist. For Mark the cleansing is no mere act of reformation by the Lord but an act of judgment by which he condemned Israel for her unfruitfulness. As a result the vineyard would be given to others. God would now turn to the Gentiles. In changing the theological emphasis of the cleansing the Evangelist witnesses once again to the fact that he is no mere collector of traditions. He is an interpreter of those traditions as well.

44. So Victor of Antioch. See Taylor, *Gospel According to St. Mark*, 459.
45. Nineham, *Gospel of St. Mark*, 298.

7

A Short Note on Mark 14:28 and 16:7

Since Lohmeyer first interpreted Mark 14:28 (ἀλλὰ μετὰ τὸ ἐγερθῆναί με προάξω ὑμᾶς εἰς τὴν Γαλιλαίαν.) and 16:7 (ἀλλὰ ὑπάγετε εἴπατε τοῖς μαθηταῖς αὐτοῦ καὶ τῷ Πέτρῳ ὅτι Προάγει ὑμᾶς εἰς τὴν Γαλιλαίαν·) as referring to the parousia,[1] several other scholars have come to similar conclusions.[2] Most scholars today agree that these two verses are Marcan redactions,[3] for the vocabulary and style are Marcan and these verses can easily be deleted from their respective pericopes without being missed. Furthermore Mark 14:28 interrupts the continuity of the peri-

---

1. Lohmeyer, *Galiläa und Jerusalem*, 10f., and *Das Evangelium des Markus*, 356.
2. Lightfoot, *Locality and Doctrine in the Gospels*, 55–65; Michaelis, *Die Erscheinungen*, 61–65; Marxsen, *Mark the Evangelist*, 75–95, and *Resurrection of Jesus of Nazareth*, 164; Bartsch, *Entmythologisierende Auslegung*, 79; Wieder, *Judean Scrolls and Karaism* , 30–51; Bailey, *Traditions*, 96; Hamilton, "Resurrection Tradition," 419–21, and *Jesus for a No-God World*, 64–65; Weeden, *Mark*, 111–17.
3. Bultmann, *History of the Synoptic Problem* , 285; Dibelius, *From Tradition to Gospel*, 190; Marxsen, *Mark the Evangelist*, 75–81; Schreiber, "Die Christologie des Markusevangeliums," 176; Grass, *Ostergeschehen und Osterberichte*, 21; Taylor, *Gospel According to St. Mark*, 549; Weeden, *Mark*, 46. Lohmeyer, *Galiläa und Jerusalem*, 29, 34, maintains that these verses are pre-Marcan. Wieder, *Judean Scrolls and Karaism*, 45, attributes them to Jesus.

cope in which it is found and is therefore clearly a foreign insertion into this traditional account.

The purpose of this chapter is to take issue with the abovementioned interpretation. The question is not whether these verses are Marcan, for it is clear that they are, but rather what Mark meant by them. Was he referring to the parousia of the Lord in "Galilee" or was he referring to a resurrection appearance in "Galilee"?[4] Several arguments have been raised in support of the former interpretation.

1. Since ὤφθη is a *terminus technicus* for seeing the risen Christ, the use of ὄψεσθε in Mark 16:7 indicates that Mark is referring to the parousia.[5] The use of the latter term for the parousia in Mark 13:26 and 14:62 lends additional support to this argument.

2. Since there existed no resurrection accounts involving a Galilean location,[6] and since Galilee has great significance for the time of Mark,[7] these verses must refer to an event imminent for the church to which Mark was writing, that is, the parousia.

3. The two events uppermost in the mind of Mark were the passion and the parousia. It is "inconceivable that a climactic event explicitly and carefully referred to by *Mark* to take place after the resurrection [14:28; 16:7] would be a resurrection appearance and not the parousia."[8]

4. It is further argued that Mark 14:28 interprets Mark 14:27, and the gathering of the followers of Jesus scattered abroad must refer to the parousia, for it is only at the

4. Another interpretation favored by some scholars sees these verses as referring to the presence of the risen Christ in the mission to the Gentiles. So Hoskyns, "Adversaria Exegetica," 147–55; Lightfoot, *Gospel Message of St. Mark*, 116; Carrington, *Primitive Christian Calendar*, 88; Boobyer, "Galilee and Galileans," 334–48; Evans, "I Will Go before You," 3–18, and *Resurrection and the New Testament*, 81; Schreiber, *Theologie des Vertrauens*, 178–79.

5. Lohmeyer, *Galiläa und Jerusalem*, 10f.; Marxsen, *Mark the Evangelist*, 84; and Weeden, *Mark*, 112 n. 14, who, however, admits that this argument is "not as solid as Lohmeyer claimed."

6. Marxsen, *Mark the Evangelist*, 82 attributes the Matthean and Johannine Galilean resurrection accounts to the influence of Mark 14:28 and 16:7.

7. Weeden, *Mark*, 112.

8. Perrin, "Towards an Interpretation of the Gospel of Mark," an unpublished work quoted in Weeden, *Mark*, 113.

parousia that the elect will be gathered together as Mark 13:26–27 indicates.[9]

5. Since Mark originally ended at Mark 16:8, it is difficult to believe that Mark 14:28 and 16:7 refer to the resurrection, for then Mark by his editorial work would be referring to a future resurrection appearance that he does not plan to include in his Gospel.

The arguments presented above are not convincing to this writer. The term ὄψομαι is not a *terminus technicus* in the New Testament or in Mark for the parousia.[10] The reason why ὤφθη is usually used to describe the resurrection appearances and ὄψομαι the parousia is not due to a difference in the quality or character of the events but due to the time of these events. The term ὤφθη is usually used with reference to the resurrection appearances because these appearances are usually spoken of in the past tense; they have already occurred. On the other hand the term ὄψομαι is used of the parousia because the parousia is always seen as a future event. When the resurrection appearances are referred to as a future event then the future tense must be used. This is why ὄψομαι is used in Mark 16:7. It should be noted in this regard that Matthew, who reports a resurrection appearance in Galilee (Matt. 28:16–20), used ὄψομαι in 28:7 and 10, so that ὄψομαι in these two instances must refer to an appearance of the risen Christ in Galilee (cf. also John

9. Marxsen, *Mark the Evangelist*, 89–90; and Weeden, *Mark*, 112.

10. Lightfoot, *Locality and Doctrine in the Gospels,* 75 correctly points out that it is not possible to argue that the verb, its tense, or its voice are used in a technical way in the New Testament. It is furthermore precarious to argue from only two clear instances (Mark 13:32 and 14:62) that this term is a *terminus technicus* in Mark for the parousia. Wieder, *Judean Scrolls and Karaism*, 30–48 maintains that "to go before" is a technical Jewish messiological idea that best applies to the parousia rather than the resurrection. The major weakness of Wieder's thesis is his neglect of the *Sitz im Leben* in which the Gospel of Mark was written. He errs in not recognizing the redactional character of Mark 14:28 and 16:7 (see 445 n. 3) and in not observing that Mark uses προάγειν five times and in Mark 6:45, 10:32, and 11:9 it is not associated with the parousia. It cannot therefore be a *terminus technicus* for Mark. (It should be noted that in none of the fourteen instances that προάγειν is used in the LXX does it have a "Jewish messiological" sense.) The same criticism can be raised with regard to Wieder's view that "Galilee" is a messiological term. Whether "Galilee" has messianic connotations in Jewish literature is not the issue. The basic issue is what this term meant to Mark. This question Wieder does not investigate.

16:16–20; 19:37; 1:51). Our first written "commentary" on what Mark meant by ὄψεσθε in Mark 16:7 therefore interpreted it as referring to a resurrection appearance.[11] The argument that ὄψεσθε must refer to the parousia is therefore invalid.

The second argument, which claims that no pre-Marcan Galilean resurrection accounts existed, is also difficult to accept. If no such accounts existed, then Matthew and John must have created independently of each other just such an account. Can we assume, however, that no pre-Marcan resurrection accounts located in Galilee existed? It is true that the Gospel of Luke does not contain such an account, but to record a Galilean resurrection appearance was probably contrary to Luke's purpose.[12] Furthermore it is doubtful that the two Gospels that report such accounts created them because of this reference in Mark. Are we to assume that Matthew created 28:16–20 just to fulfill Mark 14:28 and 16:7? It would have been simpler to have omitted these Marcan insertions than to create a Galilean resurrection account as a fulfillment of them. On the other hand if we state that Matthew did this, then we are admitting that the earliest account we possess of how these verses were interpreted indicates clearly that they were understood as references to the resurrection appearances of Jesus, and it would appear reasonable to assume that the original readers of Mark would have understood them in a similar way. Are we also to assume that the writer of John 21 created his whole account in order to demonstrate that he too knew of a resurrection account in Galilee and thus was in harmony with the Mark–Matthew tradition? It seems more reasonable to conclude that there existed two pre-Marcan resurrection traditions. One spoke of an appearance(s) in Galilee and the other spoke of an appearance(s) in Judea.[13]

11. This assumes that Matt. 28:10 and the subsequent appearance in Galilee (vv. 16–20) do not represent a lost ending of Mark. If they were part of such a lost ending, then it would be clear that in Mark 14:28 and 16:7 the Evangelist was referring to a resurrection appearance in Galilee and not the parousia.

12. Conzelmann, *Theology of St. Luke*, 93 argues that after the resurrection Galilee is no longer important for Luke. Luke's scheme does not permit any Galilean resurrection appearances. If this is correct, Luke's omission of any Galilean resurrection account is no argument against the existence of such an account(s).

13. Even if there were no such Galilean resurrection account before Mark, this would not mean that Mark could not refer to such an account here. Why should Mark be eliminated from being able to create such an account?

With regard to the arguments that the events uppermost in Mark's mind were the passion and the parousia, and that the gathering of the disciples would take place only at the parousia, it should be noted that Mark 14:26 is preceded by a passion saying. We have three clear passion predictions in Mark—8:31; 9:31; 10:33–34. Whereas the extent of the redactional element in these verses is debated, it is clear that Mark had a hand in shaping them,[14] and any claim that Mark minimizes the resurrection of Jesus is shown to be invalid once the redactional nature of Mark 8:31, 9:31, and 10:33–34 is recognized. In each of these predictions the passion and the resurrection are clearly associated and no mention is made of the parousia. To argue that the parousia is intimately associated with the passion sayings by Mark 8:27–9:8 and 10:32–40 at the expense of minimizing the passion-resurrection connection explicitly stated in Mark 8:31, 9:31, and 10:33–34 is to emphasize a minor connection at the expense of the major one. The fact is that there is not a single reference to the parousia in an explicit passion saying. Since Mark intimately ties together the passion and the resurrection in his passion predictions and since Mark 14:28 is preceded by such a passion prediction, it would seem logical therefore to interpret Mark 14:28 as another prediction linking the passion and the resurrection.

This argument is supported by the fact that the scattering of the sheep in Mark 14:27 and their later regathering are associated with the striking of the shepherd and the denial of Peter. The scattering of the sheep must therefore refer to the fleeing of the disciples in Mark 14:50–52 and to the denial of Peter in Mark 14:66–72. To maintain that this scattering would only be rectified at the parousia is unconvincing, for it was the common conviction of the early church that after the passion Jesus appeared to his disciples.[15] The Christians to whom Mark wrote received as part of their Gospel the tradition that Christ died for their sins, was buried, was raised, and appeared to the disciples and Peter. The most natural way to interpret Mark 14:28 would have been to interpret it as referring to the resurrection appearances of Jesus spoken of in the tradition, especially since the resurrection is specifically mentioned in this verse.[16]

14. See Strecker, "Passion- and Resurrection Predictions," 421–42.
15. Cf. 1 Cor. 15:3f.
16. μετὰ τὸ ἐγερθῆναί με.

It must be acknowledged that since the work of R. H. Lightfoot on the conclusion of Mark,[17] the view that Mark originally ended at 16:8 has gained support, so that in many cir-
cles this has become the dominant view.[18] Although it is
unusual for a work to end with a γάρ as Mark does according to
the best manuscript evidence, there is no linguistic reason why
Mark could not have ended in this way.[19] Furthermore the
attempts to see Matthew 28:9–10 and 16–20[20] or Matthew
28:16–17 and Mark 16:15–20[21] as the lost endings of Mark have
met with little acceptance.[22] Nevertheless it is possible that our
present text is incomplete, and if Mark originally contained an
account of a resurrection appearance in Galilee, then Mark
14:28 and 16:7 must have referred to this resurrection appearance. Yet even if Mark originally ended at 16:8 this does not
require that the passages under discussion must refer to the
parousia. On the contrary this abrupt ending may be part of
the secrecy motif, for it is at the resurrection that the secrecy
motif is lifted (Mark 9:9) and then only by the disciples.[23] Thus
14:28 and 16:7 can be understood as references to the resurrection even if Mark originally ended at 16:8.

There are several arguments, however, which make the traditional interpretation of these verses the only acceptable one.
One of these is the change of tense in Mark 14:28 and 16:7. In
the former verse Jesus tells his disciples that he *will* go before

17. Lightfoot, *Locality and Doctrine in the Gospels*, 1–48.
18. See Kümmel, *Introduction to the New Testament*, 71–72.
19. Van Der Horst, "Can a Book End with ΓΑΡ?" 121–24.
20. Goodspeed, *Introduction to the New Testament*, 156.
21. Linnemann, "Der (wiedergefundene) Markusschluß," 255–87. Cf. also
Trompf, "First Resurrection Appearance," 308–30, who argues that something
like Matt. 28:9–10 and a quotation found in Justin Martyr's Περὶ ἀναστάσεως
originally concluded Mark's Gospel.
22. See Aland, "Der wiedergefundene Markusschluß," 3–13 for a criticism
of Linnemann's thesis on textual grounds. For a criticism of this thesis on literary
grounds, see Bartsch, "Der Schluß," 241–54.
23. Fuller, *Formation of the Resurrection Narratives*, 64 states that the silence of
the women, which was part of the tradition, "has been re-interpreted by the
Evangelist in connection with this special theory of the messianic secret. For . . .
it is not until the resurrection that the secret is fully lifted, and then it is to
be proclaimed by the disciples. This is why the women may not proclaim it. . . .
The charge to the women was simply a device to point forward to the final
unveiling of the messianic secret in the two resurrection appearances, to Peter
and to the disciples."

them into Galilee. In the latter reference the disciples are informed through a message given to the women at the tomb that Jesus *is* going before them into Galilee. The change in tenses indicates that what was in the future before the resurrection (Mark 14:28), that is, a meeting of Jesus with his disciples in Galilee, is now a present reality for the disciples immediately after the resurrection. If Mark were referring to the parousia, however, there would have been no need to change the tense, for both references could have remained in the future tense (assuming that Mark is distinguishing the time of the historical Jesus and the newly risen Christ from the time of the church to which he is writing) or both could have been placed in the present tense (assuming that Mark is only concerned with the existential moment to which he was addressing himself). The change in tense is best explained by assuming that Mark is carefully distinguishing between the historical Jesus and the event of Mark 14:28 and 16:7 and the newly risen Christ and that event. This interpretation finds additional support in the use of μετά with the infinitive in Mark 14:28. This construction is found thirteen other times in the New Testament[24] and is always used with respect to an event coming shortly after the event just mentioned. Never does it refer to as long a period of time as would be necessary if the event being referred to were the parousia. Furthermore, if Mark 16:7 refers to the parousia, then we must say that before the parousia Jesus is already awaiting his disciples in Galilee,[25] but where is the parousia ever portrayed as having Jesus present in Galilee awaiting his church?[26]

Closely related to this problem is the reference to the disciples in Mark 16:7. Any reference to Jesus' appearance to the disciples

24. Matt. 26:32; Mark 1:14; Luke 12:5; 22:20; Acts 1:3; 7:4; 10:41; 15:13; 19:21; 20:1; 1 Cor. 11:25; Heb. 10:15, 26 (this may be an exception).

25. Marxsen, *Mark the Evangelist*, 86 and Fuller, *Formation of the Resurrection Narratives*, 61 correctly point out that the word means to "precede" and not to "lead."

26. Marxsen, *Mark the Evangelist*, 86, is aware of this problem but his attempt to escape it must be considered a failure. He states, "Jesus is 'already there.' This is why there is such emphasis upon his activity in this land by the Sea. To be sure, his presence is hidden, but it will shortly be manifest. Clear also is the way in which his presence in Galilee is now experienced—in the proclamation." Lohmeyer, *Galiläa und Jerusalem*, 13–14, was also aware of this difficulty.

after the event of the empty tomb would have been understood by the early church as a resurrection appearance. The
readers of Mark's Gospel had been taught from the beginning
that after the crucifixion Jesus appeared to his disciples. They
would therefore have been predisposed to interpret this passage as a reference to just such an appearance. The antiquity
of 1 Corinthians 15:3f.[27] and its possible Semitic origin[28] argue
strongly in favor of the view that the church to which Mark
addressed his Gospel would have been predisposed to think of
any appearance of Jesus to the disciples in a resurrection context
as referring to a resurrection appearance and not to the parousia, for they were not reading this work in a vacuum. If Mark
wanted his readers to understand that he was referring to the
parousia in Mark 14:28 and 16:7, he would have had to delin-
eate clearly that he was referring to the parousia, because the
most natural interpretation in the light of the tradition would
have been to see these verses as references to a resurrection
appearance. Mark, however, does not clearly indicate that these
verses refer to the parousia, as centuries of interpretation elo-
quently witness. The fact that he does not do so indicates that
Mark intended his readers to interpret these insertions in the
light of the tradition of the church.[29]

The strongest argument in favor of the traditional view, however, is the reference to Peter in Mark 16:7. In this verse the
women are commanded to tell the disciples and *Peter* to go to
Galilee where they will meet Jesus. But if Mark were written
after A.D. 65, *Peter is already dead.* Why tell the dead Peter to go
to Galilee to experience the parousia? Knowing that Peter was
dead, would any of Mark's readers have thought that a reference to Peter's meeting Jesus in Galilee referred to the future
parousia? Would Mark have expected that a message addressed
to Peter in A.D. 30 to go and meet Jesus in Galilee would be
understood as a reference to the now-dead Peter to go to Galilee
and await the still-future parousia? The answer to both of these
questions must be in the negative. It would appear that Marxsen

27. Bode, *First Easter Morning,* 103 maintains that this tradition may have
been formulated by the end of the 30s.

28. See ibid., 90–104.

29. If Mark had simply inserted the title "Son of man" into these verses,
his readers might have thought then of the parousia, but Mark does not do
this. It is not the Son of man that they are to see in Galilee but "Jesus of
Nazareth, who was crucified (Mark 16:6)."

and others have lost sight of the fact that Mark has placed the words of Mark 14:28 in the mouth of the historical Jesus and the words of Mark 16:7 in the mouth of an angel in A.D. 30 and not in the mouth of the risen Lord in A.D. 65–70. To make them the words of the risen Lord addressed directly to the reader in A.D. 65–70 is to disregard completely the context into which these words were inserted.[30] The very fact that one of these insertions is addressed to a dead apostle demonstrates that they must be understood in their historical context. They have been spoken by the historical Jesus and an angelic messenger in A.D. 30 to the disciples and Peter. They must therefore refer to events in which the disciples and Peter could participate. They must refer to a resurrection appearance and not the parousia.

It has been argued by several scholars that "Peter" is a symbolic figure in Mark[31] and that "Galilee" is more than a mere geographical designation.[32] This may be true, but whatever the symbolic significance of these terms it is clear that for Mark "Peter" was also a historical person and "Galilee" a historical place.[33] Unlike Bunyan's "Christian," Mark's "Peter"

30. Is it legitimate to see in this type of interpretation the influence of a twentieth-century existentialist philosophy? Cf. Trocmé, *La Formation*, 112 n. 10.

31. Tyson, "Blindness of the Disciples of Mark," 261–68; Trocmé, *La Formation*, 96–109; Sandmel, "Prolegomena," 298; Schreiber, "Die Christologie des Markus-evangeliums," 177–83; Weeden, *Mark*, 52–69.

32. Hoskyns, "Adversaria Exegetica," 149–53; Lohmeyer, *Galiläa und Jerusalem*; Lightfoot, *Locality and Doctrine in the Gospels*, 106–31; Carrington, *Primitive Christian Calendar*, 75–89; Boobyer, "Galilee and Galileans"; Marxsen, *Mark the Evangelist*, 54–116; Karnetzki, "Die Galiläische Redaction im Markus-evangelium," 238–72; Kümmel, *Introduction to the Old Testament*, 64–65; Wieder, *Judean Scrolls and Karaism*, 1–51; Weeden, *Mark*, 112; Best, *Temptation and the Passion*, 174–77; Schreiber, "Die Christologie des Markus-evangeliums," 171–72, and *Theologie des Vertrauens*, 170–84; Evans, "I Will Go before You," 13–17, and *Resurrection and the New Testament*, 81; Bowman, *Gospel of Mark*, 352–53. For a criticism of this view, see Burkill, *Mysterious Revelation*, 252–57.

33. In Mark 3:7–8 "Galilee" may have symbolic significance as may "Judea," "Jerusalem," "Idumaea," "beyond the Jordan," and "from about Tyre and Sidon," but for Mark these are certainly actual places as well. In Mark 6:21 Herod's leading men come from "Galilee," over which Herod Antipas ruled. Here the term has little if any theological significance and serves primarily as an actual geographical designation. It should be noted in this regard that for Marxsen the "Galilee" to which the Jewish Christians in Jerusalem are to flee is the geographical location by that name. See 115 n. 176 and 184, where the mountains of Galilee are mentioned.

had a real brother named Andrew (Mark 1:16), was also called Simon (Mark 1:16; 3:16), was a fisherman (Mark 1:16; cf. John 21:3), had a mother-in-law (Mark 1:30), was one of the Twelve (Mark 3:16), was a witness of the transfiguration (Mark 9:2–8), and denied Jesus (Mark 14:66–72; cf. John 18:15–18, 25–27). The name "Peter" may have symbolic significance for Mark, but it also stands for a historical figure. In every reference to "Peter" in Mark the reader is able to identify the name with the historical figure regardless of whatever symbolic significance the name bears with it. In every reference in Mark the reader may interpret "Peter" as signifying simply a historical person or a historical person who has symbolic significance, but in Mark 16:7, according to the interpretation which sees this verse as a reference to the parousia, the term must be understood by Mark's readers as purely symbolic and having nothing to do with the actual historical person who is now dead. If Mark had intended this, he would have had to indicate this clearly to his readers, but he did not. As a result this verse and Mark 14:28 have been interpreted from the beginning as references to the appearances of the risen Christ to the disciples and the "historical Peter."

This interpretation is supported by another consideration. Within the Christian tradition it was well known that after the resurrection the Lord appeared to Peter. This is apparent from 1 Corinthians 15:5, Luke 24:34, Acts 10:41, and John 21. Here we have at least one ancient and independent tradition relating a resurrection appearance of Jesus to Peter (1 Cor. 15:5) and possibly three. The extent to which this tradition was known is uncertain, but it is quite possible, if not probable, that it was known to the readers of Mark's Gospel, and if this was so then they would have been predisposed to interpret Mark 16:7 as referring to that resurrection appearance. For Mark to single out Peter in this insertion therefore makes good sense, if this refers to a future resurrection appearance, for tradition spoke of such an appearance, but it is hard to understand why Peter would be singled out if Mark 16:7 referred to the parousia.[34]

34. Fuller, *Formation of the Resurrection Narratives*, 63–64.

Conclusion

In the light of the discussion above it appears to this writer that the various arguments that seek to demonstrate that Mark 14:28 and 16:7 refer to the parousia are unconvincing. The conclusive argument against this interpretation is the reference to Peter in Mark 16:7. Since the Christian tradition of a resurrection appearance to Peter was well known in the church and since Peter was now dead,[35] Mark could not have expected his readers to interpret these insertions as anything but a reference to the resurrection appearance to Peter of which the tradition spoke.

---

35. If the Gospel of Mark were written before the death of Peter, then this argument is weakened, but this would require both an earlier dating of Mark and a later dating of the death of Peter than is generally accepted. Several of the scholars who maintain that Mark 14:28 and 16:7 refer to the parousia, however, clearly date the composition of the Gospel of Mark *after* the death of Peter. So Marxsen, *Mark the Evangelist*, 181—after the siege of Jerusalem began; Hamilton, *Jesus for a No-God World*, 56—after A.D. 70; Weeden, *Mark*, 159—"the beginning of the eighth decade A.D."; Perrin, *Christology and a Modern Pilgrimage*, 36—shortly after the fall of Jerusalem.

"Authentic" or "Authoritative" Sayings
What Is the Difference?

In Gospel studies one frequently comes across such terms as "authentic," "nonauthentic," "authoritative," and "nonauthoritative." There is, however, considerable confusion as to exactly what these terms mean. For instance, are "authentic" and "authoritative," "nonauthentic" and "nonauthoritative" synonyms? Are "authentic" and "nonauthoritative" antonyms?

The occasion for such terminology is the well known fact that sayings of Jesus found in parallel accounts of the Synoptic Gospels frequently differ in wording. An example of this is the words of Jesus to the paralytic he healed in Capernaum. We find the following:

Matthew 8:2—"Take heart, my son; your sins are forgiven."
Mark 2:5—"My son, your sins are forgiven."
Luke 5:20—"Man, your sons are forgiven you."

Although there is no *essential* difference among the three accounts, they are all slightly different from one another. Since it is evident that Jesus at the same time and place did not say all

147

three versions of this saying to the same man,[1] it is quite natural to seek if possible to ascertain the *ipsissima verba* of Jesus—that is, the actual words that the historical Jesus said on this occasion. The question of exactly what Jesus said involves the question of authenticity. The attempt to discern what is authentic is therefore the attempt to arrive at the exact words that Jesus of Nazareth actually said before his resurrection on this particular occasion.[2] Fortunately, historical research has provided various tools to aid in such an investigation.[3]

An example of this type of investigation by the present author appeared in *JETS* in 1979.[4] In this article I investigated Jesus' sayings on divorce and determined that the sayings of Jesus found in Mark 10:11, Luke 16:18, and 1 Corinthians 7:10–11, which contain no "exception clause," are more "authentic" than the parallels in Matthew 5:31–32 and 19:9, which both contain the famous "exception clause." In other words, the sayings in Mark, Luke, and 1 Corinthians are closer to the actual words spoken by the historical Jesus than those recorded in Matthew. This then conversely means that the Matthean versions of these sayings are "less authentic." Yet "less" or "nonauthentic" does not mean "nonauthoritative":

1. Hypothetically, of course, this is possible, but for this writer such a "solution" for the differences we encounter in the parallel accounts in our Gospels would raise far more problems than it would solve.

2. In defining "authentic" in this way we clearly reject the existential interpretation offered by Robinson, *New Quest of the Historical Jesus*, 99 n. 3: "One may however observe that material regarded as wholly 'unauthentic' in terms of positivistic historiography may not seem nearly as 'unauthentic' in terms of modern [i.e., existential] historiography. For a saying which Jesus never spoke may well reflect accurately his historical significance, and in this sense be more 'historical' [i.e., authentic] than many irrelevant things Jesus actually spoke." An ancient parallel to this way of thinking is found in Plutarch, *Solon* 27.1. Here Plutarch accepts as historical the meeting of Solon and Croesus even though he knew that they lived at different times, so that such a meeting was in fact impossible. But he accepted the "historicity" of this meeting because it was so true to the characters of both men that he would not reject it on the trivial grounds of the "so-called canons of chronology."

Robinson's definition, however, far from adding clarity to the discussion, would clearly add endless and hopeless confusion to the situation by making all questions of authenticity dependent on a subjective decision of what "turns him or her on." Whatever the weaknesses of our definition, this option has many more.

3. For a discussion of these tools, see pp. 153–87.

4. Stein, "Is It Lawful for a Man to Divorce His Wife?" 115–21.

Matthew has therefore done us a great and most useful service. Led by the Spirit, he reveals to us that when Jesus uttered these words he was not seeking in one sentence to lay down a law to cover every situation. On the contrary he was giving us a general principle rather than the "letter of the law." Is Matthew's interpretation a corruption of Jesus' teaching or a clarification of it? Our decision on this will depend on our view of the authority of Matthew and the purpose of the gospels. In my understanding Matthew's interpretive comment is every bit as authoritative and binding on the believer as our Lord's teaching, for Matthew could also in one sense say, "The Spirit of the Lord is upon me."[5]

It is important in this regard to note that the terms "authentic" and "authoritative" deal with two different dimensions of the Gospel tradition. The term "authentic" deals with the *historical* question of what Jesus of Nazareth actually said in A.D. 28–30 on this occasion in Capernaum. At times an account in Mark may be closer to the actual words Jesus spoke on this occasion—that is, it may be more "authentic" than the parallel accounts in Matthew or Luke—and at times the reverse may be true. The term "authoritative," however, deals with the *theological* question of canonicity. An "authoritative" saying is one that is canonical—that is, it possesses divine authority in that it is inspired by God (2 Tim. 3:16). An authoritative saying is, then, a saying found in the canon of Scripture, and for the evangelical this means that it is infallible. A saying in the Gospels that is authentic is, of course, authoritative as well, but a "nonauthentic" saying found in the Gospels is likewise authoritative since it is canonical and inspired by the Spirit of God. For some evangelicals this may be a difficult concept, but the Scriptures themselves teach that the role of the Spirit was not merely to help the Evangelists recall the authentic words of Jesus but also to help them understand the significance of these words by giving to them as well an authoritative interpretation of what Jesus meant.

I have yet many things to say to you, but you cannot bear them now. When the Spirit of truth comes, he will guide you into all the truth; for he will not speak on his own authority, but whatever he hears he will speak, and he will declare to you

5. Ibid., 119–20.

the things that are to come. He will glorify me, for he will take
what is mine and declare it to you. All that the Father has is
mine; therefore I said that he will take what is mine and declare
it to you. (John 16:12–15)

According to these verses the role of the Spirit was not merely
to help the disciples recall the words of Jesus. He was to guide
them into all truth and teach them many things that they
could not "bear" during the ministry of Jesus. For this writer
this involves not only the ability to recall the authentic words
of Jesus but also the provision of authoritative interpretations of those words. Both the "authentic" words of Jesus
and the "nonauthentic" interpretations of those words found
in the Gospels are therefore authoritative since they are both
inspired by the Spirit of truth.

One reason that evangelicals have trouble with the use of
these terms is that frequently in the literature "nonauthentic
is a synonym for "nonauthoritative." An example of this is
found in the writings of Joachim Jeremias:

> The gospel of Jesus and the kerygma of the early church must
> not be placed on the same footing, but they are related to one
> another as call and response. The life, acts, and death of Jesus,
> the authoritative word of him who dared to say *abba,* the one
> who with divine authority invited sinners to his table, and as
> the servant of God went to the cross—all of this is the call of
> God. The early church's witness of faith [the nonauthentic
> sections of the Gospels and the rest of the New Testament],
> the Spirit-led chorus of a thousand tongues, is the response
> to God's call. . . . According to the witness of the New Testa-
> ment, there is no other revelation of God but the incarnate
> Word. The preaching of the early church, on the other hand,
> is the divinely inspired witness *to* the revelation, but the
> church's preaching is not itself the revelation.[6]

Jeremias, by elevating the authentic words of Jesus above the
words of the Evangelists, has clearly created "a canon within

6. Jeremias, *Problem of the Historical Jesus,* 23. Cf. also Findlay, *Jesus and His
Parables,* 123, who states that "if we are convinced that Jesus was 'God manifest
in the flesh,' and that the evidence that He said such and such things is sufficient to make it probable that they actually passed His lips, we must attach
more importance to them than to all the utterances of His truly inspired followers."

the canon." The problems with such a view cannot be dealt with here, but it is difficult to understand how Jesus' infallible teachings can be more infallible than the Spirit-given infallible teachings of the Evangelists. Yet many evangelicals may in practice be closer to the view of Jeremias than they realize, for when one stands in church for the reading of the Gospels but remains seated for the reading of the Epistles, does this not imply the existence of "a canon within the canon"—that is, that the Gospels are more worthy than the Epistles because they contain the actual words of Jesus?

Finally, the question must be raised as to whether Evangelicals should investigate the Gospels in order to seek to ascertain the authentic sayings of Jesus. After all, if each of the Gospel accounts is authoritative, why bother attempting to ascertain the *ipsissima verba* or *vox* of Jesus? There are three reasons why this "quest" is both necessary and profitable. First, like Mount Everest, "it is there." There are differences in the parallel accounts in the Gospels. This cannot be denied. The student of the Gospels furthermore cannot but have a natural curiosity as to what the historical Jesus actually said on a particular occasion. Second, if we can arrive at the authentic sayings of Jesus and then note how the Evangelists give an authoritative interpretation of these words for their own *Sitz im Leben*, we shall be better able to understand their significance for us today. If we can in fact arrive at the authentic words of Jesus and at the same time also possess an authoritative interpretation of those words by the Evangelists, are we not doubly blessed in that we possess both the inspired words of Jesus and an inspired interpretation of those words as well? How much richer we are, therefore, than if we possessed three identical accounts of the authentic words of Jesus.[7] Finally, it should be noted that such an investigation can frequently serve an apologetical purpose as well, for if we can demonstrate time and time again that the Evangelists' interpretations are in continuity with and flow out of the actual words of the historical Jesus, we shall be able

7. If all the parallel accounts in the Gospels were identical in every respect, outside of some possible apologetical value (multiplicity of witnesses), would this not in effect make all but one of these accounts superfluous?

to establish bridges between the Christ of faith and the historical Jesus. The value of this should not be minimized.[8]

8. Cf. the concluding paragraph in Stein, "'Criteria,'" 253: "Finally it should
be pointed out that if by the use of these various criteria certain sayings in our
Gospels can in fact be demonstrated as being authentic and this in turn can
establish a continuity between the historical Jesus and kerygmatic Christ, there
is then no *a priori* reason to be skeptical about the general portrait of Jesus
found in our Gospels. On the contrary it would then be clear that the burden
of proof lies with those who would reject the authenticity of the Gospel
materials rather than with those who accept their authenticity. We can say
this in another way using the terminology of the law court. If by the criteria discussed above the authenticity of certain sayings and motifs in the Gospels can
be demonstrated which establish a continuity between the Jesus of history and
the Christ of faith, then we should assume that the other sayings and motifs in
the Gospels are 'innocent until proven guilty,' i.e. a saying in the Gospels pur-
porting to come from Jesus is true (authentic) until proven false (unauthentic)."

9

The "Criteria"
for Authenticity

It is evident from even a cursory reading of the literature that scholarly attitudes toward the historicity of the Gospel materials vary drastically. On the one side we have those scholars who possess a positive attitude toward the Gospel materials and state "In the synoptic tradition it is the inauthenticity, and not the authenticity, of the sayings of Jesus that must be demonstrated."[1] On the other side we have those who possess an equally negative attitude toward the materials:

> clearly, we have to ask ourselves the question as to whether this saying should now be attributed to the early Church or to the historical Jesus, *and the nature of the synoptic tradition is such that the burden of proof will be upon the claim to authenticity.*[2]

The latter view clearly presumes that the Gospel traditions are "guilty," that is, historically not true, unless they can be proven "innocent."

1. Jeremias, *New Testament Theology,* 37.
2. Perrin, *Rediscovering the Teaching of Jesus,* 39.

The Burden of Proof

The question of the historicity of the Gospel materials has been dealt with in a number of ways in the past. One popular method was to evaluate the general historicity of the Gospel materials by comparing those historical portions of the Gospel materials that have parallels in secular or non-Christian historical records and see whether these records support or tend to deny the historicity of the Gospel parallels. By this means perhaps some general attitude might develop toward the accuracy or inaccuracy of the Gospel accounts as a whole. Another attempt has been to establish if a Gospel writer was an eyewitness to the accounts he records in his Gospel. If he was an eyewitness, then this would lend credence to the historicity of his account. The problems with this approach, however, are twofold. For one, only two of our Gospels are associated traditionally with eyewitnesses and it is a much debated question as to whether any of them actually were written, as we now find them, by an eyewitness. Second, even if they were written by eyewitnesses, this does not in itself demonstrate that what they wrote are accurate historical accounts of the life of Jesus. It does not of necessity follow that eyewitness accounts of historical events are a priori accurate historical accounts! Such accounts are of course, all other things being equal, better historical records than noneyewitness accounts. We cannot, however, assume that we have proven the historicity of the Gospel accounts if we can demonstrate that behind them stands the testimony of an eyewitness. On the other hand it seems logical to assume that, if eyewitness testimony of the Gospel materials could be established, then the burden of proof should rest upon those who would deny the historicity of the events reported.

A final example that shall be mentioned with regard to the attempt to establish a general attitude toward the question of historicity and our Gospels is to evaluate the process by which the tradition was preserved and passed on. In this method, sometimes called form criticism and sometimes tradition criticism,[3] various arguments are frequently raised in support of the substantive accuracy of the Gospel accounts.

3. Technically these terms are not synonymous but in practice they essentially are.

1. The existence of the eyewitnesses during this period would have had the effect of seeing that those traditions would be faithfully preserved and that nonhistorical traditions would not be added.[4]
2. The existence of a center of leadership (the Jerusalem church) would have caused the traditions to be passed down carefully and accurately.[5]
3. The high view found in the New Testament toward the traditions (cf. Rom. 6:17—the church does not preserve the traditions but the traditions preserve the church; 1 Cor. 7:10, 12—note how Paul carefully distinguishes between what Jesus has said about divorce and what he has not said) indicates that during the oral period the traditions were carefully preserved and safeguarded.
4. The faithfulness of the early church in transmitting various difficult sayings of Jesus (cf. Mark 9:2; 10:18; 13:32; Matt. 10:5) witnesses to the reliable transmission of the Gospel materials.
5. The view that much of the Gospel material was simply created by the early church de novo to meet its religious needs and solve various religious problems is difficult to accept in the light of the fact that several of the major problems that the early church encountered never show up in the Gospel materials. Since the first and most important issue that the early church faced was the question of whether Gentile Christians had to be circumcised, one would expect to find some saying of Jesus that dealt with this issue, if the church were creating material to solve certain problems.
6. We must also not forget that the ability to remember traditions and pass them on faithfully is not limited by our present-day inability to do this or to conceive of this. The introduction of cheap writing materials into the world has had a negative impact in that it has paralyzed our abilities to memorize and to use the mind, rather than notebooks and files, as a databank.

4. For the contrary view, see Nineham, "Eye-witness Tradition," 9 (1958): 13–25, 143–52; 11 (1960): 253–60.

5. For this view, see Riesenfeld, *Gospel Tradition;* and Gerhardsson, *Memory and Manuscript.*

Although the above-mentioned attempts to establish the historicity of the Gospels are worthwhile and provide a general attitude toward the Gospel materials, when we seek to discover what the resultant general attitude is, we find no consensus at all. The present writer believes that the arguments listed above are sufficient to establish that the burden of proof ought to be with those scholars who deny the historicity of the Gospel materials. To assume the inauthenticity of the Gospel materials, unless proven otherwise, appears to be an extreme skepticism unwarranted both in the light of the various arguments listed above and a violation of a common courtesy every witness deserves.[6] A witness should be presumed innocent until proven guilty. Of course, if through the investigation of an account we arrive at a "general attitude" toward its historical veracity that is negative, then we cannot help but change the burden of proof, so that the historicity rather than the unhistorical nature of the accounts must be demonstrated. For this writer, however, this has in no way been demonstrated with regard to the Gospel materials.

Besides these general arguments, which are primarily helpful in establishing a general attitude toward the Gospel material, there exist certain tools that can be used to ascertain the historicity, or at least the historical probability, of a specific saying, teaching, or action of Jesus found in the Gospels. These "tools" or "rules of thumb" have been referred to as "criteria" by which the authenticity (or inauthenticity) of certain material can be established. Before we investigate these criteria, however, we must discuss briefly what is meant by the term "authentic."

The "Authenticity" of Jesus' Sayings

At first glance it would appear somewhat superfluous to discuss what is meant by an "'authentic' saying of Jesus," but because of the particular way in which this term has been defined by James M. Robinson such a discussion is mandatory. In contrast to the more traditional way of defining "authentic" as "being actually and exactly what the thing in question is

6. France, "Authenticity of the Sayings of Jesus," 107, states "Earlier generations of scholars assumed in their simplicity that the tradition is innocent until proven guilty, but now we are assured on every hand that it must be reckoned guilty until proven innocent."

said to be,"[7] so that an "authentic saying of Jesus" would mean "an actual saying of the historical Jesus," Robinson has defined the term according to his own existential concepts of historiography. Robinson states

> One may however observe that material regarded as wholly "unauthentic" in terms of positivistic historiography may not seem nearly as "unauthentic" in terms of modern [read—existential] historiography. For a saying which Jesus never spoke may well reflect accurately his historical significance, and in this sense be more "historical" [or authentic] than many irrelevant things Jesus actually said.[8]

In so redefining the "hopelessly ambiguous term 'authentic'" Robinson, however, has not contributed anything to clarity. To claim that a saying that was created by the early church and was therefore not uttered by the historical Jesus is an "authentic saying of Jesus" whereas an actual saying that the historical Jesus uttered is not an "authentic saying" can only lead to more confusion rather than clarification. We shall therefore define an "authentic saying of Jesus" as an actual saying that was uttered by the historical Jesus before his death. We shall leave out of the question entirely the issue of whether such a saying reveals "Jesus' existential selfhood."[9] All such existential considerations will be ignored, for the clearest way to avoid all ambiguity is to reserve the term "authentic" for only those words that the Jesus of history actually spoke.[10] Sometimes the terms *ipsissima verba* (the exact/very words of Jesus) or *ipsissima vox* (the very voice of Jesus) are used to distinguish the degree of exactness. The latter expression would be used in a saying when the words of that saying are not necessarily the exact words Jesus himself used but nevertheless accurately express his intention and meaning.

---

7. *Webster's Seventh New Collegiate Dictionary.*

8. *New Quest of the Historical Jesus* , 99 n. 3. A good example of this way of thinking is found in Plutarch, *Solon* 27.1. Here Plutarch accepts "historically" the meeting of Solon and Croesus even though they lived at different times because the meeting is so true to the characters of both men that he will not reject it upon such trivial grounds as the "so-called canons of chronology." I am indebted for this example to Hemer, "Luke the Historian," 30.

9. Robinson, *New Quest of the Historical Jesus,* 100 n. 3, 107–11.

10. So Calvert, "Examination of the Criteria," 209.

It needs to be pointed out that the term "authentic" is not to be construed as synonymous with the term "authoritative." Evangelicals would, of course, maintain that "authentic" material in the Gospels are "authoritative," for Jesus' words were, are, and will remain authoritative (Mark 13:31). Yet, if a saying attributed to Jesus in the Gospels were inauthentic, its authoritative quality would remain, for the Evangelists not only recalled what the historical Jesus said and did, but were taught by the Spirit and empowered by him to interpret what the historical Jesus said and did (John 14:26; 16:14). Thus in the Gospels the risen Christ also speaks through his Spirit by means of his prophets and apostles. These words are also authoritative even if not authentic. As a result if the inauthenticity of a saying should be demonstrated this should not be taken to mean that this saying lacks authority.

The Criteria for Authenticity

The criteria for authenticity are not new or unique, and some are of more value than others in seeking to establish the authenticity of the Gospel materials. The order in which they are presented should furthermore not be interpreted as implying any judgment as to their respective value. They are discussed in this particular order simply because in general they have been suggested in this order.

Multiple Attestation

One of the earliest criteria suggested for ascertaining the authenticity of a Gospel tradition was the criterion of multiple attestation. The basic idea behind the use of this criterion is that a word is "confirmed by the evidence of two or three witnesses" (Matt. 18:16). Essentially this criterion involves the use of literary criticism. Building upon the generally accepted solution of the Synoptic Problem, this view assumes that behind our Synoptic Gospels lie various sources—Mark, "Q," "M," and "L."[11] To these can be added the Gospel of John. Since each source is essentially a historical witness, if a particular teach-

11. "M" and "L" are symbols used to refer to the special material in Matthew and Luke not found anywhere else in the Synoptic Gospels. Whether "M" and "L" were written documents is of no major consequence. Whether written or oral they represent a different and separate tradition than Mark and "Q."

ing or activity of Jesus is witnessed to in Mark, "Q," "M," "L," and John, then the authenticity of this teaching or activity is "confirmed by the evidence of five witnesses."

One of the earliest scholars who advocated the use of this criterion was F. C. Burkitt. Burkitt states

> It appeared to me that the starting-point we require may be found in those Sayings which have a real double attestation. The main documents out of which the Synoptic Gospels are compiled are (1) the Gospel of Mark, and (2) the lost common origin of the non-Marcan portions of Matthew and Luke, i.e. the source called Q. Where Q and Mark appear to report the same saying, we have the nearest approach that we can hope to get to the common tradition of the earliest Christian society about our Lord's words.[12]

Burkitt then goes on to list thirty-one of these "doubly attested sayings."[13] An example of the application of this criterion might be the attempt to establish whether Jesus taught that the kingdom of God was realized in his own ministry. Witnesses that would support the view that the realized eschatology of the Gospels was authentic would be: Mark 2:21–22; "Q" (Luke 11:20); "M" (Matt. 5:17); "L" (Luke 17:20–21); and John 12:31. In general this criterion would appear to be more helpful in determining the authenticity of general motifs in Jesus' teaching rather than in establishing the authenticity of a particular saying.[14]

Of all the criteria to be discussed this criterion has the advantage of being "the most objective of the proposed criteria."[15]

---

12. *Gospel History*, 147.

13. Some others who make reference to this criterion are Dodd, *Parables of the Kingdom*, 26–27; Manson, *Teaching of Jesus*, 10–11; Dahl, "Problem of the Historical Jesus," 153–54; Jeremias, *Prayers of Jesus*, 115; McArthur, "Basic Issues," 47–48; "Historical Jesus Research," 118; Fuller, *Critical Introduction to the New Testament*, 97–98; Walker, "Quest for the Historical Jesus," 41–42; Calvert, "Examination of the Criteria," 217; Barbour, *Tradition-Historical Criticism*, 3–4; McEleney, "Authenticating Criteria," 433–35; Gager, "Gospels and Jesus," 260; Mitton, *Jesus*, 80–83; Latourelle, "Criteres," 619–21; Longenecker, "Literary Criteria," 219–20; Perrin, *Rediscovering the Teaching of Jesus*, 45–47; France, "Authenticity of the Sayings of Jesus," 108–110; Catchpole, "Tradition History," 176; Grayston, "Jesus," 264–65; Osborne, "Evangelical and *Traditionsgeschichte*," 119, 126; Meyer, *Aims of Jesus*, 87.

14. So Perrin, *Rediscovering the Teaching of Jesus*, 46.

15. MacArthur, "Basic Issues," 48.

A number of criticisms, however, have been raised with regard to its use. It is obvious from the start that the usual application of this criterion is based upon a particular solution of the Synoptic Problem. Recently this solution, that of Lachmann and Streeter (Matthew used Mark, "Q," "M"; Luke used Mark, "Q," "L") has been challenged and in the minds of some scholars "refuted."[16] If the "traditional" solution to the Synoptic Problem is not acceptable any longer, this will, of course, bring about a major revision of what sources lie behind the Synoptic Gospels. If the Griesbach Hypothesis (Luke used Matthew; Mark used Matthew and Luke) is correct, this would mean that we have essentially only the following sources for the Synoptic Gospel: Matthew[17] and "L" (the material in Luke not found in Matthew), for Mark's contribution would be minimal since 95 percent of Mark is found in Matthew or Luke. The criterion of multiple attestation would still be usable but would be of lesser value since we shall have lost entirely one witness ("M") and due to size (the 5 percent of Mark not obtained from Matthew) for all real purposes have lost another (Mark). On the other hand the question must be raised as to whether the appearance of the same tradition in Matthew–Mark–Luke should be considered as only *one* witness, whether Mark (à la Lachmann and Streeter) or Matthew (à la Griesbach and Farmer). Does not the fact that two Gospel writers chose to incorporate the account of another Gospel writer into their works witness to a threefold testimony to that tradition? Unless we assume that the later Evangelists were totally unfamiliar with the traditions found in Mark (or Matthew), then we must grant additional credence to the testimony of an account found in the triple tradition, for in their acceptance of the traditions in their source they give corroborative testimony to the primitiveness of those traditions.

Another criticism of this criterion is that all that one ultimately can be sure of is that, if a tradition is found in all or most of the various sources laying behind our Gospels, that

16. The man most responsible for this challenge and the revival of the Griesbach Hypothesis (Matthew was first and was used by Luke; Mark used Matthew and Luke) is William R. Farmer.

17. It is, of course, true that behind Matthew there would be sources that could serve as witnesses, but it would be for all practical purposes impossible to ascertain just what these sources were even as it is "impossible," assuming the Lachmann–Streeter thesis, to ascertain the sources used by Mark.

tradition is deeply embedded in the earliest traditions of the early church. Multiple attestation does not prove *absolutely* that the tradition is authentic! On the other hand the criterion of multiple attestation can, if we are able to establish the existence of various sources lying behind the Gospels, establish the probability that such a motif is authentic. Harvey K. McArthur states in this regard

> My own proposal would be that the order of priority should be reversed so that the criterion of multiple attestation is given first place, at least in order or procedure [instead of the criterion of dissimilarity]. Furthermore I would propose that when three or four of the synoptic sources concur in providing evidence for a given motif in the ministry of Jesus then the burden of proof should be regarded as having shifted to those who deny the historicity of that motif.[18]

McArthur's point would appear to be valid. The multiple attestation of a motif in the Gospels should place the burden of proof upon those who would deny the authenticity of that motif, for the tradition has been "confirmed by the evidence of two or three witnesses." On the other hand C. F. D. Moule has argued that the negative use of this criterion is illegitimate.[19] There is no reason or need to deny the authenticity of a tradition simply because it is found in only one source. The most that can be and should be said about such a tradition is that it is difficult or impossible to establish the authenticity or inauthenticity of such a tradition on this basis alone. To assume the inauthenticity of such a witness is to assume that anyone who testifies to any event without corroborating evidence is to be assumed a "false witness." Historical research may not be able to assume that the witness of a single source is true, but it has no right to assume that it is false. The wisest course in such an instance is to withhold judgment unless other evidence is available. This, interestingly enough, is what the Old Testament does.[20]

It would appear then that despite various objections, the criterion of multiple attestation is a helpful tool for ascertaining

18. "Historical Jesus Research," 118.
19. *Phenomenon of the New Testament,* 71. Cf. also Burkitt, *Gospel History,* 167–68.
20. See Deut. 19:15.

the authenticity of a Gospel tradition. It is, of course, not conclusive in and of itself, but its value cannot be denied. Surely the multiple attestation of a tradition places the burden of proof upon those who would argue against the authenticity of such a tradition or motif. Furthermore, if other criteria are found to support the historicity of such a tradition, then the historian *as historian* should assume that such a tradition is indeed authentic.

Multiple Forms

Closely related to the criterion of multiple attestation is the criterion of multiple forms. This criterion was first suggested as a tool for authenticity by C. H. Dodd, who listed six Gospel motifs as authentic because they appeared in multiple forms, that is, in different form-critical categories.[21] Surprisingly this criterion does not appear to have received much attention in the literature.[22] The basic assumption of this criterion is that the various forms of the Gospel materials, such as pronouncement stories, miracle stories, stories about Jesus, parables, and sayings, centered in different contexts and spheres of interest in the early church and were therefore preserved and passed down through different channels. As a result if a motif is found in multiple literary forms, that motif came from a broad section of the early church and was deeply embedded in the earliest church traditions.

An example of the use of this criterion might be to see if Jesus' teaching that the kingdom of God was realized in his ministry meets the criterion of multiple forms. Thus we shall see how broadly based such a teaching was in the Gospel traditions. In this instance it is evident that this motif is found in pronouncement stories (Mark 2:18–20; Luke 11:14–22); miracle stories (Luke 5:36–39); and sayings (Matt. 5:17; 13:16–17). It is evident from the above that the various forms of the Gospel materials portray Jesus as teaching that the kingdom of God came in his ministry. Does this, however, "prove" that this is an

21. Turner, *History and the Gospel*, 91–102. Some others who discuss the use of this criterion are McArthur, "Basic Issues," 49–50; Walker, "Quest for the Historical Jesus," 42–43; Robinson, "Formal Structure of Jesus' Message," 96–97; McEleney, "Authenticating Criteria," 435–36; Calvert, "Examination of the Criteria," 217; Grayston, "Jesus," 264–65; Meyer, *Aims of Jesus*, 87.

22. See, however, Trocmé, *Jesus as Seen by His Contemporaries,* who seeks to arrive at a coherent picture of Jesus from the "Dominical Sayings," "Apophthegms," "Biographical Narratives," "Parables," and "Miracles Stories."

authentic motif of Jesus' teachings? Again we must answer in the negative. The appearance of this motif in multiple literary forms of the materials does not "prove" conclusively its authenticity, but at least "the criterion has some value in distinguishing comparatively early from comparatively late traditions, but it is not as decisive as that of multiple attestation by a number of sources."[23] Assuming that the establishment of the early date of a tradition is a positive factor in the establishment of its authenticity, it would appear reasonable to suppose that the appearance of a tradition or motif in multiple forms is supportive, even if not conclusive, evidence for its authenticity. Furthermore if these different oral forms were passed on via different routes of transmission,[24] then a common motif in these various forms assures us not only of the primitiveness of that motif but possesses a "multiple attestation" not unlike that discussed under our previous criterion.

Aramaic Linguistic Phenomena

Another tool for authenticity that has been suggested involves the presence of Aramaisms in the Gospel materials. Since it seems certain that the mother tongue of Jesus was Aramaic, and in particular a Galilean dialect of Aramaic,[25] the presence of Aramaic linguistical characteristics in our Greek Gospel materials argues in favor of the primitiveness of those particular traditions and the more primitive a tradition is, the more likely it is that it stems from Jesus. As a result the Aramaic background of a saying "is of great significance for the question of the reliability of the gospel tradition,"[26] and "the closer the approximation of a passage in the Gospels to the style and idiom of contemporary Aramaic, the greater the presumption of authenticity."[27] Some of the earliest pioneering work done in this area was done by Gustav Dalman,[28] C. F. Burney,[29] and C. C. Tor-

---

23. McArthur, "Basic Issues," 50.
24. Cf. Trocmé, *Jesus as Seen by His Contemporaries*, 110, who states "As we have seen, all the strata of oral tradition have come to us by way of particular and limited groups."
25. See Stein, *Method and Message*, 4–6.
26. Jeremias, *New Testament Theology*, 8.
27. Turner, *History and the Gospel*, 77–78.
28. *Jesus-Jeshua*.
29. *Poetry of Our Lord*.

rey,[30] but the two people who have done the most work in this are Matthew Black[31] and Joachim Jeremias.[32]

This criterion has been applied in a number of ways to the Gospel materials. Through the work of Burney, Black, Jeremias, and others it is now evident that one form that Jesus frequently used in his teachings was antithetical parallelism. Jeremias lists over 138 examples of this form in the Synoptic Gospels alone.[33] Whereas some of these may be inauthentic, it is impossible to deny that many of these examples of antithetical parallelism come from Jesus himself. As a result, although no one would argue a priori that every example of such parallelism in the Gospels is authentic, there is good reason to believe that the probability of any example of antithetical parallelism being authentic is greater than that of other sayings not found in this form. (This, of course, must be qualified by an "all other things being equal.") By the use of this parallelism it may even be possible to arrive at the more primitive form of a saying by retranslating that saying back into a more perfect parallelism. Thus the original form of Mark 8:35 may possibly be obtained by the elimination of those words that disturb the parallelism. Note how much more balanced the antithetical parallelism becomes by omitting the words in parentheses. "For whoever would save his life will lose it; and whoever loses his life (for my sake and the gospel's) will save it."

Another way in which this tool is used is to note the presence of certain puns that are puns in Aramaic but not in Greek. There are some puns that are puns in both Greek and Aramaic (Matt.16:18; John 3:8). Puns based upon different meanings of the same word frequently carry over into other languages (see

30. *Our Translated Gospels* .

31. *Aramaic Approach to the Gospels and Acts* .

32. *Parables of Jesus; Eucharistic Words of Jesus; New Testament Theology.* Some additional references for the discussion of this criterion are Walker, "Quest for the Historical Jesus," 43–44; Fuller, *Critical Introduction to the New Testament,* 97; Perrin, *Rediscovering the Teaching of Jesus,* 37–38; McEleney, "Authenticating Criteria," 438–40; Calvert, "Examination of the Criteria," 216; Barbour, *Tradition-Historical Criticism,* 4; Longenecker, "Literary Criteria," 220, 223; France, "Authenticity of the Sayings of Jesus," 109; Osborne, "Evangelical and *Traditionsgeschichte,*" 125; Gager, "Gospels and Jesus," 260–61; Manson, *Teaching of Jesus,* 45–86; Sanders, *Synoptic Tradition,* 190–209; Latourelle, "Critères," 630–32; Meyer, *Aims of Jesus,* 87.

33. Jeremias, *New Testament Theology,* 15–16.

Luke 9:59–60; Mark 1:17; 4:9.) An example of a pun that is a pun only in Aramaic is Matthew 23:23–24.

> Woe to you scribes and Pharisees, hypocrites! for you tithe mint and dill and cummin, and have neglected the weightier matters of the law, justice and mercy and faith; these you ought to have done, without neglecting the others. You blind guides, straining out a gnat and swallowing a camel!

In the Greek New Testament this does not appear as a pun, but when retranslated back into Aramaic the pun is evident because the term for gnat is *galma* and for camel is *gamla*. Thus we have this pun: "You blind guides, straining out a *galma* and swallowing a *gamla*." The possibility that this saying arose in a Greek environment and by chance is converted into a pun when translated into Aramaic is minimal. It seems quite reasonable to conclude that Matthew 23:23–24 arose in an Aramaic-speaking environment. One of the most intensive attempts to use this linguistic criterion in order to arrive at the *ipsissima verba* of Jesus is Joachim Jeremias' work on the Lord's Supper. Jeremias[34] has sought to argue for the authenticity of the Marcan account of the Lord's Supper on the basis of some twenty Semiticisms, that is, Aramaisms, which he finds in the Marcan account.

A number of criticisms have been raised, however, against this criterion. It has been objected that the presence of such Aramaic linguistic phenomena in a tradition establishes only that the tradition arose in an Aramaic-speaking church rather than the historical Jesus, and such Aramaisms may not even be a sign of a saying's antiquity.[35] Another criticism is that the presence of Aramaisms in the Gospel materials may be due to Septuagintal influence on the part of the Greek church or the Gospel writers.[36] Whether this influence was conscious or unconscious is beside the point. Still another criticism of this criterion is that the assumption that the Gospel materials can be accurately retranslated into Aramaic is itself questionable. It

34. *Eucharistic Words of Jesus*, 118–26.
35. So Fuller, *New Testament in Current Study*, 33–34; Walker, "Quest for the Historical Jesus," 44; Perrin, *Rediscovering the Teaching of Jesus*, 37; Calvert, "Examination of the Criteria," 218.
36. Longenecker, "Literary Criteria," 223; Walker, "Quest for the Historical Jesus," 44; Sanders, *Synoptic Tradition*, 202.

would be overly negative to argue that this cannot be done, but on the other hand it may be that Black and Jeremias are a bit overly optimistic about this.

As a result of these criticisms some scholars have minimized the importance of this criterion or see it as possessing only a negative function,[37] that is, if a tradition contains non-Aramaic features then it (or at least those features) cannot be authentic. Such criticism is unwarranted, however, for at least two reasons. First, this criterion can serve a negative function only if we can assume that Jesus did not speak Greek and there is good reason to believe that he did.[38] As a result we cannot conclude with Reginald H. Fuller that "any saying of Jesus, if it is authentic, *should* exhibit Aramaic features,"[39] in that this precludes that at times Jesus may have taught in Greek. Second, such minimizing of the value of this criterion is unnecessary. Certainly it must be admitted that the mere presence of Aramaisms does not prove that a tradition is authentic. Even Jeremias acknowledges this.[40] Yet if we can establish due to the presence of Aramaisms (allowing, of course, for the possibility of Septuagintal influence on the formation of the Gospel tradition in the Greek-speaking church) that a tradition must go back at least to the Aramaic-speaking church, then we can use this criterion as supportive testimony for the possibility/probability that this tradition may have come from Jesus himself. Clearly the presence of such Aramaisms increases the probability of such material being authentic, for to have been translated from Aramaic into Greek and to have been used in Mark and/or "Q" argues at the very least for the primitiveness of such traditional material. Although the criterion of Aramaic linguistic phenomena cannot alone establish the authenticity of a saying or tradition, when used in conjunction with other criteria this criterion becomes a valuable tool and provides supportive testimony to the possible authenticity of the saying or tradition.

Palestinian Environmental Phenomena

Closely related to the previous tool is the criterion of Palestinian environmental phenomena. According to this criterion

37. Gager, "Gospels and Jesus," 260–61.
38. See Stein, *Method and Message*, 6.
39. *New Testament in Current Study*, 33–34.
40. *Problem of the Historical Jesus*, 18.

if a tradition betrays Palestinian social, domestic, agricultural, or religious customs, this argues that the tradition originated in a Palestinian environment and cannot be a later creation of the Greek (non-Palestinian) church. Again the argument here is that the closer we can trace a tradition to the time and environment of Jesus, the more likely it is that that tradition is authentic.[41] Probably no writer has used this tool more fully than Jeremias. He argues, for instance, that

> the pictorial element of the parables is drawn from the daily life of Palestine. It is noteworthy, for instance, that the sower in Mark 4.3–8 sows so clumsily that much of the seed is wasted; one might have expected a description of the regular method of sowing, and that, in fact is what we have here. This is easily understood when we remember that in Palestine sowing precedes ploughing. . . . What appears in the western mind as bad farming is simply customary usage under Palestinian conditions.[42]

It has been pointed out, however, that Palestinian environmental phenomena may not be as useful a tool as originally presumed, for not all of the teachings of Jesus or incidents in his life are so narrowly "Palestinian" that they could not have arisen outside of Palestine. Furthermore Jesus himself may have said things that betray a Greek environment more than a Palestinian one. An example of this is the saying of Jesus on divorce. "Whoever divorces his wife and marries another, commits adultery against her; and if she divorces her husband and marries another, she commits adultery" (Mark 10:11–12). Frequently the authenticity of this saying is denied on the grounds that it betrays a non-Palestinian social and religious environment, for in the saying there is the assumption that wives can divorce their husbands and this was not permissible in Judaism. This assumption has been challenged of late by some of the material associated with the Bar Cochba revolt,[43] but it seems reason-

41. For a discussion of this criterion, see Jeremias, *Parables of Jesus,* 11–12 in particular; Dahl, "Problem of the Historical Jesus," 154; Carlston, "*Positive* Criterion," 34; Walker, "Quest for the Historical Jesus," 44; Calvert, "Examination of the Criteria," 216; Downing, *Church and Jesus,* 113; Latourelle, "Authenticité Historique," 238.

42. *Parables of Jesus,* 11–12. Cf. b. Sabb. 73b; Jub. 11:23.

43. See Derrett, *Law in the New Testament,* 382.

able to assume that a Jewish wife divorcing her husband would
certainly have been an extremely rare incident whereas among
the Greeks this was not uncommon. Yet there is a realistic *Sitz
im Leben* in the ministry of Jesus for just such a saying, since
the ruler of Galilee had a wife who had done just that and John
the Baptist had been executed at least in part for having
denounced this divorce and the subsequent marriage. F. Gerald
Downing's statement that "A Palestinian first-century background is a necessary but not sufficient condition for acceptance as authentic; if it were Palestinian Gentile, the critic
should be worried but not dismayed"[44] should be carefully
noted. Whether Mark 10:11–12 is authentic or not is not the
issue at hand, however. What is important is to note that it is
conceivable and quite probable that Jesus could have said things
that reflect a non-Palestinian environment, if we assume that
Palestinian means non-Gentile or non-Greek. Thus this criterion,
like any criterion, is limited in its application.

The main criticism against this criterion is that at best it can
only root the tradition in question in Palestinian Christianity.
It cannot demonstrate that the tradition goes back even far-
ther to the historical Jesus. This is, of course, true, but the presence of such Palestinian environmental phenomena does nevertheless increase the likelihood that a tradition possessing such
phenomena stems from Jesus himself.

Tendencies of the Developing Tradition

Whereas the previous criteria serve a positive function, this
proposed criterion serves a primarily negative function. It is a
negative tool that has been proposed by the form critics. According to form-critical theory the passing on of the tradition during the oral period proceeded according to certain "laws" and by
understanding these "laws" we can determine what aspects of
the tradition are late, that is, inauthentic. Rudolf Bultmann
states

> the study of the laws which govern literary transmission, can
> be approached by observing the manner in which the Marcan
> material was altered by Matthew and Luke; and also how
> Matthew and Luke worked over what they took from the *Logia*.
> Here we observe a certain regular procedure which becomes still

44. Downing, *Church and Jesus*, 113.

more evident when we carry the investigation to a later tradition, particularly to the apocryphal gospels, and see how in these
the gospel material received further literary development. . . .
The ability to make the necessary distinctions can be developed
by studying the general laws which govern popular transmission of stories and traditions in other instances, for example, in
the case of folk-tales, anecdotes, and folk-songs.[45]

This criterion then serves as a negative scalpel to remove the
later accretions and modifications of the early tradition, but in
so doing it serves also a positive function by helping in the
recovery of the earlier form of the tradition. The earlier the
form the greater the possibility that we have an authentic saying or incident in the life of Jesus.

A possible example of how this criterion may be applied to
the Gospel materials is the parable of the lost sheep found in
Matthew 18:12–14 and Luke 15:4–7. It is generally agreed that
"Matthew" wrote his Gospel to Jewish Christians. On the other
hand it is clear that certain parables of Jesus were originally
addressed not to believers but to his opponents. In Luke 15:1–2
Luke describes the following parables as having been used apolo-
getically by Jesus to defend himself against those who mur-
mured that he received sinners and ate with them. The parable
of the lost sheep, at least according to Luke, is therefore a
defense of Jesus' behavior in eating with the outcasts of Jewish society. That this is the correct setting of the parable is evident from the fact that this seems to have been a frequent
charge leveled against Jesus (see Mark 2:16–17; Matt. 11:19;
Luke 7:39; 19:7). Furthermore there would appear to be no real
reason why Luke might have changed the audience from the
"church" to Jesus' opponents (if the parable was originally
addressed to the "church" as we find in Matthew) whereas there
is good reason why Matthew might have changed the audience from Jesus' opponents to the "church" (if it was originally
addressed to Jesus' Jewish opponents as we find in Luke). It
would appear therefore that whereas Luke seems more authentic in his setting of this parable, Matthew seeks to apply its

45. "New Approach to the Synoptic Problem," 345. For additional discussion
of this criterion, see Bultmann and Kundsin, *Form Criticism*, 32–35; McArthur,
"Basic Issues," 48–49; Walker, "Quest for the Historical Jesus," 44–46; Calvert,
"Examination of the Criteria," 213; McEleney, "Authenticating Criteria," 436–37.

teachings to his own audience, which does not consist of opponents of Jesus but rather of his followers! As a result, whereas
originally this parable of Jesus was primarily a defense of his
actions in associating with publicans and sinners, for Matthew
and his readers there is no great need for such a defense of
Jesus' behavior, and so the emphasis lies most heavily upon
the content of that defense: God's great love for the outcasts
of society and the inbreaking of the kingdom of God by God's
visiting the rejected of Israel.[46] Matthew applies this great truth
to his own *Sitz im Leben* by addressing the parable to the disciples (Matt. 18:1), the leaders of the church, in order that they
may exercise loving pastoral leadership over those in the church
community who have made themselves outcasts and apostates.
Even as Jesus sought the outcasts of Judaism, so the leaders of
the church should seek to restore to the kingdom of God its
own outcasts.[47] From the above it is evident that if we recognize
certain of the "laws" that the tradition experienced during the
oral period, such as the changing of the audience in the first
and the second/third *Sitze im Leben*, we shall be better able to
ascertain what is authentic.

The main criticism of this criterion involves the establishment of these "laws" by which the tradition was passed on. It
must be pointed out that Bultmann and the form critics arrived
at these "laws" based on a particular view of the relationship of
Matthew–Mark–Luke. If this traditional view is untenable, much
of their argument and their results will have to be changed,
for the "laws" obtained on the premise that Matthew used Mark
will be quite different from the "laws" obtained on the premise
that Mark used Matthew and Luke! E. P. Sanders has raised
some very serious questions about the whole matter of the
"laws" of the tradition.[48] Although it would be overly pessimistic to conclude that we know nothing about the tendencies
present in the passing on of the Gospel materials during the
oral period, it seems clear that no such "laws" ruled with an

46. Stein, *Method and Message*, 57.
47. For the present writer this redactional interpretation of Jesus' parable
by "Matthew" should be understood in the light of John 14:25–26, which
speaks of the Holy Spirit not only bringing the words of Jesus, the *ipsissima
verba*, into remembrance but "teaching" their significance as well. See also
John 15:26; 16:14.
48. Sanders, *Synoptic Tradition*, 272–75.

iron hand over the traditions. Tendencies during this period indeed existed, but "laws" did not! As a result we need to exercise much more care and reserve in determining what could or could not have taken place and not speak of what must have taken place. Furthermore we must also note that whereas we may ascertain certain general tendencies or rules that were operative and worked on the tradition, this does not tell us what happened in any single specific instance.

The value of this criterion has been criticized and rightfully so, but if it can be shown, by a careful application of these tendencies, that certain aspects of the Gospel traditions seem to be later additions or modifications, then the burden of proof would be upon those who argue that these additions and modifications are authentic. In stating this it is of course self-evident that we must have a clear understanding of what these tendencies in fact were, and Sanders' criticisms must be given serious consideration.

Dissimilarity or Discontinuity

Of all the criteria suggested for ascertaining the authenticity of the Gospel materials, the criterion of dissimilarity (or distinctiveness) has been heralded as the most useful. The exact origin of this criterion is uncertain, but the most important reference to this tool was clearly Ernst Käsemann's famous address to the "Old Marburgers." Käsemann suggested that

> In only one case do we have more or less safe ground under our feet [in seeking authentic material]; when there are no grounds either for deriving a tradition from Judaism or for ascribing it to primitive Christianity.[49]

Earlier Paul W. Schmiedel had made use of something similar to this criterion for obtaining his seven "Pillar Passages" that could not have arisen out of the early church.[50] Bultmann had also said,

> We can only count on possessing a genuine similitude of Jesus where, on the one hand, expression is given to the contrast between Jewish morality and piety and the distinctive eschato-

49. "Problem of the Historical Jesus," 37.
50. Schmiedel, "Gospels," cols. 1881–83.

logical temper which characterized the preaching of Jesus; and where on the other hand we find no specifically Christian features.[51]

Although this criterion is usually treated as a single tool, it consists essentially of two different parts that could be and have been separated into two different criteria.[52] The first "part" involves whether we can find in the Jewish thought of Jesus' day elements similar to the particular teaching or motif in question. If we cannot, the assumption is then made that the said material could not have arisen out of Judaism and later have been attributed to Jesus. An example of how this works is Jeremias' investigations involving the term "Abba" in the Gospels. Where did this designation for God in prayer arise? Could it have arisen in Judaism and then have been read back upon the lips of the historical Jesus? To this Jeremias gives a vehement "No."

> There is something quite new, absolutely new—the word *abba*. With the help of my assistants I have examined the whole later Jewish literature of prayer, and the result was that in no place in this immense literature is this invocation of God to be found. . . . Abba was a homely family word, the tender address of the babe to its father; O dear father— a secular word. No Jew would have dared to address God in this manner. Late Judaism never addressed God as *abba*—Jesus did it always.[53]

---

51. *History of the Synoptic Tradition,* 205. Some other scholars who discuss this criterion are Walker, "Quest for the Historical Jesus," 46–47; Cullmann, *Salvation in History,* 189; Perrin, *Rediscovering the Teaching of Jesus,* 39–43; Gager, "Gospels and Jesus," 256–59; Moule, *Phenomenon of the New Testament,* 62; Hooker, "Examination of the Criteria," 209, and "On Using the Wrong Tool," 570–81; Calvert, "Examination of the Criteria," 215–16; McEleney, "Authenticating Criteria," 440–42; Barbour, *Tradition-Historical Criticism,* 5–27; Fuller, *Critical Introduction to the New Testament,* 96–97; Longenecker, "Literary Criteria," 221–25; Osborne, "Evangelical and *Traditionsgeschichte,*" 118–19; Catchpole, "Tradition History," 174–76; Conzelmann, *Jesus,* 16; Turner, *History and the Gospel,* 73–74; Mitton, *Jesus,* 84–85; McArthur, "Basic Issues," 50–51; Zahrnt, *Historical Jesus,* 107; Bruce, *Tradition,* 47–49; Koester, "Historical Jesus," 124–36; France, "Authenticity of the Sayings of Jesus," 108, 110; Latourelle, "Critères," 622–25; Grayston, "Jesus," 264; Mealand, "Dissimilarity Test," 41–50; Meyer, *Aims of Jesus,* 81–87.

52. See Calvert, "Examination of the Criteria," 214–15.

53. "Lord's Prayer in Modern Research," 95. See, however, Vermes, *Jesus the Jew,* 211.

The use of "Abba" as a designation for God in the Gospels there-fore satisfies, according to Jeremias, the first part of the criterion of dissimilarity. Other expressions frequently suggested as meet-ing this part of the criterion are the use of "Amen" as an intro-ductory expression; Jesus' offer of salvation to the outcasts of Israel; Jesus' particular use of parables; and Jesus' use of the title "Son of man."[54]

The second part of this criterion involves the question of whether we can find in the early Christian church elements similar to the particular teaching or motif in question. If we cannot, the assumption is then made that the material in ques-tion could not have arisen out of the early church and then read back upon the lips of the historical Jesus. Ben F. Meyer has suggested that this part of the criterion alone established the authenticity of any Gospel saying. For him "the requirement of simultaneous discontinuity with Judaism and the post-paschal church errs by excess"[55] in that "Discontinuity with the post-paschal church is sufficient by itself to establish historicity."[56] H. E. W. Turner[57] has also sought to modify this criterion some-what by claiming that total discontinuity with the teachings of the early church is not necessary for even if they overlap somewhat with the Gospel materials the criterion is met as long as there exists a marked difference between the church's teaching and the sayings in question. According to this modi-fication there need not be an absolute qualitative difference to satisfy this criterion. Although Turner's suggestion seems rea-sonable, for the sake of argument we shall deal with those examples that do not even overlap. An example of this would be the use of "Amen" as an introductory expression. Since this is not found in the New Testament outside of our Gospels, this demonstrates its authenticity, for it meets both parts of the cri-terion of dissimilarity![58] Other teachings or motifs that would

54. It is quite possible that outside of Dan. 7:13 we do not possess a single pre-Christian apocalyptic Son of man reference, for 2 Esdras 13 is clearly late first-century and although the Book of Enoch is pre-Christian, the Similitudes (chaps. 37–71) probably are post-Christian. See Milik, *Books of Enoch*, 89–107.

55. Meyer, *Aims of Jesus*, 86.

56. Ibid., 86.

57. *History and the Gospels*, 73–74.

58. The question of whether "Amen" as an introductory formula is found in pre-Christian Judaism has been greatly debated of late. For a succinct discussion of the more recent debate, see Chilton "'Amen,'" 203–11.

appear to meet this requirement are the "Pillar Passages" of Schmiedel; Jesus' use of the parables; and the apocalyptic title "Son of man," which is found outside of the Gospels only in Acts (7:56).[59]

Despite the great optimism with which this tool was embraced, there has recently been a heavy barrage of criticism leveled at this tool. The most detailed and vigorous criticism has come from M. D. Hooker.[60] Some of these criticisms, however, are not so much criticisms of the criterion itself, but of the misuse of the criterion. It has been objected that the criterion assumes the inauthenticity of a tradition if that tradition does not meet its standard.[61] To be sure, some scholars have argued in this manner and are incorrect in so doing, but the criterion does not demand this conclusion! The criterion used as a *positive tool* does not deserve this criticism. A more serious objection is that this criterion eliminates the great majority of Gospel materials, because most of this material does not conflict with the Judaism of Jesus' day and the theology of the early church. This criticism, of course, is true, for there is little material that really qualifies as authentic via this criterion. But again this criticism does not in any way impugn upon the validity of the criterion for the material that meets its standards. It only points out that the criterion is limited—perhaps extremely limited—in its application. For the limited amount of material that qualifies under this criterion, however, the criterion of dissimilarity would appear to be an extremely valuable tool with regard to the question of authenticity.

A more substantial criticism of this criterion is that it presumes that we possess a sufficient knowledge of the Judaism

59. There are, of course, critics who deny the authenticity of certain "Pillar Passages," certain parables, and all the Son of man sayings. There have been and still are critics who deny that Jesus ever lived! To this writer, however, an objective use of the criterion of dissimilarity argues for the authenticity of this material.

60. "On Using the Wrong Tool," 570–81; but see Mealand, "Dissimilarity Test," 41–50, for a corrective.

61. See Fuller, *Critical Introduction to the New Tesatament,"* 96; France, "Authenticity of the Sayings of Jesus," 107; and Gager, "Gospels and Jesus," 258 who states "The proper use of the criterion cannot allow the claim that such a story [which does not meet the standards of this criterion] is inauthentic, merely that we can never be confident of its authenticity under the circumstances."

of Jesus' day and the primitive Christian community to determine if a particular Gospel tradition could not have arisen out
of these environments. Is our understanding of first-century
Judaism and the early church, however, complete enough for
concluding what could have and what could not have arisen out
of Judaism and the primitive church?[62] It is certainly true that
our knowledge of both these areas of history is incomplete, so
that to a certain extent this lack of knowledge makes our use of
this tool an argument based on silence.[63] The discovery of additional data no doubt may modify our present picture of both,
but it would certainly be overly pessimistic and negative to
assume that we are entirely ignorant of Palestinian Judaism in
Jesus' day and of the early church or that future knowledge
would change completely our present portrait of them. Certain modifications and refinements can and no doubt will take
place, but when and if our understanding changes we shall
then simply incorporate this in our use of the criterion. Again
the validity of the tool is not in question in this criticism as
long as we are cautious and exercise care in the use of the data
available for our understanding of first-century Judaism and
the early church.

Another cogent criticism of the criterion of dissimilarity is
that what is distinct in Jesus' teaching may not necessarily be
characteristic of it. Hooker points out that

> the English word "distinctive" can have two senses—as usual,
> the Germans use two words: "distinctive" can mean "unique"
> (what makes it distinct from other things, the German *ver-
> schieden*), or it can mean "characteristic" (the German *bezeich-
> nend*). In which sense is it being used here? Clearly the method
> is able only to give us the former—but what we really *want* is
> the latter; and the two are by no means necessarily the same.[64]

Hooker is clearly correct! A movement arising in some way or
other from the life and teachings of Jesus that did not have
much in common with Jesus' actual teachings would be impossible to conceive. It would be like trying to conceive of a late six-

62. See Hooker, "Examination of the Criteria," 575.
63. Ibid.
64. Ibid., 574. Cf. also Catchpole, "Tradition History," 174; and Walker,
"Quest for the Historical Jesus," 48.

teeth-century Lutheranism that was totally or even primarily "distinct" from the teachings of Luther. On the contrary one would expect that what was "characteristic" of Jesus' and Luther's teaching would be "characteristic" of early Christianity and early Lutheranism, respectively.[65] Again we must be careful, however, not to assume that a valid criticism of the misuse of this tool is in reality a valid criticism of the tool itself. The tool does not claim to be able to arrive at what is "characteristic" of Jesus' teaching, even if some scholars have falsely assumed that what was distinct was in fact the essence of his teaching. The tool is primarily concerned with ascertaining "a critically assured *minimum.*"[66] If we take into consideration the limited aim of this tool, it is possible to question how useful such a tool is since so much of the Gospel materials simply do not qualify under this tool, *but* this in no way negates the value of this tool for ascertaining the authenticity of those Gospel materials that meet the standards of this criterion.[67]

In concluding our discussion of this tool, it would appear that despite many of the criticisms raised of late, when used correctly in conjunction with its innate limitations, the criterion of dissimilarity is nevertheless a most valuable tool in the quest for the *ipsissima verba* or *vox* of Jesus. It may in fact be the single most valuable tool for authenticity, for if a saying or action of Jesus in the Gospel tradition meets the demands of this criterion, the likelihood of it being authentic is extremely good.[68] It is

---

65. Longenecker, "Literary Criteria," 224–25.

66. Dahl, "Problem of the Historical Jesus," 156; cf. also Barbour, *Tradition-Historical Criticism*, 26.

67. Thus the criticism that the Jesus of this criterion must by definition be "anti-Jewish" and "anti-Christian" is true only with regard to those scholars who deny the authenticity of any material that does not meet the criterion of dissimilarity. On such a basis the portrait of Jesus must by definition be "anti-Jewish" and "anti-Christian" and ultimately docetic. On the other hand if we accept the fact that this criterion can only produce a solid core of authentic material, the problem this criticism is directed at is greatly diminished.

68. Vansina, *Oral Tradition*, 107, states concerning African historical traditions,

When features which do not correspond [i.e. are dissimilar] to those commonly attributed to an ideal type nevertheless persist in a tradition, they may usually be regarded as trustworthy.

Cf. also Schmiedel, "Gospels," col. 1872. It should be noted that Vansina combines the criterion of dissimilarity with a form of multiple attestation ("features which . . . persist in the tradition").

true that this tool cannot necessarily deliver to us that which is characteristic in Jesus' teachings or even to produce "an adequate historical *core*,"[69] but it does give us a "critically assured minimum" to which other material can be added via other criteria. Care must be taken, however, to apply this tool more objectively than in the past, for McArthur has pointed out that some "advocates of the criterion relax its rigors when, on general grounds, they are convinced material is authentic, but that they tighten it on the other occasions."[70] It may be that the most objective way in which we can make use of this tool is to exclude from our sources for the theology of the early church all the Gospel materials and seek to arrive at our understanding of what the early church believed only from Acts–Revelation and from any noncanonical materials that may be relevant. In so doing we would avoid the kind of circular reasoning that concludes that certain sayings or motifs in the Gospels are the creation of the early church even though these sayings or motifs appear nowhere outside the Gospels. Perhaps the greatest example of this is the total rejection of the authenticity of any of the Son of man sayings by some scholars on the basis that these sayings originated in the early church. Yet the proof that the early church possessed a Son of man theology is based upon the very sayings under discussion. Without denying that the Gospels are a valuable source of information for the history and theology of the early church, it would nevertheless appear that caution would suggest that for the particular saying or motif in question we should exclude the Gospel materials from serving as sources for the theology of the early church. Such caution will ultimately bring even greater objectivity to the use of this tool.

Modification by Jewish Christianity

This particular criterion is frequently associated with the criterion of dissimilarity. Käsemann has even given the impression that this criterion functions primarily as a third part of the criterion of dissimilarity.

> In only one case do we have more or less safe ground under our feet; when there are no grounds either for deriving a tradition

---

69. Barbour, *Tradition-Historical Criticism*, 26.
70. McArthur, "Historical Jesus Research," 117; cf. Catchpole, "Tradition History," 175; Hooker, "Examination of the Criteria," 576–77.

from Judaism or for ascribing it to primitive Christianity, and especially when Jewish Christianity has mitigated or modified the received tradition, as having found it too bold for its taste.[71]

One example frequently given of how Jewish Christianity allegedly modified the original teachings of Jesus in order to fit better with its own situation is the famous "exception clause" found in Matthew 5:32 and 19:9. In contrast to the Marcan parallel in Mark 10:11–12 that reads, "Whoever divorces his wife and marries another, commits adultery against her; and if she divorces her husband and marries another, she commits adultery" and the "Q" parallel in Luke 16:18 that reads, "Every one who divorces his wife and marries another commits adultery, and he who marries a woman divorced from her husband commits adultery," Matthew has in both of these sayings the exception "except on the ground of unchastity" (Matt. 5:32) or "except for unchastity" (Matt. 19:9). In light of this twofold agreement in Mark and "Q," as well as the parallel in 1 Corinthians 7:10–11, which also lacks an exception clause, it seems reasonable to conclude that the *ipsissima verba* of Jesus lacked this exception.[72]

It is clear that as a tool the criterion of modification will serve both a negative and a positive function. The presence of a demonstrated modification will of course serve in a negative way by demonstrating that the modification is not authentic, so that whereas the absence of modification by early Jewish Christianity does not prove the authenticity of a particular saying, the presence of a modification indicates at least that the modification is not authentic. Yet William O. Walker has rightly pointed out that it is not easy to distinguish "whether, when, and by whom the traditions in question were modi-

71. Käsemann, "Problem of the Historical Jesus," 37. Cf. also McEleney, "Authenticating Criteria," 442–43; and Perrin, *Rediscovering the Teaching of Jesus*, 39, who adds to the criterion of dissimilarity the following: "and this will particularly be the case where Christian tradition oriented towards Judaism can be shown to have modified the saying away from its original emphasis."

72. Although Banks (*Jesus and the Law*, 152–53) acknowledges the exception clause as being Matthean, he does not see this addition as a weakening or lessening of the intensity of Jesus' words. He suggests the following translation on p. 156. "I say to you, whoever dismisses his wife—the permission in Deut. 24:1 notwithstanding—and marries another, commits adultery."

fied"[73] and points out that some early Christians no doubt were more "radical-rigid-bold" in certain respects than Jesus himself, so that it is conceivable (although in the case of the "exception clause" not very likely) that at times the "harder reading" may not be authentic. Is it not conceivable that certain groups in the early church, like the Judaizers of Galatians 2 and Acts 15, may have taken an even harder, more restricted line on certain issues than Jesus himself did? Such criticisms do raise doubts over the applicability of this criterion, but in theory, at least, it is of course true that if we can demonstrate that a particular tradition has been modified by the early church this not only witnesses negatively to the authenticity of the modification but also positively toward the authenticity of the tradition. The fact that the early church modified such a tradition witnesses to the probability that the tradition had such an authority and ancient pedigree that the church or Evangelist could not ignore the tradition but had to deal with it in the only other way possible—by modifying it to suit the present context. The modification of a tradition that the early Jewish church "found too bold for its taste" therefore serves as a positive testimony to the antiquity of the tradition and to its dominical lineage.

Divergent Patterns from the Redaction

This criterion is essentially the second part of the criterion of dissimilarity applied to the third *Sitz im Leben*. Whereas in the criterion of dissimilarity we assume that dissimilarity between the theology of the early Jewish church and the Gospel materials demonstrates that the material in question could not have arisen out of the early church and therefore is likely to be authentic, this criterion argues that such dissimilarity between the Gospel materials and the redaction of the Evangelists argues in favor of such material (1) not having originated from the Evangelist and (2) being of such lineage that the Evangelist did not feel free to omit it. As D. G. A. Calvert says

> the inclusion of material which does not especially serve his [the Evangelist's] purpose may very well be taken as a testimony to the authenticity of that material, or at least to the inclusion of it in

73. Walker, "Quest for the Historical Jesus," 49.

the tradition of the Church in such a clear and consistent way
that the evangelist was loath to omit it.[74]

The inclusion by the Evangelist of material that does not fit
his theological scheme serves therefore as a nonintentional witness to the antiquity and authenticity of such material. Calvert
lists as an example of this such kinds of material: positive statements about the disciples in Mark and negative statements
about them in Matthew. Perhaps a better example of the inclusion of material by an Evangelist that seems to conflict with
his main thrust would be the statement in Matthew 11:13: "For
all the prophets and the law prophesied until John. . . ." This
seems to conflict with Matthew's heavy emphasis on the permanent validity of the law found elsewhere in his Gospel (3:15;
5:17–20; 7:12; 12:5—note the Marcan parallel here; 23:1–3, 23).
This "despite the author" kind of evidence is furthermore the
very kind of evidence that historians often find most valuable.

> Nevertheless, there can be no doubt that, in the course of its
> development, historical research has gradually been led to place
> more and more confidence in the second category of evidence, in
> the evidence of witnesses in spite of themselves.[75]

An example of this kind of testimony is found in the Acts
of Paul and Thecla. Whereas the work is clearly one in which
the apostle Paul is eulogized, we find the following rather negative description of the physical makeup of the apostle.

> And he saw Paul coming, a man small of stature, with a bald
> head and crooked legs, in a good state of body, with eyebrows
> meeting and nose somewhat hooked, full of friendliness.[76]

This "despite the author" negative description of the hero of
the work is surely of such a nature that it deserves serious consideration.

74. Calvert, "Examination of the Criteria," 219; cf. also Moule, *Phenomenon
of the New Testament,* 62, 67; Riesenfeld, *Gospel Tradition,* 72; Osborne, "Evangelist and *Traditionsgeschichte,*" 123; Bareau, *Recherches,* 380, who applies this
principle to the "quest for the historical Buddha"; Schmiedel, "Gospels," cols.
1872–73; and Longenecker, "Literary Criteria," 225–29.

75. Bloch, *Historian's Craft,* 61.

76. Acts of Paul and Thecla, 3, in *New Testament Apocrypha,* 2:354.

It must be pointed out that this criterion does not and cannot demonstrate the authenticity of any of the material that meets the criterion. All this criterion demonstrates is that the Evangelist was "loath" to omit such material and that this material had therefore a firm place in the tradition of the church.[77] The assumption seems legitimate, however, that the more firm the place that a tradition had in the church, the more likely it is that such a tradition was old and well known, and the older and better known a tradition, the greater the probability that it is authentic. This criterion therefore, while not providing "proof" of authenticity, does provide corroborative testimony to other criteria that such a tradition possesses the "likelihood" of being authentic and may serve as a link in a chain of arguments that seeks to demonstrate the authenticity of the tradition. On the other hand, the criterion cannot be used negatively, for if a tradition is in support of the theme of theology of an Evangelist, this does not prove its inauthenticity unless it can be demonstrated that such a theme or theology contradicts the situation of Jesus, and if this is true it would be primarily the concern of the criterion of contradiction of authentic sayings.[78]

Environmental Contradiction

This criterion serves a negative function and argues that if a saying or motif in the Gospel materials presupposes a situation in the life of Jesus that was impossible, then the saying or motif must be inauthentic.[79] There would seem to be little debate over this criterion, for if a saying was not possible, by definition it could not have occurred! In effect this criterion is simply a tautology that states "If a saying or motif could not have been taught by Jesus, Jesus could not have taught that saying or motif." The basic problem with this criterion is that "It is difficult to assess what would be unthinkable to Jesus, and the decision must often be that of individual judgement."[80] Calvert gives as an example of this problem Matthew 22:7, which supposedly reflects a post-A.D. 70 situation. Yet he points out Beasley-Murray's argument that such a view depends upon the

---

77. Hooker, "Examination of the Criteria," 579.
78. See below pp. 182–83.
79. Calvert, "Examination of the Criteria," 212.
80. Ibid.

position one takes concerning the possibility of prophetic prediction. J. A. T. Robinson has furthermore argued, not without
weight, that

> the wording of Matt. 22.7 represents a fixed description of ancient
> expeditions of punishment and is such an established *topos* of
> Near Eastern, Old Testament and rabbinic literature that it is
> precarious to infer that it must reflect a particular occurrence.[81]

It must nevertheless be acknowledged that the presence of
non-Palestinian environmental characteristics do argue against
the authenticity of such a saying.[82] The problem is that it is
not easy to determine what could not have arisen in the *Sitz
im Leben* of Jesus. For some the statement found in Mark 10:12
is impossible in the first *Sitz im Leben* because Jewish women
could not divorce their husbands, but we have already pointed
out[83] that John the Baptist was beheaded for condemning just
such a divorce, so that it is clearly not impossible for Jesus to
have uttered such a statement. This criterion is therefore a valid
negative tool for determining inauthenticity, but possesses a
very serious handicap in that it is extremely difficult to determine what Jesus could not have said in the first *Sitz im Leben*.

Contradiction of Authentic Sayings

Like the previous criterion this one also serves a negative
function. "'A saying is unauthentic if it contradicts a recognized authentic saying.'"[84] Calvert admits that this criterion is
very limited in its application, for there are few instances when
one can say with certainty that two sayings are contradictory.
Furthermore the very nature of Jesus' teaching, which frequently
used overstatement, paradox, and hyperbole,[85] means that we
must be extremely careful that such a contradiction is not
merely formal but actual, that is, that the contradiction of the
two statements consists in the meaning of the statements. Are,
for instance, the following two statements contradictory?

81. *Redating the New Testament*, 20.
82. See above pp. 166–68.
83. See above p. 168.
84. Calvert, "Examination of the Criteria," 213.
85. See Stein, *Method and Message*, 8–12, 19–20.

> If any one comes to me and does not hate his own father and mother and wife and children and brothers and sisters, yes, and even his own life, he cannot be my disciple. (Luke 14:26)

> You have a fine way of rejecting the commandment of God, in order to keep your tradition! For Moses said, "Honor your father and your mother"; and, "He who speaks evil of father or mother, let him surely die." (Mark 7:9–10; cf. also Luke 6:27)

Or is the command "Judge not, that you be not judged" (Matt. 7:1) in contradiction with "Do not give dogs what is holy; and do not throw your pearls before swine . . ." (Matt. 7:6), which demands that one "judge" between "swine" and "nonswine" and "dogs" and "nondogs"?[86] We must exercise extreme care therefore before we conclude that a real contradiction exists between an authentic saying of Jesus and the saying that is being compared with it.

Yet we must raise several other questions. Can we assume a priori that Jesus did not make contradictory statements? On what grounds? And can we assume that what we consider contradictory could not have been seen by Jesus as standing in a certain harmonious relationship? Is it possible that the apparent contradiction between Jesus' teachings on reward and grace[87] may be more of a problem for western minds than for the oriental mind of Jesus? Such considerations should cause us to move with great caution before we say that Jesus could not have said "A" because it conflicts (in our way of thinking) with "B," which we know is an authentic saying of Jesus. On the other hand this criterion does increase the probability that any saying or motif that seems to contradict an authentic saying or motif in Jesus' teaching is inauthentic.

Coherence (or Consistency)

This particular criterion has been placed last because it is the last tool that should be applied in the quest for the authentic sayings of Jesus. Its validity is dependent on the presupposition that by wise and judicious use of the previously listed criteria historical research can arrive at authentic material, so that this "critically assured minimum" can now function as a tem-

---

86. Cf. also Luke 12:57 in this regard.
87. See Stein, *Method and Message*, 105–6.

plate by which other material may be judged to be more or less authentic. According to Norman Perrin, "material from the earliest strata of the tradition may be accepted as authentic if it can be shown to cohere with material established as authentic by means of the criterion of dissimilarity."[88] A good example of how this criterion has been used is provided by Carlston. Upon having concluded that Jesus' message was one of repentance in the light of the eschatological coming of the kingdom of God, he states concerning the parables: "An 'authentic' parable will fit reasonably well into the eschatologically based demand for repentance that was characteristic of Jesus' message."[89]

On purely logical grounds it would appear that the criterion of coherence is a valid tool, for if we can ascertain that certain sayings of Jesus are authentic, then other sayings claiming to be uttered by Jesus that are in harmony with the ideas and motifs of the authentic material are more likely to be authentic than those that are not in harmony with such ideas and motifs. Certainly coherence does not prove that the materials being considered are authentic, for the early church could have created material that "cohered" with Jesus' authentic teachings. As a result the criterion of coherence cannot serve as an absolute proof of authenticity. It must also be acknowledged that this criterion will tend to magnify any previous mistakes that might have been made in establishing certain sayings as authentic, for if the template is in error, then any product of the template will contain the same error.[90] Again, however, whereas this latter criticism is a valid one, it is not a criticism of the validity

88. Perrin, *Rediscovering the Teaching of Jesus,* 43. Cf. also Fuller, *New Testament in Current Study,* 98; Bultmann, *History of the Synoptic Tradition,* 105; Jeremias, *Unknown Sayings of Jesus,* 71; Catchpole, "Tradition History,"176–77; Calvert, "Examination of the Criteria," 217–18; McEleney, "Authenticating Criteria," 443–44; Longenecker, "Literary Criteria," 221–22; Barbour, *Tradition-Historical Criticism,* 9, 26; Gager, "Gospels and Jesus," 259–60; Grayston, "Jesus," 264; Walker, "Quest for the Historical Jesus," 49–50; Osborne, "Evangelist and *Traditionsgeschichte,*" 119, 121; Schmiedel, "Gospels," col. 1873; Latourelle, "Critères," 625–27; France, "Authenticity of the Sayings of Jesus," 108.

89. Carlston, *"Positive* Criterion," 34. Cf. also Bultmann's similar use of this approach in *Theology of the New Testament,* 4–11, and the approach of Robinson, "Formal Structure of Jesus' Message," 99.

90. So Hooker, "Examination of the Criteria," 577; Barbour, *Tradition-Historical Criticism,* 26; Osborne, "Evangelist and *Traditionsgeschichte,*" 121.

of the criterion but rather a criticism of the incorrect use of the criterion, that is, using as our standard material that is not authentic. If we can in fact ascertain authentic material in the Gospels, then this criterion is a valid one. On the other hand we must be quick to acknowledge that the criterion cannot prove absolutely that consistent material is authentic or that non-consistent material is inauthentic. What this tool can do is to provide for the historian a greater likelihood that material that coheres with authentic material is also authentic, and this in turn can become one additional argument in the chain of arguments that must be brought to bear on the material in question.[91]

Conclusion

Having investigated the most commonly suggested criteria of authenticity, we need now to come to some general conclusions as to the value of these criteria. How useful are they for arriving at our hoped for goal of ascertaining authentic sayings of Jesus? It would appear that taken alone no one criterion can "prove" that a saying in the Gospels is authentic, although one, the criterion of dissimilarity, is sufficiently functional so as to place a heavy burden of proof upon anyone denying the authenticity of any saying that meets its standards. Only the strongest kinds of negative evidence can hope to disprove the authenticity of a saying or motif that satisfies the criterion of dissimilarity. It is nevertheless the cumulative evidence of the various criteria that serves to demonstrate a saying's authenticity. If a particular saying or teaching of Jesus meets most (or ideally all) of the positive criteria listed above, then we can claim with reasonable certainty that this teaching is authentic. Each criterion serves as an individual chain in the investigative process. Some are stronger, of more value, than others in establishing the probability of authenticity. Whereas no one criterion, with the possible exception of the criterion of dissimilarity, is strong enough to tie a Gospel saying or motif absolutely to the historical Jesus, the cumulative effect of the various "chains" can bring the historian to the place that he "has to acknowledge

---

91. See Dunn, "Prophetic 'I'-Sayings," 193–96, for an interesting discussion of the importance of the criterion of coherence for testing prophetic 'I' sayings in the early church.

[this material] as authentic if he wishes to remain an historian at all."[92]

Even if, however, the weight of evidence is not sufficient to demonstrate the authenticity of a saying beyond a reasonable doubt, it may well be that there needs to be an acknowledgment of where the burden of proof lies. McArthur suggests that if a saying or motif meets the criterion of multiple attestation, then "the burden of proof shifts to those who deny the authenticity of that particular motif."[93] It may be debated whether this one criterion alone can bring about such a shift in the burden of proof for some scholars, but we must acknowledge that there is also a middle ground between the two extremes of Gospel tradition being clearly authentic or clearly inauthentic.[94] In such instances if a saying satisfies several criteria the probability of the saying being authentic will be increased and any burden of proof will surely be on those who hold a negative view of its authenticity. On the other hand, it must be pointed out once again that the failure of a saying or motif to satisfy the criteria of multiple attestation, multiple forms, Aramaic linguistic phenomena, Palestinian environmental phenomena, dissimilarity divergent patterns from the redaction, says nothing for or against its authenticity. This simply indicates that the case for authenticity cannot be established because of the inadequacy of our tools. Only four criteria can be used to argue for the inauthenticity of a saying: the criterion of the tendencies of the developing tradition, the criterion of modification by Jewish Christianity, the criterion of environmental contradiction, and the criterion of contradiction of authentic sayings. Yet these criteria must be used carefully with the important qualifications mentioned in the discussion above.[95]

Finally it should be pointed out that if by the use of these various criteria, certain sayings in our Gospels can in fact be demonstrated as being authentic and this in turn can establish

92. Käsemann, "Wunder im NT," 46.

93. McArthur, "Historical Jesus Research," 119. It is, of course, a matter of debate as to whether one should a priori assume the inauthenticity of any saying in the Gospels before the investigative process begins.

94. See Meyer, *Aims of Jesus*, 84, who states, "In the first place, there will be three columns for historicity judgments on the material: yes, no, and question mark."

95. See pp. 168–71, 177–79, 181–83.

a continuity between the historical Jesus and kerygmatic Christ, there is then no a priori reason to be skeptical about the general portrait of Jesus found in our Gospels. On the contrary it would then be clear that the burden of proof lies with those who would reject the authenticity of the Gospel materials rather than with those who accept their authenticity.[96] We can say this in another way using the terminology of the law court. If by the criteria discussed above, the authenticity of certain sayings and motifs in the Gospels can be demonstrated that establish a continuity between the Jesus of history and the Christ of faith, then we should assume that the other sayings and motifs in the Gospels are "innocent until proven guilty"—a saying in the Gospels proporting to come from Jesus is true (authentic) until proven false (inauthentic).

96. See Jeremias, *New Testament Theology*, 37.

Bibliography
of Sources Cited

Aland, Kurt. "Der wiedergefundene Markusscluß." *ZTK* 67 (1970): 3–13.

Albertz, Martin. *Die synoptischen Streitgespräche.* Berlin: Trowitzsch, 1921.

Argyle, A. W. "The Genitive Absolute in Biblical Greek." *ExpT* 69 (1957/58): 285.

Bacon, Benjamin Wisner. *The Gospel of Mark: Its Composition and Date.* New Haven: Yale University Press, 1925.

Bailey, John Amedee. *The Traditions Common to the Gospels of Luke and John.* Leiden: Brill, 1963.

Baltensweiler, Heinrich. *Die Verklärung Jesu.* Zürich: Zwingli, 1959.

Banks, Robert. *Jesus and the Law in the Synoptic Tradition.* Cambridge: University, 1975.

Barbour, R. S. *Tradition-Historical Criticism of the Gospels.* London: SPCK, 1972.

Bareau, Andre. *Recherches sur la Biographie du Bouddha.* Paris: Ecole Francaise, 1963.

Bartsch, Hans Werner. "Die 'Verfluchung' des Feigenbaumes." *ZNW* 53 (1962): 256–60.

———. "Der Schluß des Markus-Evangeliums." *TZ* 27 (1971): 241–54.

———. *Entmythologisierende Auslegung.* Hamburg: H. Reich, 1962.

Bauer, J. "ΠΟΛΛΑΙ : Luk I, 1." *NovT* 4 (1960): 263–66.

Beare, Francis W. "Concerning Jesus of Nazareth." In *New Testament Issues.* New York: Harper, 1970.

Bertram, G. "Die Himmelfahrt Jesu vom Kreuz aus und der Glaube an seine Auferstehung." In *Festgabe für Adolf Deissman.* Tübingen: Mohr, 1927.

Best, Ernest. *The Temptation and the Passion.* Cambridge: University, 1965.

Betz, H. D. "Jesus as Divine Man." In *Jesus and the Historian: Written in Honor of Ernest Cadman Colwell,* ed. F. T. Trotter. Philadelphia: Westminster, 1968.

Billerbeck, Paul, and Hermann Strack. *Kommentar zum Neuen Testament.* München: C. H. Beck'sche, 1965.

Black, C. Clifton, II. "The Quest of Mark the Redactor: Why Has It Been Pursued, and What Has It Taught Us?" *JSNT* 33 (1988): 19–39.

———. *The Disciples According to Mark.* Sheffield: JSOT, 1989.

Black, Matthew. *An Aramaic Approach to the Gospels and Acts.* Oxford: Clarendon, 1946.

Blinzler, Josef. *Die neutestamentlichen Berichte über die Verklärung Jesu.* Münster: Aschendorff, 1937.

Bloch, Marc. *The Historian's Craft.* Trans. Joseph R. Strayer. New York: Alfred A. Knopf, 1953.

Bode, Edwyn Lynn. *The First Easter Morning.* Rome: Pontifical Biblical Institute, 1970.

Boobyer, G. H. *St. Mark and the Transfiguration Story.* Edinburgh: T. & T. Clark, 1942.

———. "Galilee and Galileans in St. Mark's Gospel." *BJRL* 35 (1953): 334–48.

Bornkamm, Günther, Gerhard Barth, and Heinz Joachim Held. *Tradition and Interpretation in Matthew.* Philadelphia: Westminster, 1963.

Bowman, John W. *The Gospel of Mark.* Leiden: Brill, 1965.

Brown, John Pairman. "Mark as Witness to an Edited Form of Q." *JBL* 80 (1961): 29–44.

Brown, Raymond E. *The Gospel According to John I–XII.* Garden City: Doubleday, 1966.

Bruce, F. F. *Tradition: Old and New.* Grand Rapids: Zondervan, 1970.

Brun, Lyden. *Segen und Fluch im Urchristentum.* Oslo: Jacob Dubwad, 1932.

Bultmann, Rudolf. "The New Approach to the Synoptic Problem." *JR* 6 (1926): 337–62.

———. *Theology of the New Testament.* Trans. Kendrick Grobel. New York: Charles Scribner's Sons, 1951.

———. "The Study of the Synoptic Gospels." In *Form Criticism: Two Essays on New Testament Research.* Trans. Frederick C. Grant. New York: Harper, 1962.

———. *The History of the Synoptic Tradition.* Trans. John Marsh. New York: Harper, 1963.

Bundy, Walter Ernst. *Jesus and the First Three Gospels.* Cambridge: Harvard University Press, 1955.

Burkill, T. A. "Anti-Semiticism in St. Mark's Gospel." *NovT* 3 (1959): 34–53.

———. "Strain on the Secret: An Examination of Mark 11:1–13:37." *ZNW* 51 (1960): 31–46.

———. "The Hidden Son of Man in St. Mark's Gospel." *ZNW* 52 (1961): 189–213.

———. *Mysterious Revelation.* Ithaca: Cornell University Press, 1963.

Burkitt, Francis Crawford. *The Gospel History and Its Transmission.* Edinburgh: T. & T. Clark, 1907.

Burney, Charles Fox. *The Poetry of Our Lord.* Oxford: Clarendon, 1925.

Buse, Ivor. "The Cleansing of the Temple in the Synoptics and in John." *ExpT* 70 (1958): 22–24.

Cadbury, H. J. "Commentary on the Preface of Luke." In *The Beginnings of Christianity*, ed. F. J. Foakes-Jackson and K. Lake. London: Macmillan, 1922.

Calvert, D. G. A. "An Examination of the Criteria for Distinguishing the Authentic Words of Jesus." *NTS* 18 (1972): 209–19.

Carlston, Charles Edwin. "Transfiguration and Resurrection." *JBL* 80 (1961): 233–40.

———. "A *Positive* Criterion of Authenticity?" *BR* 7 (1962): 33–44.

Carrington, Philip. *The Primitive Christian Calendar*. Cambridge: University, 1952.

———. *According to Mark*. New York: Cambridge University Press, 1960.

Catchpole, David R. "Tradition History." In *New Testament Interpretation*, ed. I. Howard Marshall. Grand Rapids: Eerdmans, 1977.

Chilton, Bruce. "'Amen': An Approach Through Syriac Gospels." *ZNW* 69 (1978): 203–11.

Conzelmann, Hans. *Die Mitte der Zeit*. Tübingen: Mohr, 1954.

———. *The Theology of St. Luke*. Trans. Geoffrey Buswell. New York: Harper, 1960.

———. *Jesus*. Trans. J. Raymond Lord. Philadelphia: Fortress, 1973.

Cranfield, C. E. B. *The Gospel According to St. Mark*. New York: Cambridge University Press, 1963.

Cullmann, Oscar. *Salvation in History*. Trans. Sidney G. Sowers. New York: Harper, 1967.

Dahl, Nils Alstrup. "The Problem of the Historical Jesus." In *Kerygma and History*, ed. Carl E. Braaten and Roy Harrisville. New York: Abingdon, 1962.

Dalman, Gustav. *Jesus–Jeshua*. New York: Macmillan, 1929.

Daube, David. "ἐξουσία in Mark I 22 and 27." *JTS* 39 (1938): 45–59.

———. "Four Types of Questions." *JTS* 2 (1951): 45–48.

———. *The New Testament and Rabbinic Judaism*. London: University of London, 1956.

Davies, W. D. *Torah in the Messianic Age and/or the Age to Come*. Philadelphia: Society of Biblical Literature, 1952.

———. *The Setting of the Sermon on the Mount*. Cambridge: University, 1964.

———. *Paul and Rabbinic Judaism*. New York: Harper, 1967.

Derrett, J. Duncan M. *Law in the New Testament*. Darton, Longman, & Todd, 1970.

Dibelius, Martin. *From Tradition to Gospel*. Trans. Bertram Lee Woolf. New York: Charles Scribner's Sons, n.d.

Dillon, Richard J. "Previewing Luke's Project from His Prologue (Luke 1:1–4)." *CBQ* 43 (1981): 205–27.

Dinkler, Erich. "Form Criticism of the New Testament." In *Peake's Commentary on the Bible*. New York: Nelson, 1962.

Dobschütz, Ernst von. "Zur Erzählerkunst des Markus." *ZNW* 27 (1928): 193–98.

Dodd, C. H. "The Framework of the Gospel Narrative." *ExpT* 43 (1932): 396–400.

———. "The Appearances of the Risen Christ: An Essay in Form-Criticism of the Gospels." In *Studies in the Gospels.* Oxford: Blackwell, 1955.

———. *Historical Tradition in the Fourth Gospel.* Cambridge: University, 1963.

———. *The Parables of the Kingdom.* New York: Charles Scribner's Sons, 1961.

Doeve, J. W. "Purification du Temple et Desséchement du Figuier." *NTS* 1 (1954): 297–308.

Doudna, John Charles. *The Greek of the Gospel of Mark.* Philadelphia: Society of Biblical Literature, 1961.

Downing, Francis Gerald. *The Church and Jesus.* Naperville: Allenson, 1968.

Dunn, James D. G. "Prophetic 'I'-Sayings and the Jesus Tradition: The Importance of Testing Prophetic Utterances Within Early Christianity." *NTS* 24 (1978): 175–98.

Du Plessis, I. I. "Once More: The Purpose of Luke's Prologue (Lk 1 1–4)." *NovT* 16 (1974): 259–71.

Evans, C. F. "'I Will Go before You into Galilee.'" *JTS* 5 (1954): 3–18.

———. *Resurrection and the New Testament.* Naperville: Allenson, 1970.

Eysinga, G. A. van den Bergh van. *Indische Einflüsse auf evangelische Erzählungen.* Göttingen: Vandenhoeck & Ruprecht, 1909.

Farmer, William R. *The Synoptic Problem: A Critical Analysis.* New York: Macmillan, 1964.

Farrer, Austin. *A Study in St. Mark.* New York: Oxford, 1952.

Feine, Paul, Johannes Behm, and Werner Georg Kümmel. *Introduction to the New Testament.* Trans. A. J. Mattill, Jr. Nashville: Abingdon, 1966.

Findlay, James Alexander. *Jesus and His Parables.* London: Epworth, 1950.

France, R. T. "The Authenticity of the Sayings of Jesus." In *History, Criticism, and Faith,* ed. Colin Brown. Downers Grove: Inter-Varsity, 1976.

Frör, Kurt. *Biblische Hermeneutik.* München: Chr. Kaiser, 1961.

———. *Wege zur Schriftauslegung.* Düsseldorf: Patmos, 1963.

Fuller, Reginald H. *The New Testament in Current Study.* New York: Charles Scribner's Sons, 1962.

———. *A Critical Introduction to the New Testament.* London: Duckworth, 1966.

———. *The Formation of the Resurrection Narratives.* New York: Macmillan, 1971.

———. *The Foundations of New Testament Christology.* New York: Charles Scribner's Sons, 1965.

Gager, John G. "The Gospels and Jesus: Some Doubts about Method." *JR* 54 (1974): 244–72.

Gärtner, Bertil Edgar. *The Temple and the Community in Qumran and the New Testament.* Cambridge: University, 1965.

———. *Die rätselhaften Termini Nazoräer und Iskariot.* Uppsala: Appelberas Boktryckeri Ab, 1957.

Gerhardsson, Birger. *Memory and Manuscript: Oral Tradition and Written Transmission in Rabbinic Judaism and Early Christianity.* Lund: Gleerup, 1961.

Glöckner, Richard. *Die Verkündigung des Heils beim Evangelisten Lukas.* Mainz: Matthias-Grünewald, 1975.

Goetz, Karl G. *Petrus.* Leipzig: Hinrichs, 1927.

Goguel, Maurice. *The Life of Jesus.* Trans. Olive Wyon. London: Allen & Unwin, 1933.

Goodspeed, Edgar Johnson. *An Introduction to the New Testament.* Chicago: University, 1937.

Grant, Frederick C. *The Gospels: Their Origin and Their Growth.* New York: Harper, 1957.

Grant, Robert M. *A Historical Introduction to the New Testament.* New York: Harper, 1963.

Grass, Hans. *Ostergeschehen und Osterberichte.* Göttingen: Vandenhoeck & Ruprecht, 1956.

Grayston, K. "Jesus: The Historical Question." *Downside Review* 95 (1977): 254–70.

Grobel, Kendrick. "Idiosyncracies of the Synoptists in Their Pericope—Introductions." *JBL* 59 (1940): 405–10.

Grundmann, Walter. *Die Geschichte Jesu Christi.* Berlin: Evangelische Verlagsanstalt, 1959.

———. *Das Evangelium nach Markus.* Berlin: Evangelische Verlagsanstalt, 1959.

Guthrie, Donald. *New Testament Introduction: The Gospels and Acts.* Chicago: Inter-Varsity, 1965.

Haenchen, Ernst. *Der Weg Jesus.* Berlin: Töpelmann, 1966.

———. *The Acts of the Apostles.* Philadelphia: Westminster, 1971.

Hahn, Ferdinand. *The Titles of Jesus in Christology.* New York: World, 1969.

Hamilton, Neill Quinn. "Resurrection Tradition and the Composition of Mark." *JBL* 84 (1965): 415–21.

———. *Jesus for a No-God World.* Philadelphia: Westminster, 1969.

Hartman, Gerhard. *Der Aufbau des Markusevangeliums.* Münster: Aschendorffschen Verlagsbuchhandlung, 1936.

Hartman, Lars. *Testimonium Linguae.* Lund: Gleerup, 1963.

Hawkins, John C. *Horae Synopticae.* Oxford: Clarendon, 1909.

Hegermann, Harald. "Bethsaida und Gennesar." In *Judentum, Urchristentum, Kirche: Festschrift für Joachim Jeremias,* ed. Walter Eltester. Berlin: Töpelmann, 1960.

Hemer, C. J. "Luke the Historian." *BJRL* 60 (1977).

Hennecke, Edgar. *New Testament Apocrypha.* Ed. W. Schneemelcher; trans. R. McL. Wilson. Philadelphia: Westminster, 1965.

Hiers, Richard H. "Not the Season for Figs." *JBL* 87 (1968): 394–400.

Higgins, A. J. B. "The Preface to Luke and the Kergyma in Acts." In *Apostolic History and the Gospel,* ed. W. W. Gasque and R. P. Martin. Grand Rapids: Eerdmans, 1970.

Hooker, M. D. "On Using the Wrong Tool." *Theology* 75 (1972): 570–81.

Horstmann, Maria. *Studien zur markinischen Christologie*. Münster: Aschendorff, 1969.

Hoskyns, E. C. "Adversaria Exegetica." *Theology* 7 (1923): 147–55.

Ibers, Gerhard. "Zur Formgeschichte der Evangelien." *TR* 24 (1957/58): 283–338.

Jeremias, Joachim. *The Problem of the Historical Jesus*. Trans. Norman Perrin. Philadelphia: Fortress, 1964.

———. *The Parables of Jesus*. Trans. S. H. Hooke. London: SCM, 1963.

———. *Unknown Sayings of Jesus*. Trans. Reginald H. Fuller. London: SPCK, 1964.

———. *The Eucharistic Words of Jesus*. Trans. Arnold Ehrhardt. New York: Macmillan, 1955.

———. *Jesus als Weltvollender*. Gütersloh: Bertelsmann, 1930.

———. "The Lord's Prayer in Modern Research." In *New Testament Issues*, ed. Richard Batey. New York: Harper, 1970.

———. "Die älteste Schicht der Menschensohn—Logien." *ZNW* 58 (1967): 159–72.

———. *The Prayers of Jesus*. Trans. John Bowen. Naperville: Allenson, 1967.

———. *New Testament Theology*. Trans. John Bowden. New York: Charles Scribner's Sons, 1971.

Johnson, Sherman E. *A Commentary on the Gospel According to St. Mark*. London: Black, 1960.

———. *Theology of the Gospels*. London: Duckworth, 1966.

Karnetzki, Manfred. "Die Galiläische Redaktion im Markus-evangelium." *ZNW* 52 (1961): 238–72.

Käsemann, Ernst. "The Problem of the Historical Jesus." In *Essays on New Testament Themes*. Trans. W. J. Montague. Naperville: Allenson, 1964.

———. "Wunder im NT." *RGG* 6 (1962): 1835.

Keck, Leander E. "The Introduction to Mark's Gospel." *NTS* 12 (1966): 352–70.

Klein, Günther. *Die Zwölf Apostel*. Göttingen: Vandenhoeck & Ruprecht, 1961.

———. "Lukas I, 1–4 als theologisches Programm." In *Zeit und Geschichte*, ed. E. Dinkler. Tübingen: Mohr, 1964.

Klostermann, Erich. *Das Markusevangelium*. Tübingen: Mohr, 1950.

Knigge, Heinz-Dieter. "The Meaning of Mark." *Interp* 22 (1968): 53–70.

Knox, Wilfred Lawrence. *Sources of the Synoptic Gospels*. Cambridge: University, 1953.

Koch, Klaus. *Was Ist Formgeschichte?* Neukirchen-Vluyn: Neukirchener, 1964.

———. *The Growth of the Biblical Tradition*. London: Black, 1969.

Koester, Helmut. "The Historical Jesus: Some Comments and Thoughts on Norman Perrin's *Rediscovering the Teaching of Jesus*." In *Christology and a Modern Pilgrimage*, ed. Hans Dieter Betz. Claremont: New Testament Colloquium, 1971.

Kümmel, Werner Georg. *Introduction to the New Testament*. Nashville: Abingdon, 1975.

Kundsin, Karl. *Topologische Überlieferungsstoffe im Johannes-Evangelium.* Göttingen: Vandenhoeck & Ruprecht, 1925.

Lambrecht, Jan. *Die Redaktion der Markus-Apokalypse.* Rome: Päpstliches Bibelinstitut, 1967.

Lane, William L. *Commentary on the Gospel of Mark.* Grand Rapids: Eerdmans, 1974.

Larfield, Wilhelm. *Die Neutestamentlichen Evangelien.* Gütersloh: C. Bertesmann, 1925.

Latourelle, Rene. "Authenticitié Historique des miracles des Jesus." *Greg* 54 (1973): 225–62.

———. "Critères d'authenticité historique des Évangiles." *Greg* 55 (1974): 609–38.

Lightfoot, Robert Henry. *Locality and Doctrine in the Gospels.* New York: Harper, 1937.

———. *The Gospel Message of St. Mark.* Oxford: Clarendon, 1950.

Lindars, Barnabas. *New Testament Apologetic.* London: SCM, 1961.

Linnemann, Eta. "Der (wiedergefundene) Markusschluß." *ZTK* 66 (1969): 255–87.

Lohmeyer, Ernst. "Die Verklärung Jesu nach dem Markus-Evangelium." *ZNW* 21 (1922): 185–215.

———. *Das Evangelium des Markus.* Göttingen: Vandenhoeck & Ruprecht, 1937.

———. *Galiläa und Jerusalem.* Göttingen: Vandenhoeck & Ruprecht, 1937.

———. *Lord of the Temple.* Richmond: John Knox, 1962.

Loisy, Alfred. *Les évangiles synoptiques.* Haute-Marne: Ceffonds, 1908.

Longnecker, Richard N. "Literary Criteria in Life of Jesus Research: An Evaluation and Proposal." In *Current Issues in Biblical and Patristic Interpretation,* ed. Gerald F. Hawthorne. Grand Rapids: Eerdmans, 1975.

McArthur, Harvey K. "Basic Issues: A Survey of Recent Gospel Research." *Interp* 18 (1964): 39–55.

———. "The Burden of Proof in Historical Jesus Research." *ExpT* 82 (1971): 118.

McCurley, Foster R., Jr. "'And after Six Days' (Mark 9:2): A Semitic Literary Device." *JBL* 93 (1971): 67–81.

McEleney, N. L. "Authenticating Criteria and Mark 7:1–23." *CBQ* 34 (1972): 431–60.

McKelvey, R. J. *The New Temple.* London: Oxford, 1969.

Manson, T. W. *The Teaching of Jesus.* New York: Cambridge University Press, 1935.

———. "The Cleansing of the Temple." *BJRL* 33 (1951): 271–82.

Marshall, Christopher D. *Faith as a Theme in Mark's Narrative.* Cambridge: University, 1989.

Marshall, I. Howard. *The Gospel of Luke.* Grand Rapids: Eerdmans, 1978.

Martyn, James Louis. *History and Theology in the Fourth Gospel.* New York: Harper, 1968.

Marxsen, Willi. "Redaktionsgeschichtliche Erklärung der sogenannten Para-
beltheorie des Markus." *ZTK* 52 (1955): 255–71.

———. *Der Evangelist Markus—Studien zur Redaktionsgeschichte des Evangeliums.*
Göttingen: Vandenhoeck & Ruprecht, 1956.

———. *Einleitung in das Neue Testament.* Gütersloh: Gerd Mohn, 1963.

———. *Mark the Evangelist.* New York: Abingdon, 1969.

———. *The Resurrection of Jesus of Nazareth.* Trans. Margaret Kohl. Philadelphia: Fortress, 1970.

Mealand, David L. "The Dissimilarity Test." *SJT* 31 (1978): 41–50.

Metzger, Bruce M. *The Text of the New Testament.* New York: Oxford, 1964.

Meyer, Ben F. *The Aims of Jesus.* London: SCM, 1979.

Michaelis, Wilhelm. *Die Erscheinungen des Auferstandenen.* Basel: Majer, 1944.

Milik, J. T. *The Books of Enoch.* Oxford: Clarendon, 1976.

Mitton, C. Leslie. *Jesus: The Fact behind the Faith.* Grand Rapids: Eerdmans,
1974.

Montefiore, Claude J. G. *The Synoptic Gospels.* London: Macmillan, 1927.

Morris, Leon. *Studies in the Fourth Gospel.* Grand Rapids: Eerdmans, 1969.

Moule, C. F. D. *The Phenomenon of the New Testament.* London: SCM, 1967.

Moulton, James Hope, and George Milligan. *The Vocabulary of the Greek Testament.* Grand Rapids: Eerdmans, 1930.

Muddiman, John B. "The End of Markan Redaction Criticism?" *ExpT* 101 (1990):
307–9.

Müller, Hans-Peter. "Die Verklärung Jesu." *ZNW* 51 (1960): 56–64.

Münderlein, Gerhard. "Die Verfluchung des Feigenbaumes." *NTS* 10 (1963):
89–104.

Nicolardot, Firmin. *Les procédés de rédaction des trois premiers évangelistes.* Paris:
Librairie Fischbacher, 1908.

Nineham, Dennis Eric. "The Order of Events in St. Mark's Gospel—An Examination of Dr. Dodd's Hypothesis." In *Studies in the Gospels,* ed. D. E. Nineham.
Oxford: Blackwell, 1955.

———. "Eye-witness Tradition and the Gospel Tradition." *JTS* 9 (1958): 13–25,
143–52; 11 (1960): 253–60.

———. *The Gospel of St. Mark.* Baltimore: Penguin, 1963.

Normann, Friedrich. *Christos Didaskalos.* Münster: Aschendorffsche, 1967.

Osborne, Grant R. "The Evangelical and *Traditionsgeschichte.*" *JETS* 21 (1978):
117–30.

Perrin, Norman. *Rediscovering the Teaching of Jesus.* New York: Harper, 1967.

———.*What Is Redaction Criticism?* Philadelphia: Fortress, 1969.

———. *Christology and a Modern Pilgrimage.* Claremont: New Testament Colloquium, 1971.

Pesch, Rudolf. "Ein Tag vollmächtigen Wirkens Jesu in Kapharnaum (Mk 1
21–34, 35–39)." *BiL* 9 (1968): 114–28.

Ramsay, Michael. *The Glory of God and the Transfiguration of Christ*. London: Longmans, Green, 1949.

Rawlinson, A. E. J. *The Gospel According to St. Mark*. London: Methuen, 1925.

Riesenfeld, Harald. *The Gospel Tradition and Its Beginnings*. Philadelphia: Fortress, 1970.

———. "Tradition und Redaktion in Markusevangelium." In *Neutestamentliche Studien für Rudolf Bultmann*. Berlin: Töpelmann, 1954.

Robin, A. de Q. "The Cursing of the Fig Tree in Mark xi. A Hypothesis." *NTS* 8 (1962): 276–81.

Robinson, John A. T. *Redating the New Testament*. Philadelphia: Westminster, 1976.

Robinson, James M. *The Problem of History in Mark*. London: SCM, 1957.

———. *A New Quest of the Historical Jesus*. London: SCM, 1959.

———. "The Formal Structure of Jesus' Message." In *Current Issues in New Testament Interpretation*, ed. William Klassen and Graydon F. Snyder. New York: Harper, 1962.

———. "On the *Gattung* of Mark [and John]." In *Jesus and Man's Hope*. Pittsburgh: Pittsburgh Theological Seminary, 1970.

Rohde, Joachim. *Die redaktionsgeschichtliche Methode*. Hamburg: Furche-Verlag H. Rennebach KG, 1966.

———. *Rediscovering the Teaching of the Evangelists*. London: SCM, 1968.

Sanders, E. P. *The Tendencies of the Synoptic Tradition*. New York: Cambridge University, 1969.

Sandmel, Samuel. "Prologomena to a Commentary on Mark." *JBR* 31 (1963): 294–300.

Schelke, Karl Hermann. *Das Neue Testament*. Kevelaer Rhineland: Butson & Bercker, 1963.

———. *Die Petrusbriefe: Der Judasbrief*. Freiburg: Herder, 1961.

Schille, Gottfried. "Bemerkungen zur Formgeschichte des Evangeliums. Rahmen und Aufbau des Markus-Evangeliums." *NTS* 4 (1957): 1–24.

———. "Der Mangel eines kritischen Geschichtsbildes in der neutestamentlichen Formgeschichte." *TLZ* 88 (1963): 493–502.

Schiwy, Günther. *Weg ins Neue Testament*. Würzburg: Echter, 1965.

Schlatter, Adolf. *Der Evangelist Matthäus*. Stuttgart: Calwer, 1929.

Schmid, Josef. *The Gospel According to Mark*. Trans. Kevin Condon. Staten Island: Alba, 1968.

Schmidt, Karl Ludwig. *Der Rahmen der Geschichte Jesu*. Berlin: Trowitzsch, 1919.

Schmiedel, Paul W. "Gospels." In *Encyclopedia Biblica*, ed. T. K. Cheyne and J. Sutherland Black. London: Adam & Black, 1914.

Schmithals, Walter. "Der Markusschluss die Verklärungsgeschichte und die Aussendung der Zwölf." *ZTK* 69 (1972): 379–411.

Schnackenburg, Rudolf. *The Gospel According to St. John*. Trans. Kevin Smyth. New York: Herder, 1968.

Schneider, Gerhard. "Der Zweck des lukanischen Doppelwerks." *BZ* 21 (1977): 45–66.

Schniewind, Julius. *Das Evangelium nach Markus.* Göttingen: Vandenhoeck & Ruprecht, 1937.

Schreiber, Johannes. *Theologische Erkenntnis und unterrichtlicher Vollzug.* Hamburg: Furche-Verlag H. Rennebach KG, 1966.

———. "Die Christologie des Markus-evangeliums." *ZTK* 58 (1961): 154–83.

———. *Theologie des Vertrauens.* Hamburg: Furche-Verlag H. Rennebach KG, 1967.

Schulz, S. "Die Bedeutung des Markus für die Theologiegeschichte des Urchristentums." In *Texte und Untersuchungen: Studia Evangelica.* Berlin: Akademie-Verlag, 1964.

Schürmann, Heinz. *Traditionsgeschichtliche Untersuchungen zu den synoptischen Evangelien.* Düsseldorf: Patmos, 1968.

Schweizer, Eduard. "Anmerkungen zur Theologie des Markus." In *Neotestamentica et Patristica.* Leiden: Brill, 1962.

———. "Zur Frage des Messiasgeheimnisses bei Markus." *ZNW* 56 (1965): 1–8.

———. *Das Evangelium nach Markus.* Göttingen: Vandenhoeck & Ruprecht, 1967.

———. *The Good News According to Mark.* Richmond: John Knox, 1970.

Sjöberg, Erik. *Der Verborgene Menschensohn in den Evangelien.* Lund: Gleerup, 1955.

Smith, Charles W. F. "No Time for Figs." *JBL* 79 (1960): 315–27.

Stein, Robert H. "The Proper Methodology for Ascertaining a Marcan Redaktionsgeschichte." Th.D. diss., Princeton Theological Seminary, 1968.

———. "What Is Redaktionsgeschichte?" *JBL* 88 (1969): 45–56.

———. "The 'redaktionsgeschichtlich' Investigation of a Markan Seam (Mc 1:21ff.)." *ZNW* 61 (1970): 70–94.

———. "The Proper Methodology for Ascertaining a Markan Redaction History." *NovT* 13 (1971): 181–98.

———. "A Short Note on Mark XIV.28 and XVI.7." *NTS* 20 (1973): 445–52.

———. "Is the Transfiguration (Mark 9:2–8) a Misplaced Resurrection-Account?" *JBL* 95 (1976): 79–96.

———. *The Method and Message of Jesus' Teachings.* Philadelphia: Westminster, 1978.

———. "Is It Lawful for a Man to Divorce His Wife?" *JETS* 22 (1979): 115–21.

———. "The 'Criteria' for Authenticity." In *Gospel Perspectives: Studies of History and Tradition in the Four Gospels,* ed. R. T. France and David Wenham. Sheffield: JSOT, 1980.

———. "'Authentic' or 'Authoritative'? What Is the Difference?" *JETS* 24 (1981): 127–30.

———. "Luke 1:1–4 and *Traditionsgeschichte.*" *JETS* 26 (1983): 421–30.

———. *The Synoptic Problem.* Grand Rapids: Baker, 1987.

Steinmetz, Franz-Josef. "Literaturbericht." *Geist Leb* 42 (1969): 64.

Strecker, Georg. *Der Weg der Gerechtigkeit*. Göttingen: Vandenhoeck & Ruprecht, 1962.

———. Review of Marxsen's *Der Evangelist Markus*. *ZKG* 72 (1961): 143–44.

———. "Die Leidens- und Auferstehungsvoraussagen im Markusevangelium." *ZTK* 64 (1967): 16–39.

———. "The Passion- and Resurrection Predictions in Mark's Gospel." *Interp* 22 (1968): 421–42.

———. "Zur Messiasgeheimnistheorie im Markusevangelium." In *Texte und Untersuchungen: Studia Evangelica*. Berlin: Akademie-Verlag, 1964.

Streeter, Burnett Hillman. *The Four Gospels*. New York: Macmillan, 1925.

Suhl, Alfred. *Die Funktion der alttestamentlichen Zitate und Anspielungen im Markus-Evangelium*. Gütersloh: Gerd Mohn, 1965.

Sundwall, Johannes. *Die Zusammensetzung des Markusevangeliums*. Åbo: Åbo Akademi, 1934.

Taylor, Vincent. *Behind the Third Gospel*. Oxford: University, 1926.

———. *The Gospel According to St. Mark*. London: Macmillan, 1959.

Thrall, M. J. "Elijah and Moses in Mark's Account of the Transfiguration." *NTS* 16 (1969/70): 305–17.

Throckmorton, Burton H. "Did Mark Know Q." *JBL* 67 (1948): 319–29.

Torrey, Charles Cutter. *Our Translated Gospels*. New York: Harper, 1936.

Trilling, Wolfgang. *Das Wahre Israel*. München: Kösel, 1964.

Trocmé, Étienne. *La Formation de L'évangile selon Marc*. Paris: Universitaries de France, 1963.

———. *Jesus as Seen by His Contemporaries*. Philadelphia: Westminster, 1973.

Trompf, G. W. "The First Resurrection Appearance and the Ending of Mark's Gospel." *NTS* 18 (1972): 308–30.

Turner, C. H. "Marcan Usage: Notes, Critical and Exegetical, on the Second Gospel." *JTS* 25–29 (1924–28).

Turner, Henry Ernst William. *Historicity and the Gospel*. London: Mowbray, 1963.

Turner, Nigel. *Syntax*, vol. 3: *A Grammar of New Testament Greek*. Ed. James Hope Moulton. Edinburgh: T. & T. Clark, 1963.

Tyson, Joseph B. "The Blindness of the Disciples of Mark." *JBL* 80 (1961): 261–68.

Van Der Horst, P. W. "Can a Book End with ΓΑΡ? A Note on Mark xvi.8" *JTS* 23 (1972): 121–24.

Vansina, Jan. *Oral Tradition: A Study in Historical Methodology*. Trans. H. M. Wright. Berlin: Aldine, 1965.

Vermes, Geza. *Jesus the Jew*. London: Fontana, 1976.

Vögtle, Anton. "Die historische und theologische Tragweite der heutigen Evangelienforschung." *ZKT* 86 (1964): 385–417.

———. "Was Heisst 'Auslegung der Schrift'?" In *Was Heisst Auslegung der Heiligen Schrift*. Regensburg: Friedrich Pustet, 1966.

Walker, William O. "The Quest for the Historical Jesus: A Discussion of Methodology." *ATR* 51 (1969): 38–56.

Weeden, Theodore J. *Mark—Traditions in Conflict*. Philadelphia: Fortress, 1971.

Weiss, Johannes. *Die Schriften des Neuen Testaments*. Göttingen: Vandenhoeck & Ruprecht, 1906.

Wellhausen, Julius. *Das Evangelium Marci*. Berlin: G. Reimer, 1909.

Wieder, Naphtali. *The Judean Scrolls and Karaism*. London: East and West Library, 1962.

Winter, Paul. "Markus xiv 53 b, 55–64—Ein Gebilde des Evangelisten." *ZNW* 53 (1962): 260–63.

Wrede, William. *Das Messiasgeheimnis in den Evangelien*.Göttingen: Vandenhoeck & Ruprecht, 1901.

Zahn, Theodor. *Das Evangelium des Matthäus*. Leipzig: A. Deichert, 1910.

Zahrnt, Heinz. *The Historical Jesus*. Trans. J. S. Bowden. New York: Harper, 1963.

Zerwick, Max. *Untersuchungen zum Markus-Stil*. Rome: Pontifical Biblical Institute, 1937.

Index